THE HORIZON
HISTORY OF
CHINA

THE HORIZON
HISTORY OF
CHINA

BY THE EDITORS OF HORIZON MAGAZINE

EDITOR IN CHARGE NORMAN KOTKER

AUTHOR C. P. FITZGERALD

AMERICAN HERITAGE PUBLISHING CO., INC., New York

HORIZON
BOOK DIVISION

EDITORIAL DIRECTOR
Richard M. Ketchum

GENERAL EDITOR
Alvin M. Josephy, Jr.

Staff for this Book

EDITOR
Norman Kotker

ART DIRECTOR
Emma Landau

SENIOR EDITOR
Douglas Tunstell

COPY EDITOR
Kaari I. Ward

ASSISTANT EDITOR
Edwin D. Bayrd, Jr.

RESEARCHER
Carol Kerr

PICTURE RESEARCHER
Natalie Siegel

EDITORIAL ASSISTANT
Roxanne Wehrhan

EUROPEAN BUREAU
Gertrudis Feliu, *Chief*
Claire de Forbin

AMERICAN HERITAGE
PUBLISHING CO., INC.

PRESIDENT
James Parton

EDITORIAL COMMITTEE
Joseph J. Thorndike, *Chairman*
Oliver Jensen
Richard M. Ketchum

SENIOR ART DIRECTOR
Irwin Glusker

PUBLISHER, HORIZON MAGAZINE
Paul Gottlieb

Horizon Magazine is published quarterly by American Heritage Publishing Co., Inc., 551 Fifth Avenue, N.Y., N.Y. 10017. Printed in the United States of America. Library of Congress Catalog Card Number: 69-15081. Standard Book Numbers: Regular Edition 8281-0005-5; Deluxe Edition 8281-0026-8; Boxed Edition 8281-0027-6.

Published simultaneously in Canada by Fitzhenry & Whiteside Limited.

HALF-TITLE PAGE: *This T'ang dynasty marble lion, which stands less than a foot high, probably served to frighten away malevolent spirits.*
WILLIAM ROCKHILL NELSON GALLERY OF ART

TITLE PAGE: *Emperor T'ai Tsung, who ruled from A.D. 626 to 649, commissioned a painting that portrays thirteen of his august predecessors. A detail from the scroll shows six of the thirteen—some standing and attended by officials, others seated and attended by concubines.*
MUSEUM OF FINE ARTS, BOSTON-WANGO H. C. WENG

RIGHT: *This intricately wrought ceramic watchtower, discovered in a tomb, dates from the Han dynasty.*
MUSEE CERNUSCHI, PARIS-LUC JOUBERT

CHINA TODAY

Over half a billion people, including some thirty-five million non-Chinese—Mongols, Thais, Uigurs, Turks, Manchus, Koreans—inhabit modern China. Because two thirds of mainland China is mountainous or semidesert, ninety per cent of the population is concentrated in the East. The bulk of the population is settled in the three great river valleys that divide eastern China: the basin of the Huang Ho, or Yellow River, in arid northern China; the Yangtze River basin in central China; and the valley of the Hsi River in the humid, semitropical south. Chinese civilization almost certainly originated in the Yellow River valley. Eventually it spread south, down the coast and along the great river systems, carried by settlers who migrated from north China and overwhelmed the native population of the south. In recent years there has been massive migration into Mongolia and Manchuria, and vast areas of northern land have been put under cultivation.

OVERLEAF: *A chronological table summarizes almost four thousand years of the history of China.*

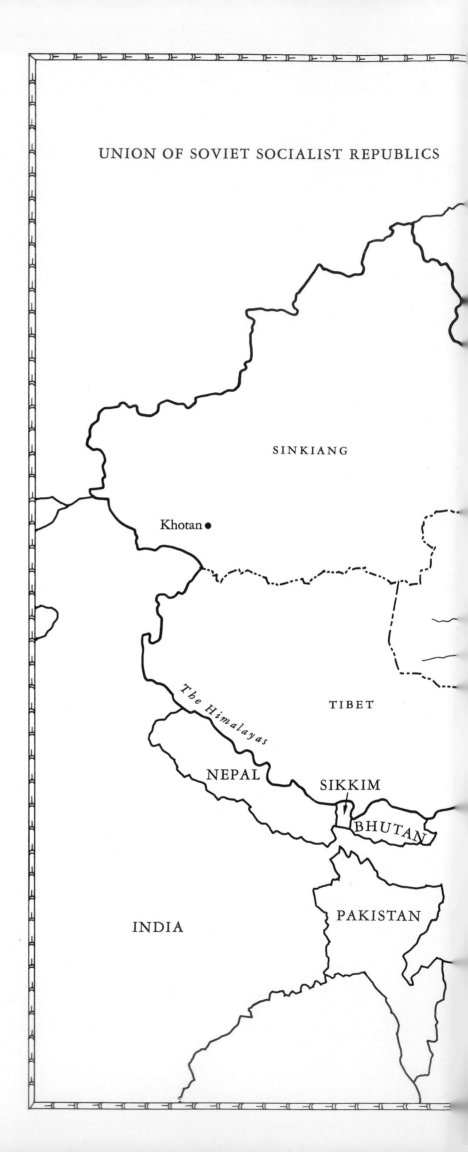

UNION OF SOVIET SOCIALIST REPUBLICS

SINKIANG

Khotan ●

The Himalayas

TIBET

NEPAL

SIKKIM

BHUTAN

INDIA

PAKISTAN

6

PERIODS	HISTORY	CULTURE	ELSEWHERE
LEGENDARY PERIOD to c. 1523 B.C. Hsia (c. 1994–c. 1523)	Period of mythical Sages Fu Hsi (2953–2838), inventor of the eight trigrams Shên Nung (2838–2698), inventor of agriculture Huang Ti (2698–2598), inventor of writing Yü the Great (died 2197), tamer of floods	Neolithic age	Old Kingdom in Egypt (3100–2160) Rise of Sumerian civilization (c. 3000) Height of Minoan culture on Crete (c. 1700–c. 1500)
SHANG c. 1523–c. 1028 capitals: An-yang; site of Ch'eng-chou	Chou Hsin (died 1027), last Shang ruler	Bronze age; casting of bronze vessels Book of Changes (I Ching) (begun c. 1100) First evidences of oracle bone inscriptions, bas-reliefs, silk, script	Height of Egyptian empire (c. 1300) Exodus of Jews from Egypt (c. 1240) Trojan War (c. 1200)
CHOU c. 1027–256 Western Chou (1027–722) Spring and Autumn Annals (722–481) *capital:* Lo-yang Warring States (481–221) *capital:* Lo-yang	Feudalism established Jung nomads overrun Western Chou (722) Feudalism begins to decline (c. 500) Wars among states of Ch'in, Ch'i, Ch'u, Chao, Han, Wei, Yüeh, Yen King of Chou dethroned by king of Ch'in (256)	Book of Documents (begun c. 1000) Book of Odes (c. 700) Spring and Autumn Annals (c. 500) Iron age begins (c. 500) Schools of philosophy flourish: Lao Tzŭ (born 604?); Confucius (551–479), Analects; Mo Tzŭ (c. 470-391) First evidences of chopsticks, crossbow, canal building	Height of Assyrian empire (c. 900–c. 600) Age of Hebrew prophets (c. 875–c. 520) Height of Etruscan empire (c. 800–c. 500) Buddha (c. 563–c. 483) Persian empire (538–333) Golden age of Athens (c. 500–c. 350) Alexander the Great conquers Egypt, western Asia (336–323)
CH'IN 221–207 *capital:* Hsien-yang	Shih Huang Ti, the "First Emperor" (222–210) Li Ssŭ (died 208), minister of state Unification of China (221) Great Wall completed (c. 220)	Burning of the books (213) Domination of Legist philosophy; persecution of all other schools Standardization of script, weights and measures	
EARLIER HAN 202 B.C.–A.D. 9 *capital:* Ch'ang-an	Feudalism destroyed; end of serfdom Liu Pang, called Emperor Kao Tsu (202–195) Emperor Wu Ti (140–87) Territorial expansion into Central Asia (c. 115)	Canonization of Confucian philosophy Taoist magical practices popular Book of Rites (c. 100) Ssŭ-ma Ch'ien (145–c. 80), Historical Records Use of coins widespread	Height of Roman empire (c. 100 B.C.–A.D. 200) Augustus, first Roman emperor (27 B.C.–A.D. 14) Jesus (4 B.C.?–A.D. 29)
HSIN 9–23	Emperor Wang Mang, "the Usurper" (9–23)		
LATER HAN 25–220 *capital:* Lo-yang	Emperor Kuang Wu (25–57) Chinese conquer Mongolia (121) Silk Road opened (c. 140) Eunuchs gain power under Emperor Ling Ti (167–189) Yellow Turban rebellion (184) Emperor Hsien Ti (190–220)	Buddhism introduced (around first century) Buddhist texts translated Invention of paper (c. 100) Lodestone and magnetic compasses used Evidences of wall painting, bas-reliefs, sculptured figures in tombs	
THREE KINGDOMS (Shu, Wei, Wu) 220–265	Period of political disunity	Pilgrimages to Buddhist sites in India	Sassanian empire in Persia (226)
NORTHERN AND SOUTHERN EMPIRES 265–589 Six Dynasties (Western Tsin, Eastern Tsin, Former Sung, Southern Ch'i, Southern Liang, Southern Ch'ên) (265–589) Barbarian Dynasties (386–587)	Period of colonization of south China Barbarians invade China (fourth century) Emperor Wu Ti (502–549) of the Southern Liang dynasty Military aristocracy emerges (fifth-sixth centuries)		Rome falls to the barbarians (410) Justinian, ruler of Eastern Roman empire (527–565) Buddhism reaches Japan (c. 550) Mohammed (570–632)
SUI 590–618 *capitals:* Yang-chou, Lo-yang, Ch'ang-an	Yang Chien, called Emperor Wên Ti (590–604) Reunification of China Yang Kuang, called Emperor Yang Ti (605–618) Grand Canal constructed	Golden age of Buddhism in China Development of Ch'an (Zen) sect Buddhist influence on art and literature Height of Buddhist cave sculpture and painting	Dark Ages in Europe
T'ANG 618–906 *capital:* Ch'ang-an	Period of territorial expansion into Manchuria, Central Asia Contacts with Japan, southeast Asia, Byzantium, Arab empire Li Shih-min, called Emperor T'ai Tsung (626–649) Professional army created Empress Wu Hou (690–705) Hsüan Tsung, called Emperor Ming Huang (712–756) Rebellion of An Lu-shan (755)	Civil service examination system made universal; rise of scholar-officials Great age of poetry: Li Po (705–762); Tu Fu (712–770) Foreign religions in China: Zoroastrianism, Nestorianism, Manichaeism, Judaism, Islam Proscription of Buddhism (845) Diamond Sutra, first printed book (868) Mass production of porcelain Tea drinking becomes common	Kingdom of Ghana established (c. 600) Rise of Arab empire (635–715) Charlemagne (768–814) Height of feudalism in Europe Golden age of Maya civilization

Dynasty / Period	Political Events	Cultural Events	World Events
FIVE DYNASTIES (Later Liang, Later T'ang, Later Chin, Later Han, Later Chou) 907–960	Period of upheaval; Mongols begin penetration of north China	Printing of Confucian classics; Footbinding introduced; First military use of gunpowder	
NORTHERN SUNG 960–1126 *capital*: Kai-feng	Chao K'uang-yin, called Emperor T'ai Tsu (960–976); Reunification of China; Wang An-shih, prime minister (1069–1086); New Laws created to reform Chinese economy; Emperor Hui Tsung (1101–1125); Chin Tatars conquer north China (1127)	Great age of figure and landscape painting; Drainage of swampland; Invention of moveable type (c. 1045), canal locks (eleventh century)	Norman Conquest of England (1066); First crusade (1096–1099); Great age of medieval Europe (c. 1000–c. 1350)
SOUTHERN SUNG 1127–1279 *capital*: Hang-chou	Sung dynasty controls the south; Genghis Khan (c. 1167–1227); Mongols begin invasions of south (1234)	Great age of figure and landscape painting; Seaborne trade flourishes; Neo-Confucian philosophy; Chu Hsi (1130–1200), commentator on Confucian texts	Mongols conquer Russia (1237–1240)
YUAN, OR MONGOL 1260–1368 *capital*: Peking	Kublai Khan (1260–1294); Marco Polo in China (1275–1292); Mongols attempt to invade Japan (1274–1281)	Civil service in eclipse; Chinese travel abroad; Drama flourishes	
MING 1368–1644 *capitals*: Peking, Nanking	Chu Yüan-chang, called Emperor Hung Wu (1368–1398); Emperor Yung Lo (1403–1424); Peking rebuilt; Naval expeditions to Indian Ocean (1405–1433?); Emperor Cheng T'ung (1436–1449, 1457–1464); Portuguese traders arrive at Canton (1514); Emperor Wan Li (1573–1620)	Revival of traditional culture; Civil service reinstated; Matteo Ricci arrives in China (1582); Novel flourishes; Widespread export of porcelain	Turks conquer Constantinople (1453); Italian Renaissance (c. 1410–c. 1550); Discovery of America (1492); Protestant Reformation inaugurated by Martin Luther (1517); Queen Elizabeth I (1558–1603)
CH'ING, OR MANCHU 1644–1912 *capitals*: Mukden, Peking	Emperor K'ang Hsi (1662–1722); Russia establishes trading rights in Peking (1689); Emperor Ch'ien Lung (1736–1795); Opium War (1840–1842); European efforts to establish hegemony in China (after 1840); T'ai P'ing Rebellion breaks out (1850); British and French take Peking (1860); Empress Dowager Tz'ŭ Hsi (1862–1908); Emperor T'ung Chih (1862–1875); Program to modernize China; War with Japan (1894–1895); Boxer Rebellion (1900–1901); Republican revolution (1911)	Imposition of queue; Imperial patronage of Jesuits; Rites Controversy (c. 1710); Opium smoking becomes widespread (early nineteenth century); China opened to missionaries (1842); Western cultural influences (after 1861); translation of Western books; Chinese study abroad; First railroad built (1896); Peking University founded (1898)	Age of Enlightenment in Europe (c. 1660–c. 1750); Chinese art and thought influential in Europe (eighteenth century); American Revolution begins (1776); French Revolution begins (1789); Industrial Revolution in Europe; Queen Victoria (1837–1901); European nations compete for colonies; Industrialization of Japan (1868–1912)
REPUBLIC 1912–1949 *capitals*: Nanking, Chungking	Sun Yat-sen, first provisional president; Yüan Shih-k'ai, provisional president (1912–1916); Warlord era (1916–1925); Chiang Kai-shek (1886–) becomes president of China (1928); Japan occupies Manchuria (1931); Long March of the Communist army (1934–1935); War with Japan (1936); Nationalist-Communist civil war (1946–1949)	Growth of industry; Western education becomes widespread	Period of scientific revolution; World War I (1914–1918); Bolshevik Revolution in Russia (1917); World War II (1941–1945)
PEOPLE'S REPUBLIC 1949– *capital*: Peking	Mao Tse-tung (1893–), chairman of Communist party; Chou En lai (1898?–), premier of People's Republic; Korean War (1950–1953); Split with Russia (1960); China becomes a major world power; Lin Piao named heir of Mao Tse-tung (1969)	Intensive industrialization begins (1958); "Great Cultural Revolution" begins (1966); Red Guards founded (1966)	Establishment of the United Nations (1945); Independence of former European colonies; First man in space (1961); Increasing influence of Asian countries

The Approach to China

"Remote" and "mysterious," these are the two adjectives that the popular mind of the West immediately applies to China. It is an old tradition amongst us to look upon China in this way, a tradition dating back to the time of the Romans and their speculation about the Seres of the East, who produced that intriguing and valuable commodity, silk. Recent political changes and conflicts have tended to reinforce the old attitude. As distance goes, China is indeed a long way from Europe or from America, but so are many other regions that have not acquired in our minds the label of "mysterious." The reason why Western man has found China so strange is that it is the only civilization the world has known upon which Western thought exercised no influence at all until modern times. It is also the only large region of the earth where Western men have never ruled.

It has seemed to Westerners that in China everything is reversed: the Chinese use white as the color of mourning; for them the left is the side of honor; writing is read vertically from the top right-hand corner downward, not horizontally from the top left corner. Chinese books begin at the opposite end of the volume to Western books. There are other examples, but what is common to all, as a moment's reflection will show, is that there are only two alternatives, either of which must be chosen. The West chose one; China the other. To avoid color as a mark of respect to the dead, mourners must either wear black or white. To honor a guest, one must seat him next to the host, on the right or on the left. One can either write across the page or downward, from left or from right. One can open a book at one end or the other; no one is likely to adopt a system whereby it is opened in the middle.

These simple examples reveal two important facts about Chinese culture: it was independent of Western influences, and it is based upon the same psychological imperatives as any other manifestation of human behavior. The Chinese may have been remote in an age of undeveloped communications; they were not really mysterious, only alien. As they built their civilization beyond the influence of the ancient Near East or the Western world, they developed many distinctive characteristics. The roots of Chinese technology and art are common to the whole neolithic world; it is the development, the evolved form, that differs. So, too, with religion and philosophy. The needs of man everywhere are similar: reassurance against death and the cruel powers of nature, and belief in protective forces more powerful than himself. These basic needs are just as apparent in the Chinese as in any other people; but the responses formulated to these needs are often peculiar to China and sharply differentiated from those that were made by men of other races and countries.

Another fallacy that is widespread in the West is that Chinese civilization is immensely old, reaching back into the most distant past. It is, in fact, in any recognizable postneolithic form, very much more recent than that of Crete. Near Eastern civilization is much older than that of China. What gives rise to the misapprehension is that the ancient cultures of Egypt, Mesopotamia, and Greece were wholly transformed or destroyed many centuries ago, whereas Chinese culture shows an unbroken continuity from the earliest times to the present. The Chinese have added to this misunderstanding because their own tradition records a fictitious history running back a full thousand years before the history for which there is factual evidence. This literary tradition was accepted without question by the early Western Sinologists, who had, of course, no means of checking the story against archeological discoveries. Thus it seemed as though China's history was four thousand years long. This tradition also gave rise to another long-standing belief about China: it is a changeless civilization that evolved a highly organized state system in remote antiquity and maintained this system almost without modification down to modern times.

The older Western histories of China, based exclusively on Chinese traditional materials, speak of a unified empire, with a territory as large as that of China today, of emperors, officials, prefectures, and provinces—all the apparatus of imperial bureaucracy that did not, in fact, even begin to take shape until the second century B.C. There were reasons why the Chinese tradition needed to emphasize an unreal unity; why the legends of ancient times should be reshaped to read like a recorded history composed in the light of what the writers of the second century B.C. saw as contemporary reality. These reasons were in time forgotten, concealed by custom and venerable tradition. It was not until very modern times that China's own historians were ready to challenge this mythical past and recognize it for what it actually is. Even Dr. Sun Yat-sen, a modern revolutionary, speaks of the "history" of the period of about two thousand B.C. as if it were

Opposite, an abandoned temple on an island in the mountainous southern province of Kuangsi stands as mute testimony to the splendor of China's past.

human society. Everyone has seen the decline of great and famous families, often within a short period of time. The founder is a man who rises from little to power and wealth; his eldest son and successor strives to maintain the property or even to increase it, but rarely has the ability to create it himself. Grandsons and great-grandsons are inclined to enjoy their prosperity rather than to expand it. Later generations are unable to retain the position that they inherit. Slowly they sink into ineffective, if often cultivated idleness. Wealth diminishes, and the end is once more poverty.

As applied to a dynasty, the theory often seems to hold much truth. No doubt this sapping of initiative and capacity is real enough; but the theory wholly ignores other factors. The Chinese historian tended to make it the total explanation of all historical change. All history depended on the moral qualities of the monarch. Economic changes, foreign invasion or pressure, social development, had nothing to do with the rise and fall of dynasties. If there were calamities, they resulted from the moral defects of the king or emperor. If there was a recovery, it could be traced to the merit of the ruler, inspired by the teaching of the Sages. The result of this moral preoccupation in presenting historical record was to view the processes of human affairs as a series of cycles: rise, splendor, decline, and fall. Nothing could escape this fate.

The Chinese historians largely escaped from the fallacy, which for so long dominated early Western historical traditions, that history is a record of the actions of great men. Instead they believed in the dynastic cycle, a theory that is at least equally misleading. The Great Man theory would put the activity of the hero in such prominence that economic change and all other factors cannot in any way limit his boundless initiative; the dynastic cycle theory would deny that any initiative or any change of circumstances can for long alter the fatal cycle of rise and fall.

The very volume and meticulous accuracy of Chinese history becomes a trap; the story is all there, told in great detail, well dated and truthfully stated. No attempt is made to cover up the failings of the great, nor to glorify their achievements in any bombastic style. So it was natural for the early Western historians of China to believe that all they had to do was translate. The Chinese had done the interpretation for them, had proved that China's was a changeless story, molded on a set pattern. This is what the Westerners had already come to believe. Here was the confirmation. Chinese historians had paid little attention to changing custom or economic growth; if sometimes they mention these processes, they do not emphasize them and very rarely relate them to the main stream of events. Early Western historians followed the same pattern. They emphasized what their Chinese authorities considered important, the moral aspects of the story—whether this or that emperor was wise or foolish, hard-working or debauched. Very rarely did they stop to inquire what was happening to the Chinese people as a whole. Were they growing in numbers, changing their social structure, or developing new techniques? Above all, no question was asked that could have implied that there had been any im-

provement since the golden age; nor were the Chinese historians concerned to treat such matters as changes in religious belief. Such changes were unwelcome. The Chinese people should be following the teaching of the Sages and of their great disciple (as they saw him), Confucius. If, in fact, the Chinese had become largely converted to Buddhism, an Indian, and therefore barbarian, creed, or had permitted the introduction of Islam and its growth among them, these things were not to be discussed or recorded in detail. If some emperor favored the Buddhists, this was reprehensible, and it would be recounted primarily to show why he later met with misfortune or why his dynasty declined. The coming of Islam to China from the eighth to the tenth centuries A.D. is never so much as mentioned in the official histories. It was not a court fashion; no emperor became a Moslem, and when in the course of time many thousands of the emperor's subjects did so, this was of no interest to the historians.

The attitudes described belong to the official histories, which are the record of the twenty-four dynastic periods into which the Chinese traditionally divided their history up to the seventeenth century. The twenty-fifth, the last dynasty, was not, of course, included in this series because, according to Chinese tradition—a tradition abandoned by the republic—its official history could not be written until it had ceased to govern. This tradition arose from a remarkable and cool appraisal of human weakness. No dynasty could be allowed to pass judgment on itself: the facts would be falsified, folly disguised, wickedness effaced, virtues claimed, and boastful untruths

perpetuated. The dynasty might, indeed must, accumulate its archives, which were carefully preserved. But this great mass of material must never be edited or published until the dynasty in question had ceased to reign. Then its successor, or, if the period of immediate succession had been short and troubled, its next well-established successor, would commission a group of the best-known and most-respected scholars to prepare and publish the official history of the late regime. No advantage could now be derived from falsification, no harm done by the truth. It was assumed, on the basis of long experience and in accordance with the theory of the dynastic cycle, that all dynasties would sooner or later decline and fall, and that all new regimes would be fresh dynasties exposed to the same political risks and ambitions as their predecessors. So history could be left to ripen till the appropriate time came for editing and publication.

Fortunately, the Chinese did not always follow official practice and allow some two or three hundred years to elapse before interesting events were recorded. The custom arose of writing unofficial histories, which, if somewhat prejudiced, were often very lively reading. Some of their material was probably to be found in the still-hidden archives of the Bureau of History, but there was also gossip and scandal that the official histories would never admit. The need for something contemporary was filled in another way, by the publication of miscellanies. These collections contain many important and interesting pieces of historical information, very often of a nature that the official histories would not have

In the year 1487 the artist Shên Chou painted a picture of himself and three friends gathered in a riverside pavilion to watch the mid-autumn moon. Their reverent attention to the beauties of nature is characteristic of the Chinese spirit and particularly of Chinese art.

Built in its present form by the third century B.C. to repel invading barbarians, the Great Wall of China snakes across the mountainous terrain that separates the birthplace of Chinese civilization, the Yellow River plain of east-central China, from the steppe of Mongolia to the northwest. Almost a million square miles— about one third of all Chinese territory—is mountainous. The land north of the Wall was not always desert;

Beyond the Great Wall

during periods of increased rainfall, the steppe became lush pastureland. Occasionally, crop farming was also feasible, and Chinese peasants migrated across the Wall to stake out new farms. Generally traffic went the other way, for south of the Wall lie the vast and often fertile territories of "China of the Eighteen Provinces," whose carefully tended fields and prosperous cities beckoned to nomadic northern tribes.

EMIL SCHULTHESS, BLACK STAR

Eighty-five per cent of China is arid or inaccessible steppe, desert, or mountain. As a result, China's arable lands must be intensively cultivated in order to feed its burgeoning population. In the temperate highlands of

Yünnan in southwestern China—where less than ten per cent of the land can be cultivated—all food-producing acreage is carefully terraced and irrigated. The flooded rice paddies shown below yield two crops a year.

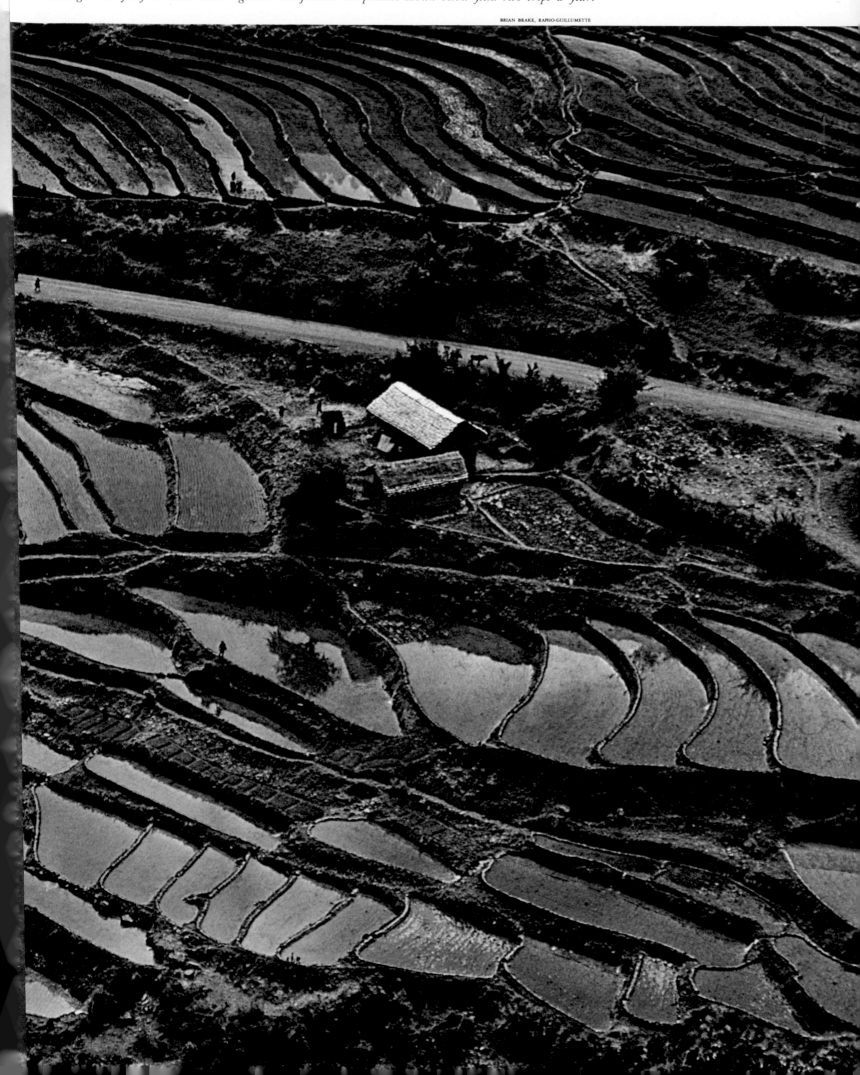

I Land and Language

Poems inscribed in fine calligraphy often appear in Chinese landscape paintings. This scroll, entitled Spring Plowing, *dates from the fifteenth century.*

Before the fall of the Chinese empire of the Ch'ing, or Manchu, dynasty in 1912, it was customary to define "China Proper" as the eighteen provinces inside the Great Wall. The three provinces of Manchuria, as well as the great outer dependencies of Mongolia and Tibet and Sinkiang, were treated as territories under the sovereignty of the emperor, but they were not part of his Chinese dominions. There were historical reasons for this distinction, which ceased to be meaningful when the Chinese republic was proclaimed and all the outer territories were incorporated. Outer Mongolia, beyond the Gobi desert, soon broke away, and has subsequently been recognized as an independent state. "China" today, according to international law, means all of the Manchu empire except Outer Mongolia. Including Tibet, Sinkiang (Chinese Central Asia), Inner Mongolia, and the three provinces of Manchuria, it comprises a region of continental size, approximately three million square miles. By comparison the United States is only slightly larger, and without the detached states of Alaska and Hawaii, a little smaller.

Historically and culturally, "China" usually means the old China within the Great Wall, the area inhabited by the vast majority of the population, which has expanded beyond this region only in modern times. This China of the Eighteen Provinces, as it is usually named in China itself, is a diverse region stretching from the Mongolian border, with its very cold winter, down to the tropical lands of Kuangtung and Hainan Island. It is exposed to almost all types of climate and produces every variety of crop.

Based on differences in climate, it has been customary to divide China into three major zones, which correspond roughly with the three great river systems. North China is the basin of the Yellow River, with the mountain zone reaching up to the Great Wall, which runs along the Mongolian border. Central China, or the Yangtze provinces, is the basin of the Yangtze River, divided from the northern region only by relatively low ranges of mountains. In the east the two regions merge in the valley of the Huai River—an indeterminate zone that in times of strife has been the scene of major military confrontations. If the Low Countries were "the cockpit of Europe," so the Huai valley has been the cockpit of China, and for the same reasons: the strategic importance of the area and its easy accessibility from the north and the south. South China includes the provinces lying along the coast south of Shanghai, Chekiang and Fukien, which do not form part of the major river basins, and also the most southerly provinces, Kuangtung, on the coast, and neighboring Kuangsi, and Kueichou and Yünnan to their west. The south China provinces are marked off from those of the Yangtze basin by steep and difficult mountain ranges, giving this region a distinct history and a characteristic culture.

But there is another, and historically most important, way of dividing China: between east and west, which is also, in general terms, between mountain and plain. The dividing line is particularly sharp in the northern part of China. Peking lies at the foot of the mountain ranges: west of that city they stretch, unbroken, to Tibet and beyond; eastward the flat plain extends to the sea. Except in the hilly Shantung peninsula, the land is flat all the way from Peking down to the Yangtze valley. The present line of the main railway from north to south runs not far from the base of the mountain ranges; from one side of the train the mountains are always visible, from the other side there is never a hill in sight. In the central region the land pattern is rather different. The great Yangtze splits through a mountain zone and creates its own flat valley, intensely fertile and never very wide. From the

river itself one can usually see the ranges to the north or to the south. Near the river's mouth silt has filled in a wide area of what was once shallow sea; on it isolated hills rise, showing very plainly that anciently they were islands.

South China has no plains of great extent; the delta of the West River below Canton, on which a huge population is concentrated, is the largest and almost the only considerable area of flat country. But the division between west and east is real nevertheless. The western provinces of Kueichou and Yünnan are high mountain country, averaging 4,000 feet in the first province, and from 6,000 to 8,000 in the second. Lofty ranges run from west to east across both provinces. The coastal provinces of Kuangtung and Kuangsi, centered on the fertile valleys of the West River and its tributaries, are lower. The hills are less imposing; the valleys flat. Historically there was little intercommunication between the two coastal provinces and the western mountain provinces. The latter were more easily reached from the north, from the Yangtze valley, although this route (that taken by the modern motor road, the Burma Road) is high and difficult.

Fukien and Chekiang, on the east coast, were always rather detached, especially the former, which was more accessible by sea than by land and which remained without a rail connection with the rest of China until a few years ago. Both provinces have high and rugged mountains in the interior and small, fertile plains around the river mouths on the coast. Pressure of population in these fertile pockets has driven the people to migrate elsewhere in large numbers. Many millions of Fukienese ancestry now dwell in Taiwan, Indonesia, Malaya, and Thailand. They form the majority among the overseas Chinese. The surplus population of Chekiang found it easy to move northward into the ample lands of the lower Yangtze provinces, and modern Shanghai, near the mouth of the Yangtze, is almost a Chekiang colony.

It is within this framework that the story of the Chinese people unfolds. It is at once obvious that although China has grown into a huge united state—an empire for more than two thousand years—there was little in the geographic setting to encourage this development. It may rather be said that the Chinese topography, sharply divided by mountain barriers, would be more likely to have nourished the growth and rise of separate nation-states, inhabited by people broadly akin, but differing much in speech and culture. Perhaps the main factor preventing this development was that one area, the northern plains and the Yellow River valley, is large and homogeneous enough to dominate all China. The provinces of Shantung, Hopei, Honan, Shansi, and Shensi are contiguous and for the most part separated only by rivers that serve to link as much as to divide. This meant that any state controlling this very large region, more than seven hundred miles from east to west and not much less from the north to the Yangtze valley, was stronger than any other possible combination of Chinese states and tended to dominate all neighbors.

For a few centuries after 481 B.C. the northern region was divided among many states usually antagonistic to each other; consequently it was in this period, and only in this period, that a few southern kingdoms were formed that for a time could maintain independence or even challenge northern domination. The idea that there was a fundamental difference between north and south China, and that unity was accidental and division natural, gained currency in the West during the confused period following the fall of the Ch'ing dynasty in 1912. It was derived from some very transitory circumstances and finds

no basis in Chinese history. Because the republican revolutionaries were based in Canton, and there were many Cantonese among the overseas Chinese, southerners seemed more accessible to modern ideas (and for a time they were) than their northern countrymen, who remained broadly indifferent to the new doctrines. As soon as the spread of modern ideas and Western techniques became equalized in north and south, the apparent predominance of Canton in the revolutionary government waned. The massive manpower and resources of the north restored a balance that has been traditional throughout Chinese history. Very few and very brief were the regimes ruling a united China from a southern capital: the Ming dynasty for twenty years, the Kuomintang for ten. All long-lasting dynasties based themselves at a northern site, even the few that originated in the south.

Separate nation-states had, therefore, little chance of developing so long as the north was united under one rule. The best chances for separate development were in the western mountain provinces—Kansu, Shensi, Ssŭch'-uan, and Yünnan. Of these, Kansu was always exposed to the raids of the nomadic Tatars of the Mongolian steppe, and too poor to sustain independence for long. Shensi, centered on the Wei River, a tributary of the Yellow River, was better placed to become the conqueror of the eastern plains than to remain in isolated independence, and such has been its role for many centuries. It was from Yenan in north Shensi that the Communist regime spread till the Communists were able to gain military control over the eastern plains, and so over all China. The first unifying empire in China was established by the kingdom of Ch'in, which was based in Shensi.

Ssŭch'uan, very isolated by mountains to the north, the Tibetan massif to the west, and the gorges of the Yangtze to the east, has

Twenty miles northwest of Peking lies the Valley of the Thirteen Tombs, where rows of carved marble animals mark the burial site of the Ming emperors.

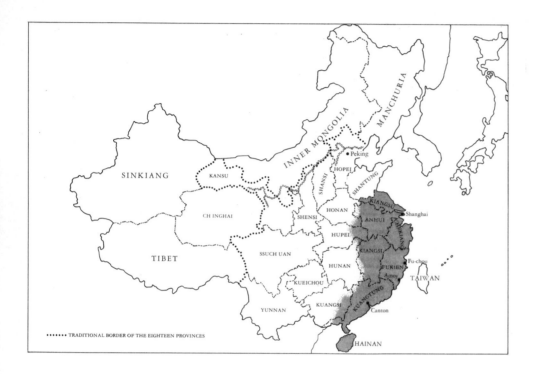

.... TRADITIONAL BORDER OF THE EIGHTEEN PROVINCES

Throughout China of the Eighteen Provinces much of the population speaks Mandarin, but in the southeastern region of the country (shaded area) a variety of dialects is found. Tibet, Sinkiang, and Manchuria have traditionally been inhabited by non-Chinese, although Chinese settlers are now concentrated in southern Manchuria.

often, as in the last war, been the refuge of hard-pressed regimes that have lost control of eastern China. It is rich and lush, able to sustain a great population; but it has never been a center of conquering power—perhaps because its people were too well off at home to wish to go elsewhere—and it has easily been controlled by any strong government based in the north. Yünnan was too remote to contend for wide authority, and with its great mountain ranges, too disunited to sustain a permanent independence. For some centuries Yünnan did support a well-organized kingdom independent of China, but the kingdom was under strong Chinese cultural influence and could never expand; ultimately it was incorporated into the empire.

The Yangtze valley, so large and rich, also might have been the heartland of a powerful kingdom; it was for a time in antiquity. The river provides easy communication to all the valley's provinces. The land is fertile and rela-

tively free from risk of flood or drought. But the Yangtze valley, because of its great length, is vulnerable to attack from the north. Separate regimes based in Nanking, the traditional capital of the Yangtze provinces, have survived only so long as there was disunity in the north. In early times the region's vulnerability was partly due to the fact that central China, like the southern zone, was still very much less populous than north China. The colonization and settlement of the Yangtze provinces was a long process. Only when it was complete in the twelfth and thirteenth centuries A.D., and the north subjected to destructive invasions from nomad peoples, did the central region come to balance the north. It gained an economic preponderance that has continued, although the contemporary development of mineral resources in the north promises to restore the old relationship.

The coastal provinces of south China were not a part of "China" before the first century B.C.; their people were akin to the Vietnamese. These provinces were incorporated into the Chinese empire under the Han dynasty in the first century B.C., but remained an essentially colonial region for several centuries thereafter, until fuller settlement in the T'ang period (seventh to tenth centuries A.D.) resulted in a greater assimilation of the original inhabitants. To this day Cantonese, unlike all other Chinese, call themselves *Tong Yan*, "men of T'ang," not *Han Jen*, "men of Han," which is the name all other Chinese use for themselves.

Although some cultural features remain diverse, and the spoken language is not uniform, there has been no firm basis for the growth and development of separate nations on the Chinese subcontinent. Despite apparent diversity, the topography really imposed unity, and the development of Chinese civilization tended to reinforce trends toward unity and to discourage those that made for divi-

A pottery gristmill shelters laborers operating machines that (from left to right) husk rice, grind corn, and winnow wheat. Rice is the typical crop of south China; corn and wheat grow in the north.

sion. To the Chinese, division became synonymous with weakness and strife; unity meant strength and peace. A writer of the fifteenth century opens his famous historical novel, the *Romance of the Three Kingdoms*, with the observation: "The empire when long united tends to break up; and when divided strives once more for unity."

There are no reliable figures for the Chinese population dating from before the first century B.C., which is earlier than available statistics for a large population elsewhere in the world. The Chinese began to take a count of heads at this time in connection with taxation purposes. It was not, as was long believed, a simple register of taxpaying families, each listed by the head of the family. Discoveries in the ruined sites of Han forts in the desert lands of Sinkiang and northwest Kansu provinces have shown that all members of a family, including young children, were listed. But there was an important distinction: the list was confined to taxpaying classes, thus excluding the aristocracy, much of the official class, and no doubt also the rather small class of slaves. The total recorded in the first century B.C. was over sixty millions. A century later it was rather less, not much exceeding fifty millions. This does not mean that the population as a whole had been reduced, but only that the number of taxpayers had diminished, for many millions had managed to get themselves out of paying taxes by becoming tenants on the tax-free estates of nobles.

On the evidence of these returns and other sources it is clear that in the first centuries B.C. and A.D., during the Han empire, the population was heavily concentrated in what is now north China. Population in the Yangtze valley was lighter, but increasing; in the far south it was still sparse. The Han empire, China's first long period of unity, saw a steady colonization of the Yangtze valley; but the colonization hardly affected the far south. Soon after the fall of the Han in the early third century A.D. the empire was invaded by the Tatars and divided into a northern part ruled by dynasties of Tatar conquerors and a southern part ruled by Chinese emperors from Nanking. This period of the Northern and Southern Empires, as it is called, saw a further massive colonization of the fertile Yangtze provinces. Many thousands of northern landowners migrated with their followers to the territory still ruled by their countrymen. On the other hand, the Tatar conquerors in the north were too few to make any deep impression on the huge Chinese population over which they ruled. The military aristocracy was Tatar in origin, but soon intermarried with Chinese aristocrats. The mass of the invading tribesmen seems to have become absorbed.

Intensive settlement of the far south had to wait until the T'ang dynasty, when Kuangtung and neighboring Kuangsi were colonized in strength by Chinese settlers from the north, many of whom were political exiles. The far south was in the T'ang period a kind of Chinese Siberia. The last area to be incorporated fully into the empire and settled by Chinese was the southwest, Kueichou and Yünnan provinces, which did not receive any large number of settlers until the last five hundred years, during the late Ming and the Manchu dynasties. To this day a very considerable part of the population of these provinces, and of Kuangsi, consists of so-called national minority peoples—Miao, Nosu, Chuang, Thai, and others—who continue to live either in the hill

Calligraphy, a refined and complex art, requires special tools, many of which are art works themselves—like the pressed-carbon inkcake (center), the porcelain and jade brushes (top), and the brush stand (bottom), shaped like a plum bough.

defined by Prime Minister Chou En-lai. Mandarin divides into subdialects: the Peking colloquial; the Yangtze, or southern, as it is called in Peking; and the variant forms spoken in Ssǔch'uan and Hunan. No person who has learned one of the forms of Mandarin Chinese would have any real difficulty in making himself understood in China, though he may find the speech of peasants hard to follow. The value of Mandarin is that all educated people can understand it, and this is as true in the southern dialect zone as in the rest of the country.

The major dialects of the coastal region are not innumerable; there are, in fact, only seven of them. The most northerly is the language of Wu, as it is known to history, although it is more often now called Shanghai dialect, because it is the prevailing speech of that great city. "Wu" is the ancient name for the Yangtze delta country of Kiangsu, where this dialect has long flourished. It differs much less from northern Standard Chinese than the other great southern dialects do. Next comes "Hokch'iu," which is the pronunciation in its native form of the city called Fu-chou, capital of Fukien province. This dialect has no great range beyond this city and its environs, but it enjoys a certain prestige as a result of its association with a famous city. It is also said by some linguists to preserve a near approximation to the pronunciation of the Han period (third century B.C. to third century A.D), when the province was first incorporated into China. Most of the population of Fukien speaks a dialect called Hokkien, named from their pronunciation of the word "Fukien." This is one of the major dialects of the south and of the overseas Chinese in southeast Asia. It is centered on the port of Amoy, and therefore it is often called Amoy dialect by foreigners. A little further south comes "Teochiu," which is how the name of the city of Ch'ao-

chou is pronounced by its inhabitants. Teochiu is also a major dialect, spoken more widely beyond China than within it.

Cantonese is the "Mandarin" of the south. The speech of the great and ancient city that has always been the unquestioned center of south China is distinguished, almost alone among the great dialects, by having a colloquial literature that has required the invention of some new ideograms. There are numerous country variations of Cantonese dialect, but the accent of the city itself is universally recognized as the pure form. It has definite links with the pronunciation and speech forms of the T'ang dynasty in the seventh century, the period when Canton was settled by men from the north. It is possible that a T'ang Chinese, returned today, would find Cantonese intelligible, but would not follow a word of what was said in his northern city of origin. A characteristic of Cantonese, familiar to the West, is to prefix the word "Ah" to the surname of anyone of whom one is speaking. It is not the equivalent of "Mr.," but rather less determinate. The usage is now found only in Cantonese; but several contemporary reports of speech by great persons of the T'ang court show them using "Ah" in precisely this way.

Hainanese, called Hailam by its speakers, is the dialect of the large island of Hainan in Kuangtung province. It is not closely related to the speech of the nearby mainland, but rather to that of Fukien, some hundreds of miles to the north. It seems possible that Hainan was settled by sea from Fukien, and not from Kuangtung. If so, Hainan at a remote period was the first settlement of overseas Chinese from Fukien. The last major dialect is called Hakka, a word that means "guest families" or "migrants." The Hakka speakers were in origin northern Chinese who fled south in great numbers before the terror of the Mongol invasions in the thirteenth century A.D.

Using a brush similar to the one on the opposite page, the famous Ming dynasty Emperor K'ang Hsi writes at a desk, in front of a picture of dragons.

Later they mixed with some of the native non-Chinese hill tribes and adopted elements of their language to form the new dialect. Hakka is still not so far removed from northern Standard Speech as to be wholly unintelligible to northerners. All these southern dialects are now spoken by as many, or more, people overseas as in their original districts. On the other hand, most of them are quite beyond the grasp of speakers of Standard Chinese.

The fact that dialects are spoken along the southeast coast and among overseas Chinese communities is often given more significance than it deserves by commentators who do not appreciate that all Chinese, of no matter what dialect, is written in one uniform script, equally intelligible to all who can read. Until forty years or so ago very many dialect speakers could not read. This was particularly true of the overseas migrants, who were mostly from poor peasant families. Dialect differences were therefore a real barrier, and in overseas communities this tended to create pockets of one or another dialect group. Men went by preference to the region where their speech was used. The spread of literacy, recently sharply accelerated, has reduced the importance of the dialects as a divisive force. At the same time the existence of the major dialects is a strong reason for the Chinese to retain their peculiar ideographic script.

The nature of the Chinese ideographic system can be easily grasped by comparing it with another ideographic system, which we all take for granted: the system of numerals called Arabic, but in reality of Indian origin. This is in world-wide use. When a speaker of English, French, Russian, or Hindi wants to write "five," he does not have to use the spelled word of his own language; he writes 5. The figure 5 is an ideogram or "character," divorced from sound, but carrying a meaning that is known to all who have learned simple

arithmetic, no matter how they pronounce the word 5 stands for. The meaning, moreover, has nothing whatever to do with the form of the ideogram. When we wish to write "fifty," we combine two ideograms and write 50, and so on for the largest and most complex numbers. Mathematics also uses a variety of other ideograms, such as +, =, —, and x. The Chinese made this invention also, and at a very early date, apparently independently; but they applied it to the whole range of language. Not only numbers but also words were rendered by an ideogram.

The basic principle of Chinese script is to use one ideogram for each word. It can be inferred that in remote antiquity the script was simple picture writing, although no examples have survived. Every concrete object was represented by a more or less stylized picture. A small number of Chinese ideograms, standing for obvious everyday objects, still retain enough of their simple pictorial construction

35

WILLIAM ROCKHILL NELSON GALLERY OF ART

midable obstacle than it was in the days when education was dominated by a scholar elite, who refused to simplify the laborious task of writing that they themselves had mastered. The difficulty of mastering the script gave standing and distinction to men who could read. In practice only those who could read fine literature and classical texts obtained the respect due to the educated man. Those who could merely get through a popular novel, write letters home, or keep accounts hardly considered themselves able to read, and would not have claimed such ability in the presence of a real scholar. Today mass education programs have created a huge class of readers, but they are readers who would be floored by the classical texts and by much of the scholarly literature of the past. For, apart from the need to recognize a great many ideograms to read such literature, it is also necessary to know how words have changed meaning over many centuries and to master a terse style that uses words with great precision and skill.

Because spoken Chinese is largely monosyllabic and has many homophones, the language employs combinations of words to elucidate meaning. One does not just say *chin* for "gold," for there are many other *chin* words with differing meanings. One says *huang chin*, "yellow gold," to clear up any doubt. But in writing Chinese this sort of qualification is unnecessary. The ideogram for "gold" is distinct and cannot be confused with other ideograms.

Perhaps the main reason for retaining the ideographic script is to preserve the unity of the nation. If it were abandoned, Cantonese, Hokkien, Teochiu, Hailam, and Hokchiu,

along with a number of less common dialects, would become, in effect, foreign languages, wholly unintelligible to speakers of other dialects or to the three quarters of all Chinese who use Mandarin. A second reason against adopting a new script is that it would result in the loss of all previous literature. Transliterating would not be the simple task of rendering ideograms into an alphabet. The terse style of traditional literature, the numerous homophones, could not merely be put into their alphabetic equivalent; they would not convey meaning for more than a few words together. It would be necessary to translate them into modern Chinese, to transliterate them. Such a task is obviously impossible—and it is pointless, for the quality of the original would be wholly destroyed.

For the benefit of Westerners a number of systems of Romanization have been developed for Chinese script. The earliest Sinologists were Jesuit missionaries in the late seventeenth and the eighteenth centuries. Because a great many of them were French, the earliest Romanizations render Chinese names and words in an orthography that could be understood by French readers. When the English, Dutch, and other Westerners came on the scene, they introduced their own versions, conforming to their own languages. Confusion threatened to be worse than if no system at all were in use. In the nineteenth century the predominance of French and English influences in Chinese scholarship moderated this babel to some degree. Many European scholars continued to use the Jesuit system. The English invented their own, which has gained great currency.

40

The English system is known as Wade-Giles, from the two scholars, both diplomats, who devised it in the second half of the nineteenth century. It was a noble but perhaps mistaken endeavor to render Chinese sounds as accurately as possible into a Romanized form that would be meaningful for all Western readers, no matter what their native language might be. This was impossible for the obvious reason that certain European languages give different values to the letters of the Roman alphabet. Unfortunately the initial consonant pronounced like the English *Ch* is very common in the Chinese language. By assigning *Ch'* to that consonant, Wade and Giles made it virtually certain that the French and other Continental scholars, who pronounce those letters in a different manner, would not follow their system.

There were other problems. The Chinese language has two forms of the *Ch* sound and two forms of the initial *T* sound. One is hard, and one "breathed," or soft. Wade and Giles render the hard *Ch* with *Ch* and indicate the soft *Ch* sound as *Ch'*. The same plan is used for the initial *T*. This has caused much difficulty for the English reader. "Chang" is not pronounced as it would appear to be from the way it is written, but as "Jang." "Ch'ang" is pronounced as we would normally expect "Chang" to be, for *J* in English is a harder sound than *Ch*. According to Wade and Giles, "Tien" is pronounced "Dien," whereas "T'ien" is pronounced with a *T* sound.

Wade and Giles failed to take into account the time-saving devices of the popular press. Hardly ever will a newspaper print these apostrophes, which their readers probably would not understand. So "Chang" and "Ch'ang," "Tien" and "T'ien," as well as very many other words, get the same simple treatment and appear without any apostrophe. In their hope of making a system useful to speakers of all European language, Wade and Giles gave peculiar and non-English values to many of the vowels. They ended by producing a system that has to be specially learned and could never be grasped without instruction. "Chou En-lai" is not "chow" to rhyme with "plow," or "En" to rhyme with "pen," or "lai" to rhyme with "say," but more nearly "Joe Un-lie."

For more than a century the Chinese themselves ignored all these attempts. They needed no Romanization. But gradually, as contact with the West increased, the need for an official system of Romanization became increasingly apparent. For a long time no Chinese government tackled this problem. The Post Office system was allowed to grow in a completely haphazard fashion, following rough approximations of the dialect forms, and elements of both the Wade-Giles and the French systems. Towns with the same name would appear with two spellings. What was "Pei Hai" in north China would be "Pak-hoi" in the Cantonese-speaking province of Kuangtung. Chinese scholars produced good and elaborate systems that rendered the tones of the Chinese language in Romanized spelling, but none of these systems was officially adopted. It was not until the Communist People's Republic was established that an official commission was given the task of devising a system that would allow the Chinese to render proper names and other words alphabetically.

For centuries China's educational and governmental bureaucracies were dominated by a scholar elite—a group of well-educated men who refused to permit any simplification of the highly complex system of Chinese writing they had mastered. Such scholar-officials are shown taking their leisure in a Yüan dynasty handscroll, Composing Poetry on a Spring Outing.

41

The Chinese had come to realize that an alphabetic system could be a useful aid to the rapid learning of the ideograms, and thus a tool in the campaign against illiteracy. Before the invention of the new system, the Chinese had difficulty reading foreign words and names, for their rendering by ideograms was very inefficient. Some foreign names, such as "Leigh" or "Hann," are easily converted into Chinese ideograms. Others, such as "Roosevelt" or "Russell," are almost impossible to render precisely. There is no initial *R* in Chinese and no final *T* or *L* (or many other letters). In Chinese documents these names appear translated as "Lo Ssu Fu" and "Lo Ssu." The reader needed to know more than how to read Chinese to make sense of these renderings.

The commission decided, before 1956, that they would not recommend the use of the Russian Cyrillic alphabet, but that the Latin alphabet would be used, "because it is the most widely employed." They then decided upon a system of Romanization that is in general more practical than either Wade-Giles and its derivatives, or the French system. It avoids the trap of unusual non-European initial consonants—such as the one Wade-Giles renders by *Hs*; for this sound it uses an *X*, and so the Chinese word for a county, *hsien*, in Wade-Giles, now becomes *xien*. The Latin alphabet and this system are now taught in all Chinese schools in the People's Republic. They are used to render place names, as on railway platforms, for the benefit of non-Chinese readers, and for rendering foreign words that appear in a Chinese text. The new custom of writing Chinese from left to right, horizontally across the page, facilitates the interposition of words in the Latin alphabet. In the past they would have to be written vertically, which was a nuisance both to printer and to reader. The new Chinese Romanization only attempts to render the sounds of Mandarin, not those of the dialects. It is now educational policy to teach Mandarin speech in all schools, as a second language for dialect speakers.

The decision, inevitable in the circumstances, to continue the use of the ideographic script, means that the ancient Chinese art of calligraphy can still flourish—and along with it traditional Chinese culture, with which this art is so inextricably linked. Either the Chinese keep their ideographic script and their culture (however they may choose to interpret it today) or they start afresh, without literature or tradition. No government, not excluding the enthusiasts of the Great Proletarian Cultural Revolution, has hinted at adopting the second daunting alternative.

A Ch'in dynasty earthenware sculpture shows two limp-limbed scribes with writing implements between them.

42

Kaogu Xuebao, 1959, NO. 9

2 The Dawn of China

(to 200 B.C.)

This bronze mask was discovered at An-yang in eastern China in the tomb of a ruler of the Shang dynasty—one of the earliest periods of Chinese history for which we have archeological evidence.

ACADEMIA SINICA, TAIPEI; COURTESY JAMES BURKE, *Life*

Knowledge of the real history of the Chinese people, as opposed to the traditional fictions, shows that it is much more recent than that of many of the other great ancient civilizations. Neolithic sites and artifacts do not antedate 3000 B.C. The Chinese bronze age cannot be shown to be earlier than 1500 B.C., but this date may change when fuller investigation has uncovered more sites. At the present time archeological knowledge of early China rests on very few fully excavated sites. Yet it must also be recognized that, although we have no record of Chinese civilization earlier than 1500 B.C., there is much to suggest a continuity between the earliest historical period and the long age of prehistory.

The historical cities of the Shang dynasty (from around 1500 to 1028 B.C.) are built on much older, prehistoric strata of occupation, running back to the neolithic period. In some few cases the artifacts used in Shang times are directly related in form and function to those found on neolithic sites. The old Chinese belief that their civilization developed in north China, without foreign influence, is on the whole strongly borne out by archeological discovery.

In the traditional history the Shang is the second dynasty. To the archeologist and modern historian it is the first of which there is clear evidence. The Shang kingdom was situated in northern China; two of its capital cities have been discovered at Ch'eng-chou and An-yang in Honan, both in the valley of the Yellow River. Tradition places the origin of the kingdom west of these cities, but this has not yet been confirmed by archeology.

The Shang sites have yielded very fine bronze vessels (used, it would seem, in religious rites), some stone carving, much pottery of high quality, and carved antlers and tusks. Animal remains in the tombs show that the Shang people were in touch with the east coast of China, and that the elephant was still to be found in some part of the country—most probably in the jungle that then covered the Yangtze valley. The tombs have also yielded inscribed oracle bones and tortoise shells, with the first-known examples of the Chinese written language.

Among the early Chinese, oracles were taken by writing a question on a tortoise shell or on the shinbone of an ox and then touching the shell or bone with a hot metal rod; the cracks thus made were then "read" by the priests to give an answer to the question asked of the oracle, who was, it seems, always a royal ancestor. "Should the king go hunting on such and such a day?" Answer: "Yes, favorable; so many stags, boar, or other game will be obtained." "Should the king go to war with such and such a people?" Answer: "Favorable; he will have victory and take many prisoners." Not all the answers were in favor; some advised against such expeditions.

These records are of great interest, but they leave many gaps in our knowledge of the Shang kingdom and its history. We do not know exactly how far it extended, or who were the neighbors against whom it waged war. The early ideograms are not always decipherable, especially when they refer to place names that have not survived. Many attempts to deduce the nature of the Shang social system, and to learn whether it was founded on slavery or serfdom, have been made from this material, but the evidence is very slender. It is clear that war prisoners were an important part of the spoils of victory, but how much the economy was based on slavery supported by war is quite uncertain.

The Shang culture was advanced in bronze metallurgy, and the Shang bronzes are not only beautiful but demonstrate a highly developed skill in casting. It is not at all easy to cast in a clay mold a bronze vessel weighing three fourths of a ton. Shang bronzes, and those of the succeeding Chou period, were cast in molds and not by the lost wax process, which prevailed in the ancient Middle East. Thus it would seem that metallurgy, or at least metallurgic techniques, developed independently in China.

It is clear that the earliest inscriptions so far found, at An-yang, are a relatively developed system of writing, a long way from simple picture writing. It proved possible to read these early records without much difficulty, although the form of the ideograms is archaic. There is thus a direct continuity between the oldest-known Chinese written inscriptions and the literature of the present time. This is unique and is the most-striking proof of the continuity that is so characteristic of China. There is every reason to think that the Shang kingdom was an early form of the Chinese state, and that its people were the ancestors of the Chinese, particularly of those that inhabit Honan and Hopei.

It may be that the Shang kept much fuller records than those found on the oracle bones. They had developed a system of writing that enabled them to keep such records, but none has survived. Probably in the Shang period, as in post-Shang times, books were written on strips of wood or bamboo, materials that rot away. All the Shang sites so far known were destroyed by floods of the Yellow River and buried deep in silt. These conditions quickly destroyed wood and textiles, although they favored the preservation of hard materials, such as bronze, stone, bone, and pottery. What is known of the history of the Shang is dependent, therefore, on the interpretation of the official history. The Shang, we are told, fell into decline after a long period of prosperity and finally came under the sway of a cruel tyrant, King Chou Hsin. According to the traditional history, he indulged in shameless orgies

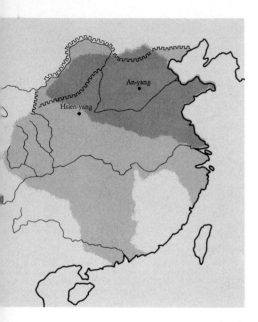

The Shang domain covered much of northern China (dark-shaded area). Approximately the same territory was governed by the early Chou; this area remained the center of Chinese culture during the Warring States period (481–221 B.C.), which began around the time of Confucius' death. With the establishment of the Ch'in dynasty in 221 B.C. came territorial expansion. From their capital at Hsien-yang, the Ch'in ruled a vast territory, including the old Shang domain and much of south China (the light-shaded area).

(which, as described, seem much more like fertility rites) and wantonly killed his ministers and loyal advisers if they crossed his will. Eventually, a man named Wen—the Chief of the West and the lord of Chou—threw off the Shang yoke. Wen's successor, Wu, led a great army eastward, defeated King Chou Hsin, sacked his city, and conquered the Shang kingdom. He was then recognized as king. His kingdom, centered on the present province of Shensi in northwest China, was called Chou, after the name of the state from which he had originated.

The fact that the Chou kingdom conquered and replaced the Shang kingdom is certainly historical; nor need there be any doubt that this victory was gained by King Wu. But it is far from certain what the true relationship had been between the king of Shang and the Chief of the West: whether it had been a feudal tie or whether the Chief of the West was really an independent tribal leader, perhaps ruling a people of somewhat different stock who had recently come under Shang cultural influence. These problems cannot be solved until more archeological work is done, especially in the west, the home of the Chou rulers.

It is certain that once in power the kings of Chou ruled—in name at least—over a very wide territory. Their kingdom stretched from Shensi eastward to the coast, and southward to the northern rim of the Yangtze valley, distances of more than six hundred miles each way. To control this great kingdom, the Chou kings instituted a system of fief holding, which has been called the Chinese feudal system.

The entire kingdom was divided into fiefs, some very large and some, it seems, quite small. It is probable that the largest feudatories, such as Ch'i in modern Shantung, were not in a real sense subordinate to the king of Chou, but were, rather, semi-independent tribes or kingdoms that had allied themselves with the Chou to overthrow the Shang. Most of the fiefs were given to the king's brothers, sons, and other relatives. When a fief-holder was not related, a fictitious kinship link was invented for him. The essence of the Chinese feudal system, as distinct from those that later arose in Europe and Japan, was that it was conceived of as an extended family system. The king was the head, the father. His brothers and cousins of the same generation, his sons and their cousins, and so on in a widening circle of kinship, were all members of the ruling family. As such, they each deserved a fief, or part of the family "property." They were accountable to the king for its government. They also had to raise followers and lead them in war if the king required. This last was the main way in which Chinese feudalism resembled that of other countries and ages.

The Chou took over from the Shang their writing, bronze culture, and religious system, although there is evidence to suggest that they also brought in their own practices and their own gods. Very soon the records become less scarce. Long inscriptions on early Chou bronze vessels record the investiture of noblemen with new fiefs won in war from the still-dissident supporters of the Shang and from other peoples in eastern China. These inscriptions tend to show that the clear-cut victory related by the traditional history is a considerable simplification. The Chou conquest, in eastern China at least, was slow and never complete. The Shang retained a large state, called Sung, which owed a nominal allegiance to the king of Chou.

What is known of the early Chou period, from around 1025 to 722 B.C., is rather sketchy. There is a much larger and longer series of bronze inscriptions than appear from the Shang era, but only a few of these throw direct light on the history of the age. There is

the traditional history, much of which is founded on a surviving early work, the *Shu Ching*, or *Book of Documents*, which is, in part, of early Chou date. Yet often the traditional history provides little more than a pedigree with a few facts added. This lack of record is to be explained in part by the fact that the early or Western Chou period ended in 722 B.C. with a catastrophe, the capture of the capital and its destruction by invading nomads. After the nomadic Jung people had overrun the Chou homeland in Shensi, the reigning king of Chou moved eastward and established his new capital at Lo-yang in Honan. The king appointed a lord to control the western borders and expel the Jung nomads. This he and his successors did, thus establishing in the ancient Chou homeland the foundation of a new kingdom, called Ch'in, which one day was to conquer all China.

As a result of the Jung invasion, royal power swiftly declined. In the age that is now called that of the Spring and Autumn Annals, from the ancient book that records some of its history, the Chou king in Lo-yang became a respected but almost powerless figure, investing feudal lords and carrying out ancient ceremonies, but exercising little real influence. The great feudatories began to lord it over the lesser ones; later they suppressed them and annexed their territory. Curiously enough this age of decline, which one might expect to be poorly recorded, is the first period when accurate and well-dated history appears in China. This may be an accident; such records could well have been kept earlier in the old Chou capital in western China. But Lo-yang survived much longer without suffering sack and ruin, and consequently its records survived also. Within a century of the move to the east, there is a relatively complete and detailed chronicle of the main events of the era. Toward the end of the Spring and Autumn

Annals period Confucius was teaching, and other philosophers were expounding their ideas. Literature was rapidly expanding, and the full light of history illuminates the scene.

It is thus possible to obtain a clear and detailed understanding of the nature of Chinese feudal society, at least as it was when beginning to decay. All political power was held by the aristocracy, and in particular by the lord of each fief. Whether he held a high rank, such as that translated as duke, or a low one, such as that we call lord, he was the effective sovereign, only remotely responsible to the king, who was quite unable to enforce his own authority. All the king could do, and often did, was to sanction the aggression of one fiefholder against another to punish an erring lord. Since the transgressor often won the battle, this method of disciplining feudal lords had its defects.

In a polygamous society kinship was widely diffused. A large class of aristocrats was cre-

Meat, grains, and occasionally even deceased children were buried in Chinese tombs in funerary urns, such as the polished earthenware one above, which was made around 2000 B.C. The wide ruff of the masked figure below, dating from the same period, suggests that the piece may have served as the lid of another mortuary urn.

Unluckily, one king was so determined to make his favorite lady laugh, she being of a glum disposition, that he had the fires lit for no cause. He achieved his aim of amusing the lady when his princes and lords arrived post-haste in warlike array. But thereafter nobles were not inclined to take these summonses very seriously. Incidents of this kind, carefully recorded, stand as warnings to future rulers not to trifle with the powers of government, but to treat their subjects with sincerity.

According to the *li*, war must be conducted on restrained lines. Wars between the feudal lords were frequent and could not be suppressed by the king; but for many centuries they were fought more for sport than for permanent conquests. The nobility rode in chariots, with footmen attending them; cavalry had not yet been adopted by the Chinese. It was considered wrong—unsportsmanlike—to attack a warrior who had been thrown from his chariot; one should wait until he could remount it or get another.

There were other rules that were observed, at least sometimes. It was considered contrary to the *li* to attack an army when it was crossing a river; the right thing to do was to wait until it had formed up on the bank. This neglect of obvious strategic and tactical advantages demonstrates that war was not yet a very serious matter. Several instances of the observance of such rules are given in contemporary or near-contemporary chronicles. If the consequences were sometimes disastrous to those who observed the *li*, they were not always so; the historians are happy to record occasions when the prince who behaved correctly scored a resounding victory.

By the time of Confucius, around 500 B.C., this decorous mode of behavior was yielding to sterner and more cruel conduct. In large part this was caused by the rise to power of two states that did not wholly share the cultural

ated, men who held land under the duke or lord, just as he supposedly held his fief under the king. Aside from being the landowners, the aristocracy, called the *chun tzu*, the "sons of lords," were the warriors and the scholars. One could also say they were the priests, for no professional priesthood developed in China, and the aristocratic class performed priestly functions. In sharp contrast to their counterparts in feudal Europe, the Chinese nobility were literate. A class with such a strong position in society naturally left little on record that did not concern it. We know a great deal about feudal aristocratic society and very little about the peasantry who worked the land.

In feudal times, as depicted in ideal colors by the early Chinese writers, the conduct of the nobility was regulated by the *li*, a term that has usually been translated as the priggish "rules of propriety," but that would be better explained as a mixture of courtesy and chivalry sanctified by religion. According to the *li*, every lord must be entirely loyal to the "Son of Heaven," the title that only the king of Chou could assume. The lord must come to his aid when beacon fires burn on the mountaintops.

heritage of the Middle Kingdom, as the central group of feudal states under the king of Chou were now known. One state was Ch'u in the Yangtze valley, the other was Ch'in in the northwest, the region of the present-day provinces of Kansu and Shensi. Both states were somewhat alien. Ch'u contained many peoples who would today be styled as national minorities. Its spoken language was markedly different from that of the Middle Kingdom. The underlying culture of Ch'u was of southern origin. The state had a long undefined southern frontier adjoining barbarian lands, into which it was expanding. Ch'in, likewise, had incorporated foreign tribes, perhaps of nomadic stock, and was often at war with the wild nomads of the Inner Mongolian steppe. In their frontier wars, where no *li* was observed, the two border states learned a harsher style of warfare. When they turned their arms on their neighbors in the Middle Kingdom, they used the new methods—and were often victorious.

Ch'u had never admitted the suzerainty of the king of Chou. The ruler of Ch'u was styled "king" in his own country, but his title was not accepted by the men of the Middle Kingdom. His pretensions were a frequent cause of quarrel. The duke of Ch'in did not usurp any higher title for many years, but once he did assume the royal title, his action was imitated by the leaders of the other great feudal states. The lifetime of Confucius witnessed the beginning of the end of Chinese feudalism. Before he died around 480 B.C. small states were being annexed by their neighbors, and wars were becoming dangerous exercises in ambition rather than noble pastimes. Members of the old aristocracy, sometimes displaced by the fall of their own prince or driven into exile by jealous rivals, began to wander from court to court, offering their services and their schemes to any ruler who would employ them. The old

local loyalties were breaking down.

In 403 B.C. the collapse of the large state of Tsin in north-central China was the signal for the intensification of struggle and continuous warfare, which has earned for this age the name of the Warring States. The period lasted for two hundred sixty years, from around 480 to around 220 B.C., and presents a most complex story of intrigue, aggression, and treachery. There are certain dominant features that are clear enough. The object of policy and of war was to win a position of complete supremacy, which at first was conceived of in terms of hegemony over the other states, then as outright conquest and the creation of a great unified empire.

All the weaknesses and vices of the sovereign state system—as seen in our own time—are most clearly illuminated in the story of the Warring States. Selfish policy, failure to unite to resist aggression, ruthless exploitation of victory gained by treachery, the pursuit of transitory advantages that are not of basic importance, all these traits appear in the history of the Warring States of China. Since the historians believed that they should record errors as a warning to future rulers, we have in the history of the times a more candid chronicle of political folly than any other culture has produced—including our own.

The main contestants were Ch'u, the great southern kingdom, and Ch'in, the northwestern power. In between, and for long a check to their ambitions, were Ch'i, a powerful state on the seacoast of Shantung and Hopei, and Han, Wei, and Chao, the states that had partitioned the fallen Tsin. These three states, called the Three Tsin, were smaller than their rivals, but more thickly inhabited, much richer, and more advanced in civilization. Thus they were able to remain in the contest until the end, although none of them had any real hope of coming out the victor.

By its size and by its long record of successful northward expansion, Ch'u seemed likely to be the winner at first. Its success was frustrated by the rise of two new southern kingdoms, Wu in the Yangtze delta region, between modern Nanking and Shanghai, and later Yüeh in present-day Chekiang province, which was peopled by the same stock that later spread southward down to the coast to Vietnam. Wu challenged the supremacy of Ch'u in the Yangtze valley and inhibited its advance. Ultimately Yüeh challenged Wu, and after an epic struggle, wiped out the Wu state. But the resources of the still thinly-settled south were insufficient for prolonged war and for the foundation of an empire. This proved to be the weakness of Ch'u as well as of Yüeh. Ch'in, meanwhile, had been steadily seizing territory from its eastern neighbors, the Three Tsin—Han, Wei, and Chao. They tried to form leagues to stop Ch'in. Appeals to Ch'i on the seacoast were not always heeded. Ch'i had no frontier with Ch'in and did not feel concerned. In this its ruler made a great error.

The last phase of the Warring States era, coincident with the long reign of the king of Ch'in, Chao Hsiang (302–251 B.C.), marks the ascendancy of Ch'in and the increasing weakness of its rivals. These states survived, although they were frequently invaded, suffering ruinous slaughter, and were forced to yield territory. Often they were mutually hostile, and although they sometimes united, they never effectively opposed the progress of Ch'in. In 256 B.C. Ch'in actually dethroned the last king of Chou and ended that ancient dynasty. The event was no longer of least importance. The king of Chou had been a nominal ruler in a single city for several generations.

The final victory of Ch'in was not reserved for the great, ruthless conqueror Chao Hsiang.

It was left to his successors, above all to his grandson, who is known to history as Shih Huang Ti, the "First Emperor." There is a very strong probability that this future conqueror of all China was illegitimate, the son of a merchant, and not the real heir of the royal house of Ch'in. There had been brief troubles at court when old King Chao Hsiang died, and his immediate successors were short-lived. One of these, King Chuang Hsiang, had been sent as a hostage to the court of Chao when a young man. It was there that he became enamored of a beautiful girl, the concubine of another man, Lü Pu-wei; he carried her off to Ch'in, with, it is said, the consent of Lü Pu-wei himself. Shih Huang Ti was born to this woman eight months later, but rumor alleged that the child was the son of Lü Pu-wei and not of Chuang Hsiang, who later became king.

Shih Huang Ti is one of the great villains of the Confucian historians; he is the man who burned the books and suppressed the schools of philosophy. It is to be expected that the scholars would dig out and report any discreditable story about this hated figure; but there is at least some evidence that the tale of his origins may be true. When grown to man-hood, the king learned what men said of his birth. His mother had not lived the pure life that Chinese custom expected of a widow; she had remained on very friendly terms with Lü Pu-wei, who had been loaded with titles and honors. The king confined his mother to a secluded country palace and ordered Lü Pu-wei to leave court to reside on his own estates. Shortly afterward he wrote to Lü asking some awkward questions, including: "What connection do you have with the royal house that entitles you to bear the rank of prince?" He then ordered Lü Pu-wei to retire to Ssǔch'-uan. Lü preferred to take his own life rather than go into exile. Shih Huang Ti could thus not actually be accused of parricide.

Once he had established his authority at home, the king of Ch'in resumed the onslaught against his surviving rivals. In ten years he achieved their total destruction by a series of ruthless aggressions in which his generals commanded in the field, for Shih Huang Ti was not himself a warrior. In 231 B.C. the state of Han was conquered and the royal family exterminated. Chao was the next and received similar treatment. Wei followed in 225 B.C., and again the royal house was wiped out. Next Ch'in attacked its greatest surviving

A foiled attempt to assassinate Shih Huang Ti, builder of the Great Wall, is shown on a Han dynasty tomb bas-relief. In the detail above, taken from a rubbing of the original carved relief, the assassin retreats (left) after plunging his sword into the pillar at center instead of into the emperor (right). Beside the pillar lies a box containing the head of one of the emperor's mortal enemies—a gift from the would-be assassin, brought to gain an audience with Shih Huang Ti.

51

The turquoise-inlaid bronze sword at left dates from around 300 B.C. The bronze dagger-axe beside it, probably used in religious ceremonies, may once have been fixed to a wooden handle.

foe, Ch'u, and overcame it in 223 B.C. This time the royal house was merely carried off into captivity. Yen, a kingdom based on present-day Peking, was destroyed in 222 B.C. No mercy was shown its royal house, which a few years earlier had plotted to have the king of Ch'in assassinated, and had nearly succeeded. Last of all Ch'i, in the east, seeing no hope, surrendered. Its royal family was taken captive to Ch'in; they were left in misery and are said to have perished from starvation and neglect. At no time in the record of the conquests of Ch'in was there any example of mercy, humanity, or greatness of heart. Chinese historians recording the violent end that soon thereafter befell the Ch'in point out that they reaped what they had sown—men of blood ended in a bloodbath.

Though the period was one of savage wars, it was also a time of great intellectual activity. The age of the treacherous, scheming ministers and ruthless warrior-monarchs was the same age as that of the philosophers and writers whose works are the classics of early Chinese literature. It is characteristic of Chinese culture that the worlds of the sword and the pen are not remote from each other. The well-known writers and teachers of the Warring States period include ministers in the service of warlike kings; and many philosophers sought and obtained positions of influence at the courts of these rulers. The philosophers were one and all politically minded. Whether their theories called for the unification of world by force, or by love, or by inaction, they were all engaged in the great problem of their day, which was no longer the restoration of a ruined feudal system but rather the establishment of the proper basis on which a universal empire could be built.

The term that came into use for "empire," *t'ien hsia*, meaning literally "under heaven," that is, the whole known world, itself gives

evidence of the way thought was now turning. It is also important to remember that "empire" and "emperor," which the Western nations have used for the Chinese institution, are rather misleading, as the original Chinese words do not have the military connotations that our terms derive from their Roman origin. The emperor of China was not an *imperator*—a commander. He was something much nearer to a pope. His priestly function was more important than his military authority, which was delegated to generals. The words *huang ti*, which are translated "emperor," mean "august ruler," and there is good reason to think that in high antiquity the word *ti* originally meant "ancestor." It was the father image rather than the military image that lay behind the Chinese conception of a world ruler. The empire, the "under heaven," was the human family—simply a great family enlarged to embrace all mankind and presided over by the father, the "august ancestor." The thinking of the philosophers was social as well as political; it was necessary, they believed, to find the right social structure from which to project the political form of the state and determine its moral basis for rule. Most agreed that the family provided a proper model for the state.

The Ch'in conquest not only unified China by destroying all the separate kingdoms, but it also brought about a very far-reaching social revolution. The new state was organized on a centralized basis. The former kingdoms were ruled by military officers from Ch'in and divided up into new units, called commanderies, which were rather less than one-third the size of modern Chinese provinces. The new empire covered not only the old Middle Kingdom of Chou but also the Yangtze valley and the far western provinces of Ssŭch'uan and Kansu, which Ch'in had annexed. Soon some authority was imposed on the far south—the coast down to Canton and the region around that city. Only the southwestern region of modern China remained beyond the reach of Ch'in power. To secure this vast domain, Shih Huang Ti, or the "First Emperor," as the conquering king of Ch'in now styled himself, had the aristocracy of the fallen kingdoms transported to Ch'in, where, it seems, they were allowed to live under surveillance. No local leadership potentially hostile to the conqueror must be left in the provinces. Some of his counselors advised him to re-create the feudal kingdoms and endow his own numerous sons with them, but this policy was firmly opposed by Li Ssŭ, Shih Huang Ti's chief minister.

Li Ssŭ was not a native of Ch'in, but came from Ch'u, a country that he had left as a young man to seek fortune as a wandering scholar. He was a firm adherent of the Legist school of thought, which believed in government by harsh laws and opposed as useless all activity but agriculture and war. In Ch'in these views were welcome, and Li Ssŭ soon rose high in the service of the king. He opposed any restoration of feudalism, no matter who would be the beneficiaries. He argued that the ancient model of the Chou kingdom was a false guide to follow, for times were different. Chou feudalism had, in time, led to the complete loss of the royal authority and ended in the ceaseless strife of the Warring States. He suspected that those who spoke in favor of restoring feudalism were secret supporters of Confucian doctrine, which he abhorred as the antithesis of his own views. A forceful man and an able administrator, he exercised great influence over the new emperor.

The emperor decided not to restore any fiefs, but to keep the empire united under his direct authority. When, some years later, the conservatives once more raised the question and again cited their antique precedents, Li Ssŭ still more forcefully denounced them. Having the emperor's support, he proposed a

way to stop agitation for the restoration of feudalism: all the books of the schools opposed to the Legists and all historical records except those of Ch'in were to be surrendered to the magistrates, under pain of harsh penalties, to be burned.

Li Ssŭ's advice was taken; a law proscribing all literature, with just a few exceptions, was passed and enforced. Scholars who resisted or hid their books were put to death. The schools of philosophy came to an end, teaching of their doctrines was forbidden, and all education was entrusted to the magistrates and regional officials, who taught only Legist doctrine. For centuries there has been much debate on the question of how far this proscription was effective. The decree was issued in 213 B.C. In 210 the First Emperor died, and within a very few years after that the Ch'in empire collapsed into utter chaos. The enforcing of the decree in any organized manner cannot have lasted more than five years, but twenty or more were required before it was repealed under the new Han dynasty.

It is certain that much of the old literature did perish, and a great deal of what has survived is in the form of fragmentary and reconstructed texts. But it is not certain that the disappearance resulted directly from the Ch'in burning of the books. In the turbulent years that followed the collapse of Ch'in, many libraries, including the imperial one at the capital, were sacked and burned. It does seem that the books most revered by the Confucians were singled out for destruction by the First Emperor. On the other hand, the Confucian scholars risked their lives to hide these works and keep them from being destroyed by the agents of the emperor.

Having destroyed the intellectual basis of the opposition, the Ch'in government set about enforcing its own system, based on the Legist principle of harsh laws, with the ut-

More lavishly decorated than the weapons opposite, this ceremonial axe, which may have been used in Shang dynasty sacrifices, has a jade blade and a handle heavily inlaid with turquoise.

53

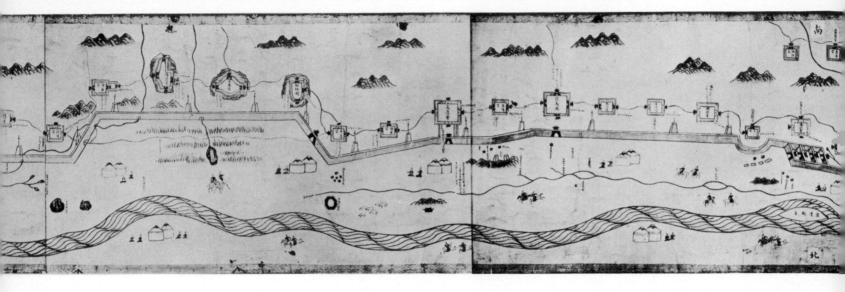

most rigor. The whole country was ruled with an iron hand. Huge numbers were condemned to forced labor for trivial breaches of the law and were sent to build the Great Wall along the northern frontier. This vast construction, which still tops the mountain ranges between the sea at Shan-hai Kuan and the borders of the deserts of Sinkiang, fourteen hundred miles to the west, was not entirely the work of the First Emperor. Earlier, northern kingdoms had built stretches of it to guard the passes against nomad incursions. Ch'in built long connecting sections to link individual walls, and completed the huge project. Later writers condemned the project for the cruelty practiced on those forced to labor at it as much as they did the burning of the books.

The question of how far the Wall was, in fact, a useful defense has also been debated. There can be no doubt that such a rampart did check nomad raids. It is not easy to get horses over a twenty-foot wall, and still harder to make a rapid retreat with large flocks and herds of captured animals when such an obstacle lies in one's path. Raiders who hoped to penetrate deep into China had to try to capture one of the passes; but these were guarded by strong garrisons in walled fortresses. The length of the Wall along the mountaintops was not manned in strength—it would have required an army of millions—but it was patrolled by watchmen, who could signal from one of the wall's numerous towers to the garrison forts when raiders were seen approaching. Therefore the Wall had a real military value against nomadic horsemen. Subsequent rulers may have been grateful to the First Emperor for undertaking this gigantic construction, but it remained unpopular, and the em-

peror of Ch'in was not given any public praise for his work.

Having pacified the whole country, defended it from invasion with the Wall, uprooted the aristocracy, destroyed the schools of philosophy, put the scholars out of employment, and removed their influence on education, the First Emperor could find time for other far-reaching plans. Roads were built to connect his capital, Hsien-yang in Shensi, with all parts of the empire. Weights and measures were standardized. There was a reform of ideograms, imposing on the whole empire the forms that were used in Ch'in. Commerce, of which the Legists did not approve, was restricted and heavily taxed. Agriculture, which they regarded as one of man's more justifiable activities, was encouraged.

Perhaps unintentionally, a most significant reform was undertaken, which proved to be of long-lasting importance. Under feudalism the lord owned the land, and the peasants were his serfs, bound to the soil and required to fight for him in time of war. The new laws allowed any man, rich or poor, to own a farm, so long as he paid a land tax. Feudal holdings were broken up. The result was that in the last years of Ch'in, and still more in the succeeding Han empire, there arose the social structure that was to persist in rural China for more than two thousand years, until it was overturned by the Peoples' Republic: the landlord-tenant relationship. Rich and powerful men bought up the land, and leased it to tenants to farm. Some peasants managed to acquire their own farms, but exposed to the risks of flood or drought, they were often forced eventually to sell out to a rich landlord. It can be argued that the free purchase and sale of land is a so-

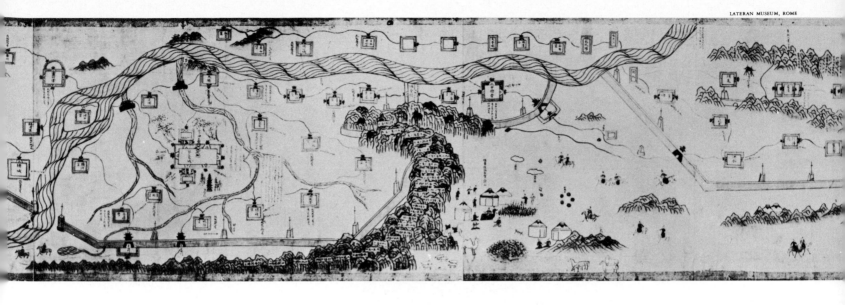

cial advance on serfdom and feudalism; it can also be shown that the tenant peasantry suffered as much, perhaps more, under the new system than they had under the old, when at least they were owned by someone who wanted to preserve his property alive and in working order.

The First Emperor, who, fearing assassination, lived in utmost seclusion, liked to travel nonetheless and see the world he had conquered. He made two major journeys, to the south and the east—to the Yangtze valley and the east coast country—being particularly attracted to the latter region because it was the native land of an active cult of magicians, who promised him the drug of immortality. This was to be obtained, they assured him, only from the Immortals who inhabited the enchanted isles of the Eastern Sea. It was necessary to make suitable offerings to the Immortals before they would part with the drug, and this could only be done if the emperor sent an expedition, under the command of a magician, an expedition made up of costly presents and of several hundred young boys and girls who were particularly pleasing to the Immortals. The emperor believed this tale and fitted out the expedition under the leadership of one magician. It sailed away, never to return. (It has long been conjectured that the coast people already knew of Japan, and that the enterprising magician took himself and his young followers off to that country and there founded a settlement.)

On his second journey to the east coast the emperor fell ill and died. This event, in 210 B.C., brought about the crisis that was soon to destroy his empire. The crown prince was far away on the northern frontier; he disagreed

with much of the severity of his father's policy, and although there had been no open breach between father and son, the crown prince would obviously not give his trust to those ministers who had inspired the harsh laws under which the empire groaned. One of the few men close to the emperor, who could see him at all times, was the chief eunuch, Chao Kao. He had reason to dislike the crown prince and had won the confidence of a younger son of Shih Huang Ti, a vain and frivolous youth, who happened to be in the east with the emperor when he died. In his last hours Shih Huang Ti had written and signed a decree appointing the crown prince his successor, and ordered it to be sent off immediately. But Chao Kao held it up. He then approached the minister Li Ssŭ, who was also with the emperor, and after pointing out that he, Li Ssŭ, could expect at best disgrace and discharge if the crown prince came to the throne, persuaded Li Ssŭ to join in a secret plot.

A false decree was sent off to the crown prince, ordering him to take his own life. The commander in chief on the northern frontier, General Mêng T'ien, was ordered to come to the capital for investigation, it being alleged that he and the crown prince had formed a conspiracy against the emperor. The younger son was then acknowledged as emperor, but the death of his father was kept secret, and the court hastily set out for Hsien-yang, the capital of the Ch'in empire, a city which lay more than six hundred miles to the west.

The dead emperor was placed in his traveling sedan, with drawn curtains. No one was allowed to attend him except Chao Kao. It was summer; the corpse began to decay, and

Three quarters of the Great Wall's length is accurately mapped on an eleven-foot-long scroll dating from the eighteenth century. Like the small section seen above, the entire scroll is drawn from an alien's point of view— looking across the Wall from the barbarian-inhabited north (bottom). The meandering Yellow River bisects the military map, which indicates precise distances between one town and another, and gives details of each garrison's strength, names of barbarian chieftains, and locations of wells in arid areas.

55

Sacrifices—human as well as animal—were common in prehistoric China; the lid of this bronze vessel depicts a sacrificial ceremony. The vessel contained cowrie shells, used as a medium of exchange.

to conceal this embarrassing fact, the conspirators had a cart of rotting fish follow the imperial sedan, between it and the soldiers of the guard. No one dared to inquire why His Majesty should choose to be accompanied by such an unpleasant cargo. Thus it was not until after the court had reached the capital that the death of the emperor was announced. Meanwhile, the crown prince, deceived by the false decree, had insisted on carrying out the First Emperor's supposed order, and had taken his own life. General Mêng T'ien, being more suspicious, tried to raise the army against the usurpers, but it refused to follow him. He was arrested and put to death. The younger son was placed on the throne, with the title Erh Shih Huang Ti, the "Second Emperor." When his father had assumed the title Shih Huang Ti, the "First Emperor," he had intended that

subsequent rulers should be styled "Second Emperor," "Third Emperor," and so on for "ten thousand ages"—for the idea that the house of Ch'in should lose the throne was not to be admitted.

Chao Kao was now the intimate counselor of the new emperor, who was wholly unfit to govern. He left everything to his eunuch favorite. Li Ssŭ, alarmed by the reckless conduct of affairs, began to remonstrate, but Chao Kao kept him from seeing the emperor. For the first year of the new reign all seemed well. The Second Emperor even made his own progress to the eastern provinces, but the fact that the strong hand of Shih Huang Ti was gone was soon recognized by the millions of malcontented subjects who had suffered under his harsh rule. The harshness was increased in the new reign, for Chao Kao urged his master to apply the laws more rigidly still and increase the penalties for breaking them.

Suddenly revolt broke out, started by a simple officer who was charged with the task of conducting criminals to exile. He was delayed by bad weather, and knowing that no excuse for unpunctuality would be accepted, chose to rebel rather than submit to the death penalty. He enlisted to his cause the criminals who had been placed under his control. Almost at once he was imitated in all parts of the country. Everywhere the people rose; within a few weeks the whole empire was in confusion. Chao Kao kept the news of these events from his master. When Li Ssŭ declared that this policy of deception was fatal, the two conspirators quarreled. Chao Kao accused Li Ssŭ of treason, had him arrested and later put to death. From that moment on all was lost for the Ch'in. There was no one competent to take command against the rebellions. Able officers were in charge of large forces, but Chao Kao feared to employ them. He still kept the emperor in total ignorance of what was going on throughout the vast empire.

When this finally proved impossible, Chao Kao decided to rid himself of a master who would reproach him for his perfidy. Having brought men disguised as rebels into the palace, he roused the deluded emperor in the middle of the night, showed him the alien-looking soldiers in the courtyard, and declared that rebels had surprised the palace. The only thing the emperor could do to avoid a horrible death at their hands was to take his own life before he was captured. Erh Shih Huang Ti believed him and drank poison. Chao Kao then put another young prince on the throne. Since this time more than half the empire, including all the conquests of Ch'in, were in open revolt, he decided that the new monarch could not be styled "emperor," but merely "king of Ch'in"; apparently he hoped to appease the rebel leaders by surrendering most of the empire to them and abolishing the rank of emperor.

The young prince was rightly doubtful of Chao Kao's loyalty. He took an early opportunity of summoning him to an audience, at which he had the unsuspecting eunuch slaughtered. But it was too late. Within a few weeks one of the rebel leaders advanced almost unopposed upon Hsien-yang and captured the city. The ephemeral king of Ch'in surrendered. He was spared by the rebel leader Liu Pang; but later he was massacred together with all other members of the royal house by that rebel's superior officer, Hsiang Yü. These two leaders, Liu Pang and Hsiang Yü, were soon to quarrel and contest the supreme power. Liu Pang, the victor, became the founder of the great Han dynasty.

The first intention of the rebels was to restore the fallen feudal kingdoms. Scions of their royal houses or purported royal heirs were discovered in hiding and placed upon their ancestral thrones. But the real power lay with the rebel leaders who were not men of royal descent. Liu Pang was a peasant who had become a village headman. Hsiang Yü was an aristocrat from Ch'u, in the south, and the descendant of a family of hereditary generals in Ch'u. But most of the soldiers of fortune who joined the fray were of obscure origins.

Nothing could long prevent an all-out struggle for power among the rival rebel leaders. For his share of the spoils Liu Pang had received the land of Han, one third of the kingdom of Ch'in. He took an early opportunity to dethrone the other two "kings" and to seize all Ch'in for himself. It was a strong base, guarded by the mountains, and known as the Land within the Passes. Hsiang Yü tried to oust him, but he was too harassed by other aspirant chiefs in the east to give his full attention to Liu Pang. Hsiang Yü had set up the puppet king of Ch'u as an emperor, but before long dethroned him and put him to death. He then assumed the supreme power himself, but not the title. A war of four years followed in which Hsiang Yü, a brilliant tactician, won the victories, and Liu Pang, the cunning peasant, won the campaigns.

Liu Pang was shrewd and persistent, holding steadily to his main purpose, and not diverted by seeming easy opportunities. He won the confidence of his followers, and he treated the people of his newly acquired kingdoms with justice, reducing their taxes while diminishing the harsh penalties of Ch'in law. He was a very capable organizer but not a brilliant warrior. Hsiang Yü, on the other hand, was an aristocrat by birth, with all the virtues and defects of his class. He was a huge man, handsome, brave, generous when in the mood, cruel and savage when crossed. A poet of some distinction, ambitious and impatient, he lacked strategic insight, but he rarely lost a battle. He had concentrated on pacifying the

This painted wooden figure of a man was found in a late Chou dynasty tomb.

east and north of China, thus allowing Liu Pang to consolidate the west. In four years the story of Ch'in's expansion, which had taken nearly three hundred years to achieve, was re-enacted, for the Han kingdom of Liu Pang now played the role of Ch'in, and Hsiang Yü in the east was cast in the part of the old rulers of the eastern kingdoms. Ultimately Liu Pang conquered the north, then turned south and crushed Hsiang Yü in the valley of the Huai River, between the Yangtze and Yellow rivers. Hsiang Yü broke out of encirclement; but without followers and unable to avoid pursuit, he took his own life.

The rebellions against Ch'in had been raised to abolish the tyrannical rule of the new empire. But their result was the refoundation of that empire by the king of Han, who at once took the imperial title. The real work of the Ch'in, the unification of China and the destruction of the feudal state system, could not be undone. By the end of the war between Liu Pang and Hsiang Yü it does not appear that anybody really wanted to restore the old order. The first Han emperor did make some gestures toward local feeling, partly because he had to try to conciliate powerful generals who had fought for him. These men were rewarded with kingdoms that were neither so independent nor so large as the old ones and that were safely wedged between imperial territories. Within a few years Liu Pang eliminated all the generals and decreed that only members of his own family could hold a fief. Before many generations had passed, fief-holders had little more than honorary titles; various devices for reducing their status, such as dividing every "kingdom" equally among all the late king's sons (and there could be many), diminished their power to insignificant dimensions.

For the first two generations the policy of the Han rulers was pacific. The country was greatly devastated and exhausted by the long wars, with only the brief interval of the Ch'in empire as a respite. The Ch'in period had been one of very harsh oppression and had done little to restore the ruined economy that Shih Huang Ti had inherited.

The first Han emperor, Liu Pang, who is known to history as Han Kao-tsu, a posthumous title meaning the "high ancestor of Han," was probably almost illiterate; he had no interest in scholars or books. If he did not enforce the Ch'in proscription, he equally did nothing to encourage the revival of learning or the recovery of the lost literature. The court was rather more inclined to Taoism than to classical literature, and it was to be several years before the Confucian scholars acquired a dominant influence over the government and education. Had the Han dynasty proved as short-lived as the Ch'in, it may be doubted whether the Confucian historians would have granted it much praise. It was the later reigns, when Confucianism was in favor, and the long duration of the new empire that won the approval of the Confucian scholars for the Han dynasty.

China did not take assured form until fifteen hundred years from the earliest recorded period of Chinese history. During that long interval it was really divided among several kingdoms, large and small, which were very loosely associated in a cultural union. Even the idea of a unified empire covering the whole Chinese world cannot be shown to have emerged until the fourth century B.C. The fact that once formed, it proved to be the most enduring political system, and ultimately became the normal state organization, proves that the cultural relationship among the old regions of China was most powerful, and that there was no lasting basis in ethnic differences or in regional characteristics for the development of several separate "Chinese" nations.

army marching across the deep valleys and rugged peaks of the Yellow River region on their way to Ch'ang-an.

MUSEUM OF FINE ARTS, BOSTON, WILLIAM AMORY GARDNER FUND AND ANNIE ANDERSON HOUGH FUND

3 The Sages

A bronze incense burner, dating from the Sung dynasty, shows a water buffalo and its rider, who is thought to be the sage Lao Tzŭ, founder of Taoism.
WORCESTER ART MUSEUM

In most countries of the world the myths of the creation, the story of early mankind, and the legends of the antique heroes form part of the religious system, enshrined in epics and in drama. Whether this was ever the case in China seems doubtful; there such stories are found not in epic poems but in history, history written very many centuries after the alleged events and presented as if verifiable source material existed. Except for a small number of bas-reliefs, themselves no earlier than the first century B.C., nearly the only sources for the Chinese myths and legends are the writings of the historian Ssŭ-ma Ch'ien, who flourished around the turn of the first century B.C., and those of later historians who copied him or, occasionally, varied his tales. In the writings or recorded sayings of the Chinese philosophers, such as Confucius, some reference to the legendary Sages of remote antiquity can be found; but the connected story of these Sages and of the legendary heroes occurs only in the official history.

At an early date the distinction between Chinese and other civilizations becomes apparent. To the Chinese it was the story of mankind, not the action of the gods, that mattered. In order to make the early legends acceptable to a society infused with a humanistic outlook, the legends were recast as history. According to this history, the people of the world—which meant northern China—lived like animals at first, without shelter or clothing. They preyed on other animals for food and had no knowledge of gods or of the arts. They were not the noble savages of European tradition, but brute beasts. A Sage arose among them whose name, Yü Tsao, means "shelter maker"; he taught the people to form encampments and make shelters of branches and timber. A successor invented fire and cooking, and he in turn was followed by a personage named Fu Hsi, dated as living around 2950 B.C., who proclaimed himself the first monarch and instituted many of the basic customs of Chinese society. He had a fixed residence at Ch'eng-chou in Honan, a town that exists today. He forbade the intermarriage of people with the same patrilineal ancestry. He invented music and extended his kingdom—already described as an empire—to the eastern coast. In this history practically the only characteristic of Fu Hsi that is not normally human is his long reign, which lasted 115 years.

Fu Hsi was succeeded by Shên Nung, the "Divine Cultivator," who invented agriculture and made the Chinese abandon hunting for farming. His reign, which lasted 140 years, also witnessed the first occurrence of war, in the form of a rebellion against him in 2698 B.C., led by his successor Huang Ti, the "Yellow Emperor." Huang Ti virtually dethroned the aged Shên Nung, and then suppressed numerous rebellions against his own authority—as many historical emperors were later to do. Under Huang Ti the art of writing was invented and the collection of historical material begun; this perhaps explains why Ssǔ-ma Ch'ien treats his time as fully historical, while remaining somewhat cautious about his predecessors. Many other arts and inventions arose under Huang Ti's patronage: architecture, astronomy, sericulture, boats, bridges, carts, bows and arrows and other weapons of war. He was a severe but just ruler who extended his kingdom down to the Yangtze valley.

Huang Ti is considered the ancestor of all the royal and feudal families of later classical China. He and the early monarchs who followed him did not inherit their positions. They were chosen by the grandees of the court. Sometimes, as with Huang Ti's own successor, a son was chosen. More often the new king was a grandson of the old and a descendant of Huang Ti through the female line rather than the male. Succession through a female line was so much at variance with Chinese monarchical institutions in the historical period that it is tempting to believe that in reporting it Ssǔ-ma Ch'ien was incorporating into his history a very strong and ancient Chinese tradition of matrilineal succession to the chieftaincy.

After an interlude of undistinguished successors, Huang Ti was followed by the two famous Sages, Yao and Shun, both of whom traced their descent from him through the maternal line. The Chinese tradition made Yao and Shun the models on whom all rulers should base their conduct. Much of what is recorded about them takes the form of a rather didactic exposition of the virtues and precepts of good government. Their acts were constantly cited as examples by scholars exhorting later emperors to mend their ways. At the death of the second of the two Sages, Shun, his relative Yü, who had already become famous as a great engineer of flood control (there is hardly a river in China that he did not tame), became emperor, the first ruler of the first dynasty, the Hsia. At his death the people insisted on placing his son, a worthy man, on the throne, and thus they established the hereditary principle that remained standard in China.

This in brief is the outline of the Chinese mythical age as it was recorded in the Han period, from the third century B.C. to the third century A.D. It contains some very interesting and revealing details of the ideas that prevailed when Ssǔ-ma Ch'ien wrote. The story of mankind's rise from savagery to civilization over a period of about five hundred years follows a logical sequence. Animal-like savages are successively taught to clothe and shelter themselves, to organize their matrimonial customs, to grow crops, build

The legendary first monarch, Fu Hsi, is credited with many inventions, among them the eight symbolic trigrams (foreground).

houses, make carts and boats and weapons of war. Their Sage rulers gradually institute a more elaborate government and extend the boundaries of civilized rule. It is difficult to escape the thought that these processes were, in fact, being applied by the early Chinese rulers in the outlying territories of the far south, and that what men knew to be happening in these regions supplied a model for what they believed to have happened among their own ancestors.

Yet the reconstruction of the myths and legends to form a connected historical record was not purely a work of imagination. It was based on some documents of considerable antiquity and probably also on commonly accepted oral traditions. The earliest literature with any reference to the Sages of the remote past are the *Shu Ching*, or *Book of Documents*, part of which dates from around 1000 B.C., and the *Shih Ching*, or *Book of Odes*, which is some three hundred years later. In the recorded sayings of Confucius and of other philosophers of the fifth and third centuries B.C. there are mentions of the Sage rulers, but there is no connected account of their reigns and acts.

One important point must be remembered in assessing the documentation of early Chinese civilization: that is that few books earlier than the third century B.C. have survived. All early Chinese literature is known only from copies made by successive generations of scribes and scholars. Late in the third century B.C. the Emperor Shih Huang Ti made the continuity of Chinese literature even more precarious by ordering most books in China burned in order to keep his subjects from reading about the reigns of his wise predecessors. The ancient Chinese wrote with a stylus on strips of wood or smooth bamboo, both of which are very perishable. They did not write on baked clay tablets, and in the early period made few inscriptions, if any, on stone. They did inscribe precious bronze vessels, but in the Shang dynasty, which is traditionally dated as ending in 1028 B.C., bronze inscriptions were extremely short, of three or four characters only, and give little more than the name of the vessel's owner. These facts explain the artificial character of the surviving Chinese legends and the relative paucity of genuine materials for the history of early China. Much has no doubt been lost that was accessible in the age of Confucius, around 500 B.C.

Traditionally—and it was a very long tradition—Confucius was the author or editor of the earliest surviving works, which together are considered the Chinese classics and which have held a predominant role in Chinese culture for millenniums: the *Shu Ching*, or *Book of Documents*, the *Shih Ching*, or *Book of Odes*, the *I Ching*, or *Book of Changes*, and the *Ch'un Ch'iu*, or *Spring and Autumn Annals*. In addition there was the *Lun Yü*, or *Analects*, which is a record of Confucius' personal teaching, compiled by his original disciples. Hardly any of this traditional attribution is now accepted. Confucius probably venerated the *Book of Documents*, some five hundred years old in his time, and his followers probably preserved copies and made fresh ones; but there is no reason to accept the opinion that he compiled the *Shu*. The same is true of the *Book of Odes*. These poems, which appear at first sight to be simple country songs, date from the eighth and seventh centuries B.C. and are the work of a court aristocracy imitating folk poetry with considerable sophistication. The odes are frequently rather licentious and far from moral in their general tone.

Confucius, a man of aesthetic tastes, certainly loved the *Shih*; therefore later ages attributed to him the collection of this anthology and tried to find good reasons why the sage should have included poems that clearly refer to illicit love. The rationalization they arrived at was that these odes came from degenerate states and were included as warnings. The *I Ching*, or *Book of Changes*, is primarily a book of divination, and has been used until modern times for this purpose. It may date from around 1100 B.C. Attached to it are appendixes, which are philosophical explanations of the work. They were long believed to be the contribution of Confucius, but it is now clear that they date from some five centuries after his death. Only the *Analects* can be said to be the work, albeit indirectly, of Confucius himself. It is a collection of his sayings and teaching, and is accepted as basically the work of his immediate disciples, although it was probably expanded in later times, perhaps from oral tradition. Almost all that is certain about Confucius' life and teaching comes from the *Analects*.

The greatness of Confucius does not rest upon the attributed authorship or editorship of well-known works, but on his method and his approach to moral problems. Confucius broke away from the traditional ritualistic attitude toward religion and morality. Until his day if one performed the correct rite, one's duty was done. It did not matter whether the person who performed the rite was a virtuous man or a bloodthirsty tyrant; if the rite was properly performed, it was efficacious. This is an ancient belief, common in many parts of the world. The significance of Confucius was that he taught that the effectiveness of rites depended on the spirit in which they were performed. Man must be guided by morality, by virtues, and not just by the knowledge of how to perform rites. In later ages, when this view was so generally accepted that it no longer seemed significant, the immensity of Confucius' advance was forgotten. As Confucius left so little in writing, his followers felt it neces-

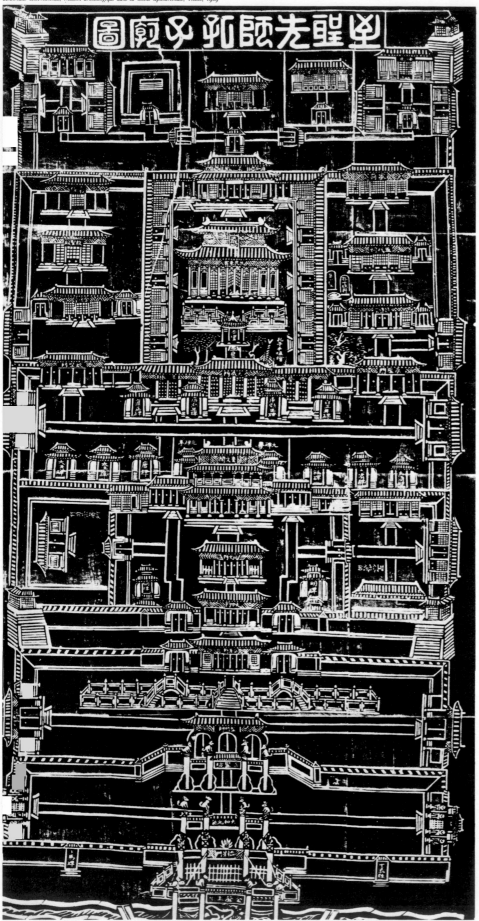

The complex temple of Confucius, built near the sage's tomb in the province of Shantung, is depicted in the modern print at left. Confucius is shown opposite, clad in billowing scholar's robes, in a stone rubbing that dates from the nineteenth century.

sary to uphold his prestige by assigning some monument to him. So the belief arose that he wrote or edited the ancient texts that his school venerated and that he himself had revered. The belief, in effect, proved his achievement.

Confucius did not have a successful life as men then measured success. Born in 551 B.C. into an aristocratic family in the state of Lu (in the present-day province of Shantung), he obtained a very unimportant post at the court of his prince, for his kin had little influence. Resigning his post when he realized its lack of significance, he taught for a while in Lu, his disciples being young men of the aristocracy who later filled important posts in Lu and other states. Society was aristocratic; no member of a lower class could expect a post of authority or power. Confucius made a deep impression on these young aspirants for government and command. They received his ideas, which enjoined a new attitude to duty: it should be carried out with loyalty, restraint, sincerity, and benevolence. The rulers needed men who could be counted upon to be loyal and sincere in a violent and treacherous age; they came to appreciate that the young Confucians were men of this stamp. Confucius never received patronage, but his disciples rose high in government service, and as a whole, displayed in office the qualities that Confucius had matured in them.

He himself set off to travel through China in search of a righteous prince who would put his teaching into practice. In Wei, a neighboring and renowned state, whose duke was of the highest lineage, he found the ruler corrupt and degenerate, his wife incestuous—with her husband's knowledge and consent—and the government run by an able but evil minister. Passing from there to Sung, the sage was nearly the victim of a jealous nobleman who tried to have him assassinated.

Thence he went to Ch'en, one of the small and weak southern states of feudal China. Ch'en was in daily risk of being annexed by its southern neighbor Ch'u, the great power of the Yangtze valley. Its weak prince and distracted counselors had little time or inclination to listen to moral philosophy. But in neighboring Ts'ai, then under occupation by the king of Ch'u, Confucius found at last a worthy ruler, the duke of She, who was not a sovereign in his own right, but a relative of the king of Ch'u, acting as viceroy in Ts'ai. The duke was renowned for his justice and virtue. Confucius was not disappointed in him. They had long conversations and only differed on one important point. Confucius held that a man's greatest and first loyalty must be to his parents and kin; the duke thought that it was owed to the king. But as the duke was a close relative of his own king, the point was perhaps of less difference than the two philosophers seem to have believed.

Later Confucius returned to Lu. There he taught in peace for the last years of his life, respected but not employed by the government. He died tranquilly in his native city. His life (551–479 B.C.) coincided with the declining age of Chinese feudalism, a period of violence and treachery, when great states were beginning to seize and annex their small neighbors, old virtues were falling into disuse, and new ambitions were stirring. The period of the Warring States, beginning at the time of Confucius' death, was to herald the final agony of the old society. Confucius lived at a turning point in Chinese history. His life and teaching cannot be understood unless this fact is grasped.

His whole effort was directed toward trying to arrest a swift decline in political practice and public morality. Obviously he failed; but he accomplished something that he may not

OVERLEAF: *In a modern print, Confucius and seventy-two of his disciples are shown assembled in the temple dedicated to the sage. The figure of Confucius, much larger than the others, is at top.*

EDOUARD CHAVANNES, *Mission archéologique dans la Chine septentrionale,* PARIS, 1909

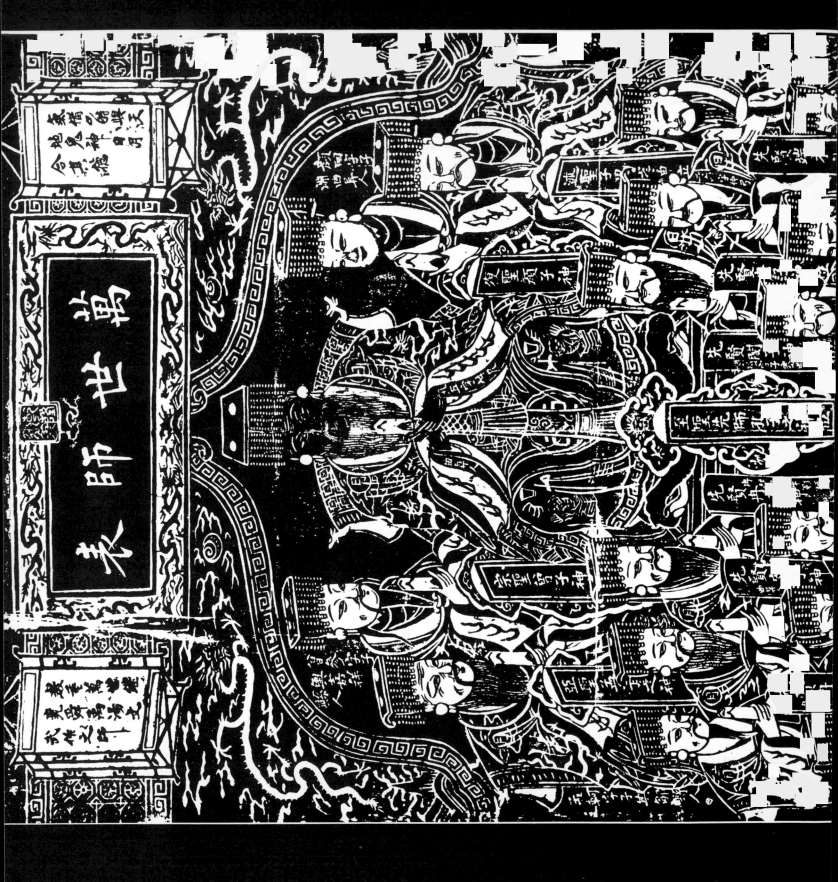

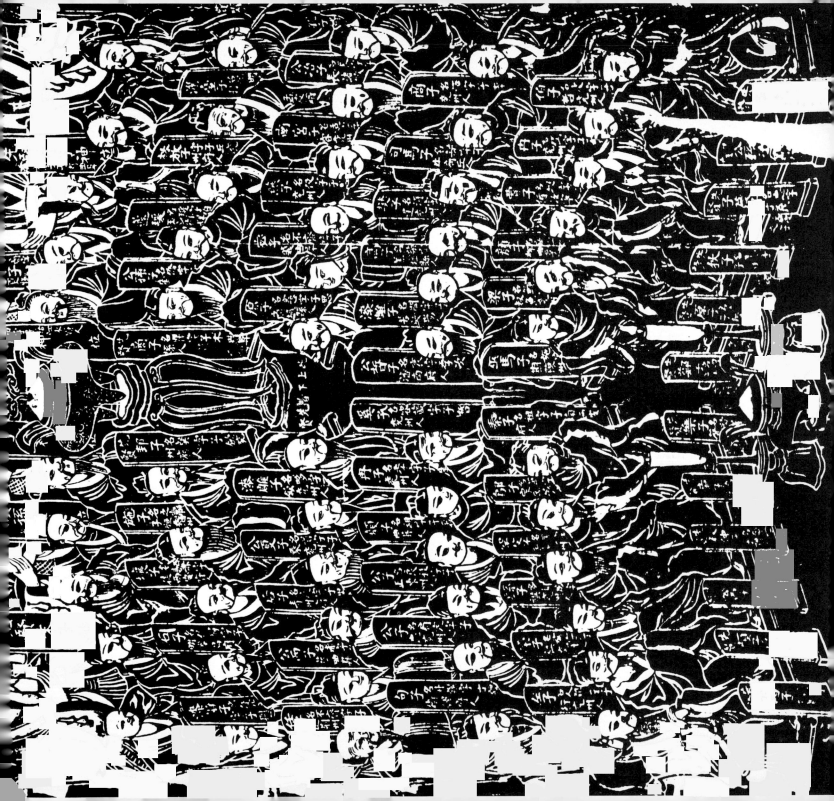

閑來隱几枕書眠夢入
壺中別有天彷彿若
夷親面目大還真訣得
親傳晉昌唐寅為
東原先生寫圖

have expected to achieve. He left behind a new understanding of ethics, an ideal of the aristocrat as a man of morality: just, sincere, loyal, benevolent, and owing his high esteem to the possession and practice of these virtues, not to his birth or wealth. In this sense Confucius created the image of the official who held his post by learning and knowledge, virtue and diligence, rather than by blood or purchase. This was to become the standard of the future Chinese civil service, an ideal always revered, sometimes attained, and never repudiated.

In the next generation rival schools of thought appeared. There were the Taoists, who taught that all power was tyranny, all law a mark of decline in virtue. They believed that the real happiness of mankind involved a return to the simplest manners. Leaving aside the whole apparatus of state and government, men could seek identity with the Tao, the Way, the way of nature, and by conforming to its secret and obscure dictates, live in harmony with their natural surroundings. Nonaction, the Taoist specific, does not mean passive inaction, but rather a conscious attempt to identify with nature and to refrain from opposing by action the true cause of events. Taoism had a great following in clas-

sical China, perhaps in reaction to the violence of the period, and it retained followers in later ages. A great many of them were not true philosophic Taoists, but believers in the *elixir vitae*, or the drug of immortality, and in other magical formulas. Taoist magic was based in part on allegories used by ancient Taoist writers to illustrate the condition of the sage who fully conformed to the Tao and in part on traditional magical cults that seem to have flourished among the common people, particularly along the eastern seaboard. The Taoists were fond of illustrating their doctrine that nonaction was more important than action by pointing out that emptiness is often the quality that makes an object valuable. An empty bowl is useful because it can contain a liquid; the nave of the wheel (the hole through which the axle is fitted) is the really essential part of the wheel.

Another school of thought in ancient China was founded by Mo Tzŭ, a near contemporary of Confucius. He taught a novel doctrine for his land and period, that of universal love. Love of all men was, he said, the only way to construct a just society. Love would put an end to war, the great curse of the time; it would diminish aristocratic arrogance and pretension, raise the condition

of the poor, bring about a society where crime and punishment would fade away. Mo Tzŭ hated waste; he disapproved of war because the resources squandered on campaigns could be better employed on public works, such as irrigation and flood control, which would bring benefits to all men. He equally disapproved of costly ceremonies, funerals, and marriages, of which, it must be confessed, Confucius approved. Confucius thought such ceremonies were needed to inculcate proper respect and the observance of filial piety and family solidarity—virtues on which he believed society was founded, and which he taught as fundamentals of the true morality. Mo Tzŭ claimed that such ceremonies were wasteful—that the poor became indebted in trying to perform them, and that the rich competed in ostentatious and useless display and then paid for it by extorting the costs from their peasants. It would seem probable that both philosophers had some right on their side.

During his life Mo Tzŭ was much more successful than Confucius. He set up a large organization to propagate his teaching and appointed a successor to head it. For some generations the Mohists were an active force in society, but they never captured the im-

agination of any ruler. Pacifism was certainly not a reality in the age of the Warring States, and universal love seemed too all-embracing an ideal to have practical application. Confucius, basing his teaching on the social reality of clan allegiance and family solidarity, had been on firmer ground and had appealed to that commonsense outlook that has, it would seem, characterized the Chinese people from their beginnings. The teaching of Mo Tzŭ, in some ways a forerunner of the Christian message, waned and died out in China. After the foundation of the early empire little is heard of it. Mohism's few surviving books have had to be reassembled from citations and corrupt texts.

During the Warring States era, in the fourth and third centuries B.C., there arose a new school of philosophy that has left a certain body of literature and a bad reputation to posterity. The School of the Law was founded by men from the civilized and advanced states of the Honan region in eastern China, but found acceptance only in the northwest, in the warlike realm of Ch'in. The Legists, as followers of the School of the Law were called, took the opposite view to Confucius in all respects, teaching that strict laws rather than traditional rites should control the people

Painted to illustrate a Taoist poem, a sixteenth-century scroll shows a Taoist scholar sleeping in his thatched cottage (center). The scholar dreams that he has attained immortality through magical practices; at left, he is shown blithely floating off over the mountains to the land of Immortals.

71

and that the only activities worth fostering were agriculture and war. The former fed the armies, which would in turn aggrandize the kingdom. No other occupation was worthwhile, and most were actually pernicious.

Commerce, which made men greedy, was condemned by the Legists—so were art, literature, philosophy, and poetry. These merely served to distract men from their true duty and weaken the state. In the state of Ch'in, where Legists ran the government, feudal privilege was suppressed. All men, even princes of the blood, had to submit to the same harsh laws, from which there was no appeal. The population was regimented, no free travel was allowed, innkeepers had to report to the officials on their guests, and any traveler who did not carry a travel permit was arrested and charged with sedition. Very severe penalties, of which the mildest were mutilation and exile to forced labor, were imposed on all who broke the law. It was argued that if all men feared to break the law, peace and order would prevail. Whether the king was a strong ruler or a weakling would not matter; his ministers, ruling by the law, would maintain order. Strangely enough, some of the sources of this doctrine are to be found in the quietist teaching of the Taoists and in the pacifist doctrines of Mo Tzŭ. The Taoists condemned ceremony, rank, and privilege. Their philosophic objections to complex society accorded with the teaching of the School of Law. Mo Tzŭ had also condemned as wasteful many of the arts that were considered superfluous by the Legists, although they were dear to Confucians. The Legists ignored his pacifism but borrowed his ideas on regimentation and his anti-aestheticism.

As if to prove the validity of the Legist approach, it was Ch'in, where Legist doctrines were enforced, that succeeded in conquering all other states and founded the first empire.

Then the Legist doctrine was put into practice throughout China with the utmost rigor. In less than two decades it produced the massive revolt that destroyed Ch'in, brought the Han dynasty to power, and forever discredited the School of Law. Yet although the teaching of this school was eventually repudiated, Legist thought remained an influence in Chinese society. It made the law a hated word, and as a result, China developed no civil law. Law was confined to the criminal branch, where it retained much of the severity and cruelty of Legist practice. Authoritarian government, the complete supremacy of the monarch, the dissolution of feudalism, and the rise of an imperial bureaucracy are other developments that were inspired to some degree by Legist ideas. It can be said that while later China adopted Confuciansim as the ethical and moral basis of society, it retained some Legist concepts in the actual practice of government.

There were other schools of philosophy of which little trace now remains. All had been persecuted during the brief domination of Ch'in, and only the strongest were able to recover when that regime was overthrown. Taoism, while never regaining its former influence, survived, although it turned increasingly to magic, alchemy, and mysticism. Confucianism became the recognized teaching, but gathered up some ideas and practices that had not been part of its founder's thought.

The most important of these was the concept that the cosmos was governed by the interaction of the two principles named yin and yang—the positive and negative, male and female, dry and wet, hot and cold, sunny and shady aspects of nature. Yin and yang are simply ordinary Chinese words meaning, respectively, the shady side and the sunny side of some natural feature; the south slope of a mountain is the yang side, so is the north bank of a river, which faces the sun. Thus the words are common in place names. Their wider use as philosophical terms arose in the fourth century B.C. in connection with a doctrine that taught that the harmony of nature was maintained by the ceaseless balance of yin and yang.

The two forces are not antagonistic—no connotation of good and evil is attached to them—and they move in a harmonious flux, symbolized by the device of a circle divided into two equal parts by a curving line. Disturbances in nature, floods or other calamities, were believed to indicate a temporary imbalance in yin and yang. Before long this belief was extended to include disturbances in human conduct. Gross misrule, savage cruelties, or luxurious debauchery in the monarch indicated a disharmony of yin and yang, which was then made manifest physically in drought, flood, earthquake, or other natural phenomena. This interpretation was widely accepted, and later became part of orthodox Confucian doctrine. It had great influence once the empire was established. The monarch was the sole ruler of the Chinese world; he had no rival, no equal. He alone bore the responsibility to Heaven for the maintenance of harmony on earth. He held the Mandate of Heaven, but only for as long as he ruled with sincerity and righteousness. Throughout Chinese history this doctrine was generally believed, and served as a powerful moral restraint on the autocrats. There is some evidence to show that on many of them the moral restraint was effective.

Akin to the yin-yang doctrine was a very ancient idea that eventually became formalized: there is no continuing prosperity, nor unending misfortune. "Good and evil have their rewards; life and death have their limits." There will be an inevitable end to prosperity; its time of decay must come. So, too, bad luck must change; there will be no permanent

The five-clawed feet of the dragon (above) identify him as a symbol of the emperor, the Son of Heaven. Nonimperial dragons had four claws.

73

*In the seventeenth-century painting opposite, a group of schol-
ars studies the yin-yang symbol, whose interlocking halves represent the opposite but complementary forces of the universe.*

misery. The world moves in slow cycles, governed by yin and yang. It is useless to struggle
against these cosmic forces; the wise man will
recognize their operation as ineluctable and
accept his lot in life. If happy and well-to-do,
he should know that a day of decline is coming and that excess of indulgence and exploitation will only hurry it forward. If poor and
miserable, he must wait in patience for the
equally inevitable upward turn of fortune.

Man in China was faced by a hostile and,
often, destructive nature. Drought and flood
were frequent and beyond human control.
There was no visible benevolence in the powers of Heaven, but a certain rhythm could be
perceived. Bad times are sure to pass; good
years are sure to come again. It was perhaps
natural to transfer this just observation of nature to the character and conduct of human
affairs. No dynasty will rule for ever; it will fall
into ruin. But another will rise in its place and
go through the same cycle.

None of the Chinese schools of philosophy
was religious in a way familiar to Europeans
or western Asians. They did not teach that the
high gods intervened in man's affairs or that
they could be invoked to do so by prayer.
Sacrifice was a rite that helped to maintain the
balance of yin and yang; it was not an offering
to a personified deity. In fact the Chinese did
not conceive of their great gods as personalities. Heaven was a vague supreme power, the
source of the weather that so deeply affected
the lives of men. No image was made of
Heaven. One of the terms for Heaven, *shang
ti*, which Christians translated as "emperor
on high" or "God," did not mean God at all.
Originally it probably meant only "supreme
ancestor," that is, the first royal ancestor to
whom the sacrifices of the ancestral cult were
made. Gods were vague powers; ancestors had
once been men, and as such, their spirits could
be invoked to help their descendants. The es-

sential humanism of the Chinese outlook,
with man ever in the forefront and other
powers admitted but not personified, shows
through the early literature of all schools.

The works or sayings of the philosophers
comprise most of the literature that has been
preserved from the feudal period, before the
burning of the books under the Ch'in empire.
Little history or poetry has survived. The
Ch'in inquisitors who supervised the book
burning had little desire to preserve the histories and annals of the states that Ch'in had
conquered. They looked on poetry as an art
that softened hearts and made men unfit for
war. Confucius would have agreed with them,
but for that very reason he would have encouraged poetry rather than condemn it.

After the restoration of the books under
the Han dynasty, there appears a marked
change in the character of Chinese literature.
In the feudal period, before the Ch'in conquest, philosophy and the contention of the
various philosphical schools had been the
main intellectual concern; history had taken
second place. After the Han dynasty was firmly
established, Confucians won the leading place
in the esteem of the new emperors, and Confucianism became the orthodox doctrine of
the Chinese world. Intellectuals turned their
attention toward the writing of history. The
disputes of the schools faded away; their questions were, in effect, settled. Many centuries
were to pass before a new age of philosophic
debate arose in which the interpretation of
Confucian texts, rather than the comparison of
Confucianism and rival systems, formed the
subject of discussion.

Perhaps the disputes of the schools had
been related to the contemporary struggles of
the Warring States. The world was in flux, and
it was as urgent to find new doctrines to control a new age as it was to shape that age by
force and conquest. Under the Han empire the

75

The lid of a Han dynasty bronze censer, inlaid with gold, silver, and turquoise, is shaped to suggest the mountaintop home of the Taoist Immortals.

political problem was solved, at least on broad lines. There was a united empire, ruled by a single sovereign, whose power was exercised through officers of a civil service, whom he could appoint, promote, transfer, or dismiss at will. Confucian learning was the key to office-holding, which now, after the fall of feudalism, became the normal ambition of men of means and education. Consequently, the urge to discuss strange doctrines or to revive those that had fallen into oblivion was not present. Such speculations seemed irrelevant to the needs of the new age. On the other hand, the tremendous events that had marked the conquest of China by Ch'in, the subsequent overthrow of the Ch'in state, the rise of the Han dynasty to supreme power, and the construction of a new society inevitably focused intellectual interest on history. How had these things come about? Were they really altogether new? Or, as the scholars were soon to argue, were they the long-delayed restoration of a pristine unity that had been enjoyed in the dim past?

The most important Han historian was Ssŭ-ma Ch'ien, whose great work, the *Shih Chi*, or *Historical Records*, was compiled in the

first century B.C. Its author held a post at the court of the Han Emperor Wu Ti. He had access to the library of the palace, which evidently contained some of the few surviving copies of ancient historical texts. Ssŭ-ma was a magnificent editor. He includes every source he can find, quotes it word for word, and sometimes, when two ancient authorities present varying versions, cites both, leaving it to his readers to decide which they find the more convincing. His purpose was to record the whole history of the Chinese world from its beginnings down to his own time, and this he did. Naturally the value of his work is uneven. His record of and comments on the reign of Emperor Wu are invaluable. He did not love his sovereign, and lets this be seen. His collection of the surviving historical records of the feudal states provides the greater part of what is known of their history. But as he works back into the far past his materials begin to fail. Although his early history of the Chou dynasty can to some degree be corroborated by bronze inscriptions, much of it is conjectural.

Ssŭ-ma Ch'ien is the best known of the great Han historians, but he was not the first. He has cited and quoted works, now lost, that were written immediately after the fall of Ch'in. But his own work was to be the model for all later histories. Another model was Pan Ku's *History of the Former Han Dynasty*, written early in the first century A.D., about a century after the death of Ssŭ-ma Ch'ien.

Most subsequent Chinese histories cover only one dynasty as their subject. This may be long, two hundred years or more, or very short, a decade or so. The plan that Pan Ku adopted for his book was to divide it into three separate sections: annals, biographies, and monographs. Annals are simply an arid record of dates, of imperial acts and travels, and of natural portents. They are meticulously dated, often to the day. They supply a chronological framework and little more.

Then come the biographies, more than two hundred in number. They are detailed accounts of the birth, parentage, lives, and acts of people of all types: loyal officials, rebels, conspirators, bandits, ladies of the palace, actors, and writers—a gallery of men and women who were thought to have played significant roles in the society of their time. Each biography deals with one person; other people only receive passing mention, even when their acts were intimately connected with the career of the biography's subject. To get a full picture of a particular event, it is therefore necessary to read the biographies of all the people who were connected with it.

In addition there are what the Western historians have called the monographs, long essays, each dealing with a single subject of importance that concerned the government, the system of land tenure, the army, the rites of the state cult, astronomy, flood and irrigation control, and so on. The monographs deal strictly with the matter in hand and do not trouble to give any dates. Innovations and changes may be mentioned as occurring in such and such a reign, but to discover their exact date and to relate them to acts of policy or the consequences of war, it is again necessary to consult the annals and the biographies of several eminent statesmen. Many subjects that the modern historian would consider very important find no place in the monographs, or elsewhere. There is no connected and general economic history. Commerce receives no special treatment and only casual, often deprecatory, mention.

This method of writing history does not provide an easy approach for modern historians. It often seems to lack the artistry of such ancient writers as Herodotus or Livy; but it is more accurate and far better dated than

they are, and at times, in the biographies, it furnishes many vivid passages.

Another difficulty this method of writing history presents, perhaps unintentionally, is that it reinforces the prevalent idea of the dynastic cycle. Since history was confined in each work to the story of one dynasty, showing how it rises, flourishes, declines, and falls, there is a strong tendency to cast all history into a dynastic pattern. The general advance of society, the growth of commerce and technology, changes in religion and society, are not seen in long perspective; if mentioned at all, they appear only in the narrow context of a single dynasty. Another consequence of the method, which seems strange in a nation so devoted to historical studies, is that the Chinese did not devise an overall chronology until modern times. Every reign is self-contained, and events are dated as occurring in the first, second, and so on year of such and such an emperor. Even the dynasty as whole does not have a continuous system. The annals do not mention the first and fifty-fifth year of the Han, but, rather, disconnected series of regnal years. By late Han times this system was still further fragmented by the custom of changing the emperor's name at irregular periods during his reign, so that even one reign may have three or many more reign periods, each separately dated. Without the use of conversion tables, it is therefore very difficult to relate one age of Chinese history to another. Before the introduction of the Christian calendar by the Communist regime (which prefers to style it "the calendar in general use"), Chinese scholars needed to be very well read to understand the chronological framework of their country's history.

The early and classical literature of China had an immense and long-continuing influence on the whole course of Chinese civilization. It was revered, but it was never attributed to divine authorship. Confucius was a man, and one who often made it plain that he considered human affairs much more urgent than the worship of gods or speculation upon the nature of the divine. The ancient history, a fiction, if a pious one, was taken for truth and held up as a model of an age that all must strive to restore. In time there arose another type of literature, which was in part based on Buddhist legend and in part on Taoist tradition. This literature had a more popular origin than the productions of the scholars; it reflected the folklore of the people, and it grew slowly into a body of romantic fiction, still very often retaining the strong historical bias of the Chinese mind, but largely independent of the moral imperatives that constrained the official literature patronized by the court and practiced by the scholar-officials.

History was written to show the governing class of the age what kind of conduct they should emulate and what faults and vices they should avoid. The good and the bad deeds of past rulers must be equally recorded, for both are examples that contemporaries must note and posterity should study. It was assumed that future or present conditions were similar to those of the past, however remote. History was a mirror in which the ruler could see himself, could see what he should do to carry out his duty, and what he should refrain from doing if he hoped to retain the Mandate of Heaven. It came to be taken for granted that the moral character of the monarch set the tone of the age; his ministers were likely to follow his example, and the common people would take the great men as their models. "As the wind blows, so the grass bends." The reward of moral virtue was prosperity; the penalty for vice was disaster. The rise and fall of dynasties was the pattern of history, a pattern set by the moral strength and weakness of their leading men.

Of China's three great religions, Taoism was the most concerned with man's place in his natural environment and with his ability to live harmoniously with the forces of nature. In China landscape painting, known as shan-shui, or "mountain-water," evolved in direct response to the Taoists' reverence for mountains and rivers. These elements *dominate* Asking about the Tao in the Autumn Mountains, *the Sung dynasty scroll at right, painted by Chü-jan.*

THE FORCES OF NATURE

Chinese cosmology associated extraordinary virtues with rather ordinary animals, several of which are featured on the Han dynasty slip pottery plate below. Ranged around the outer rim of the plate are four kneeling human figures bearing offerings and four common domestic animals. The pig and the ram were sacrificial beasts; the duck was an emblem of felicity, and the rooster of masculinity. The fish and crane, which appear at center, often symbolized wealth and longevity.

The Chinese traditionally believed that water and the weather were controlled by beneficent dragon gods. In ancient times human victims were sacrificed to the river god in the hope of preventing floods and ensuring proper rainfall. Dragons are still associated with water. One of China's most widely celebrated holidays is the dragon-boat festival, when thousands of wooden representations of the river spirits, such as the cumbersome dragon boat below, ply the waterways.

Three spiritual powers—the rulers of Heaven, Earth, and Water—stood watch over the Taoist world, bringing happiness to man, forgiving his sins, and shielding him from harm. Originally each god personified also a vast but undefined period of time, but eventually that conception was modified. A detail of an eighteenth-century painting shows the Taoist divinity of Earth, representing summer, being borne in a litter surrounded by fan bearers. In the god's train is a retinue of ladies, celestial musicians, and attendants bearing fluttering banners.

4 The Family

A painting from the twelfth or thirteenth century shows women of the imperial household bathing and dressing four of the emperor's numerous offspring.

In Chinese society the family has always played a primary role. This is, of course, true of other societies, but in China the family had a special significance, for it was the model on which the structure of the state came to be based, and it was the focus of the most important aspects of religious life. We know very little of social structure in China in earliest times; but it is clear that by the beginning of the feudal period the aristocratic families were tightly organized in noble clans. What we know of peasant customs suggests a less rigid organization, having features in common with some of the free-mannered national minority peoples living in the mountains of southwest China. If it is true, as some authorities suggest, that peasants chose their mates at a spring fertility festival, marrying girls only if they were with child, this practice passed away before long. Stories from the early historical period suggest that sometimes even the aristocracy was not as strict as one might expect. One famous minister of the state of Ch'i is said to have allowed his guests free access to his inner apartments, and in consequence had "a hundred sons." These examples of free living may well have been recorded in condemnation of immoral manners, rather than as a report of social customs. Eventually, more exacting standards came to prevail, standards whose dissemination was generally credited to the teaching of Confucius and the example of his disciples.

The norm for the Chinese family was evolved in the late feudal age. Much of the family's structure and custom derived directly from the model of the aristocracy. In feudal times nobles practiced exogamy—total avoidance of marriage between people with the same patrilineage. Toward the end of the feudal period and in the early empire this practice became obligatory for all people, and with it came the adoption of surnames. The noble clans had not had surnames as the term is now understood, but they did have clan names, and always married outside their clan. The clans seem to have been few in number and did not embrace the mass of the people, who had no claim to noble blood.

Surnames were sometimes derived from the family's home region, or from an office held, or from a city or town. It seems that the Chinese never used the common form of surname found in the West, son of so and so. Yet they were the first people known to use the surname as it is now customarily used in most parts of the world: handing down the father's surname to the children, both male and female (who also received a given name analagous to the Christian name among Europeans). There can be no doubt that the motive for the adoption of surnames was the spread of the noble custom of exogamy to other classes. To make sure people of the same patrilineage did not marry, it was necessary to establish a clear distinction for each family line. The surname provided a method for doing this. No Wang can marry another Wang, no Li can marry a Li, and so on. Even when the people bearing a specific surname had become innumerable and could be found in all parts of China, the rule still held. Exceptions would be admitted only if it was shown after an exhaustive inquiry that bride and groom, though of the same surname, came from parts of the country so remote from one another that no kinship was possible. Naturally, only the wealthy could afford to go through all the trouble and expense of such an inquiry.

Another device to get around the restrictions of exogamy was adoption. If a man had no son and could not adopt one of the sons of his brother or cousin, he could adopt the son of his sister or of another female relation and give him his own surname. It was then legal, if not very common, for this youth to marry a girl with his own native surname, which he no longer bore. The exogamous family did not put any obstacle in the way of the marriage of people who were closely related so long as their relationship was matrilineal. Therefore cousins could marry if they were not related through their fathers; and because a married woman and her siblings no longer had the same surname, their children could marry each other. Such marriages were popular, especially among the wealthy; the practice was called *ch'in shang tso ch'in*, to "pile relationship upon relationship."

Careful registers were kept for very many generations among upper-class families, and it is not uncommon for families to trace their descent for more than a thousand years. In such families no two children of the same surname and generation, however distant the relationship, bore the same given name. There are no common "first" names in China. Every child had a personal name so distinctive that he could not possibly be confused with any other child. This was accomplished in one of several ways. If one son was called Kuo-pao, his younger brother would be given a variant name, such as Kuo-chu. It was then clear that both sons and all other boys with a name containing "Kuo" were members of one generation in that family. Thus their place in the family, an important matter in ancestral rites and ceremonies, could be immediately distinguished. Sometimes the distinctions were made by choosing names written with only the slightest variation. A third method, favored by some scholarly families, was to give one child two consecutive words from a well-known classical text as his personal name, give the next child the next two words, and so on through the whole text if the family was sufficiently numerous. People so named had some very odd appellations, with meanings such as "can say" or "he did." The common

A group of elaborately coiffed and costumed women gathers to fuss over a small child in this seventh-century domestic scene.

people used simpler methods, very often resorting to mere numerals. A ninth child would be called Wang Chiu, "Wang Number Nine." If the family was distantly related to a great clan, the clan elders would choose an appropriate name.

The father of the family was the ruler; he could order his sons to work at whatever tasks he chose. He could determine their profession, decide upon their education, punish them, and at least in earlier times, even put them to death for just cause. The father's power of life and death over children was never fully legitimized; the magistrates and the imperial law were not very willing to concede it and seem only to have sanctioned it when the case was extremely serious.

Girls were married at the age of sixteen, or as soon thereafter as possible. Once a girl was married, she was in complete subjection to her mother-in-law. Her young husband had little say in the home and could do little for her. Her sole compensation was the hope of bearing sons, which would raise her prestige in the family, and of becoming a mother-in-law herself one day. In rich families the practice of concubinage was not only permitted but fairly common in imperial times. There was, however, a sharp distinction in social class between the principal wife and the concubines. They were strictly subordinate to the principal wife, who was the social equal of her husband. It was common, especially in more exalted circles, for concubines to be chosen from families of retainers, tenants, and other respectable households, but some were pretty girls taken from the teahouses or even from the streets. It was a high honor to be chosen as concubine for the emperor, and he had many of them. Although concubines were of lower social status, their children were equal before the law and in family custom to the children of the principal wife. They were the sons and

daughters of their father, and that is what counted. It was usual for one of the sons of the principal wife to become head of the family; but if there were no such sons or if the only one was feeble and ineffective, the son of a concubine could take over the leadership of the family.

The fact that polygamy, in the form of concubinage, was legal has often caused misunderstanding of the Chinese family system. Although concubinage was legal, it was expensive. Concubines could own property, and if they were, as often, "star" singers from the entertainment world, they demanded a large dowry from their prospective husband before consenting to enter his household for ever. They then had to be maintained, and their requirements of clothing and jewelry could be exacting. The institution of concubinage was far beyond the means of the poor. Even among the middle class of small landowners, merchants, and shopkeepers it was very restricted. The great majority of Chinese families were monogamous by economic necessity. This explains why concubinage is now condemned as a typical reactionary feudal institution and suppressed by law.

The great official, or wealthy landowner, or merchant who had several concubines found many disadvantages to the institution. His family was often too numerous to be supported easily. His network of relatives by marriage became more widespread; they and their clients, friends, and distant relatives came to expect employment, preferment, and often outright maintenance at his expense. Even the largest fortunes were quickly eroded in this way. There are few examples of a Chinese family remaining very wealthy for many generations. The need to find support for large kin groups was one cause for the accumulation of land by official families, to the detriment of the peasantry. Ultimately it resulted in social

unrest that undermined many dynasties.

Concubinage caused a great deal of trouble and intrigue at court. Emperors not infrequently preferred concubines, chosen at their pleasure, to their wives, chosen for reasons of state; often they wanted a concubine's son to inherit the throne. Many sanguinary palace plots revolved around this situation. Another problem that frequently arose was caused by the families of the empresses. There was only one sovereign in the Chinese world; he had no equal. He could not marry into his own patrilineal family, and so he had to marry the daughter of a subject. This made the empress' family of the first importance, especially if the empress gave birth to a son, who would be emperor one day.

The ambition of these consort families constantly upset the tranquillity of the Han empire and finally contributed to its ruin. Almost all the empress' families tried to usurp the throne or were accused of trying to do so. Each new one attempted to oust its predecessor from power and put its own members into office. Indeed, almost all consort families were exterminated by their successors. In later dynasties the problem seems to have been less serious. The consort families used their influence to secure good positions for their relatives, but not to conspire for supreme power or aim at the throne itself.

It has been pointed out that the family was the model for the whole system of government. The emperor was the father; the people

87

were his children. The country was family property, all, in theory, owned by the emperor, just as in a private family all property came under the control of the head. As a result there was in a sense no private property in China as there is in our society. Family property could not be alienated without the consent of the heads of all the family's branches; no one man owned it or was able to dispose of it at his pleasure. A farming peasant family with some land of its own operated within the family property system as far as its means allowed; that is to say, the head of the family, consulting his adult sons and brothers, would be free to dispose of property or to acquire more if he could. However, the kinship property system could not be maintained far beyond the immediate family as was possible among the well-to-do. It is not entirely clear how the family property system worked among families that owned little or nothing—among day laborers, who worked for their food and lodging and had almost nothing left over. This was the condition of many millions in the late empire, after a huge increase in population in the seventeenth and eighteenth centuries. Such poverty had probably been less common in earlier centuries, however.

There was a very strong aversion to parting with land and a powerful urge to add more to the family holding. For centuries land was re-garded as the only safe investment, and its ownership was the mark of social status. The strong attachment of the Chinese to their hereditary lands had a religious basis. In feudal times a prince or lord could only hold his rank if he was in absolute control over some territory, however small. There he maintained altars to the gods of the soil and to his ancestors. So long as their rites could be fulfilled, he was a lord. If his estates were annexed, sacrifices were no longer made at the altars. Their discontinuance was believed to cause the extermination of the ancestral spirits and to signal the lord's or prince's fall from rank and fortune. Some of these concepts, like many others of feudal origin, were adopted by the successors of the feudal lords, the class of landowners, who remained the main element in the Chinese social structure from the creation of the unified empire in 221 B.C. until the Communist revolution.

A family was always said to come from such and such a district in one of the provinces. Actually, if they had been officials for several generations, their real home was usually in the capital, Peking or its forerunners, K'ai-feng, Lo-yang, or Ch'ang-an. Often people had never so much as seen their ancestral home, but remained attached to it by a spiritual link. If they had spent their childhood there before setting out on an official career

METROPOLITAN MUSEUM OF ART, FLETCHER FUND, 1947, A. W. BAHR COLLECTION

during which they were forbidden to serve in their native province, they would return home in old age or in sickness, if possible. For there was a strong belief that the native air was wholesome to its sons, and that the consumption of the produce of the native soil and the water of the home streams would cure many diseases. Even in modern times students studying abroad were often sent parcels containing packets of home produce, flasks of home water, and small quantities of the ancestral soil, to use as medicines. Property was thus more than wealth; it was spiritual treasure also.

Although the poor were very exposed to the vicissitudes of war and famine, they also tried to hold property from generation to generation. In some well-protected and out-of-the-way regions, far from the routes over which armies passed, it was not uncommon to find simple peasant families who had held the same farm for very many generations. At the end of the nineteenth century, when the British occupied and leased the territory of Wei-hai-wei at the tip of the Shantung Peninsula, British officials found that about half the farming population had held the same land for more than seven centuries; families that had been there only three or four centuries were regarded as newcomers. The Chinese farmer, rich or poor, often had a far longer and better-documented connection with his lands than

the proudest landowning nobility of Europe had with theirs.

The family was the natural center of the ancestral cult. In the view of many students of Chinese society this cult was the real religion of the people, and fundamentally more important than Buddhism and the local polytheism that finally gathered under the umbrella of Taoism. It was undoubtedly the most ancient religion of China. What may have been only a royal cult in Shang dynasty China became a feudal and aristocratic cult, and later a popular and universal religion. Every family had its ancestral altar, furnished with the tablets of the ancestors, lacquered wooden boards in gilt or red frames on which were written the names of ancestors. Usually the names extended back no more than three generations. The altar held no image or picture. Ancestral portraits could be hung elsewhere, but they did not have religious significance.

Large clans, whose branches often included peasant families, maintained an ancestral temple or shrine either on the original estate in the home district or in a city nearby. At certain seasons of the year leaders of the clan celebrated ceremonies in the temple. Here, too, were kept the registers of the members of the clan. Some of these covered a very long period of time, running back more than a thousand years. Usually, the records were less

Clan feeling was strong throughout China, and family gatherings were frequent; the one depicted in this late Ming dynasty scroll is attended by members of several generations, including the youngest. Riding off at left are two elders mounted on donkeys.

89

complete, for wars or other calamities often interrupted record-keeping or destroyed the shrine. If the clan had the resources, the shrine might be rebuilt. If it did not, that clan would lose coherence and cease to maintain registers.

The ancestral temple of a wealthy clan was also used as a school, or the clan maintained a school in other premises, providing education for its members, whether rich or poor. It was in the interest of the clan to do this. Every intelligent boy might rise through the official hierarchy to a position of great power and wealth, which would open economic and official opportunities for other members of his clan. This system of clan education was one of the mainsprings of social mobility, making it possible for the poorer members of the clan and their children to rise in the social scale and enter the privileged class of the literati.

There were some important variations in family custom and clan practice in different parts of the country. The clan system was strongest in the south. This in part may be a result of the fact that the south was originally a colonial area, settled by immigrants from the north, many of whom had withdrawn from war-torn regions under the leadership of a prominent member of their clan. He established his followers on lands that were almost uninhabited; there their cohesion tended to persist. In the south it is not uncommon to find every village wholly inhabited by families of one clan, bearing the same surname. It was also common, and still is among overseas Chinese, for a business or bank to employ only members of the proprietor's clan, often only those from his native district. In the north the situation was somewhat different. Place names such as Chang-chia-chuang, "farm of the Chang family," show that what are now large towns or villages were once the property of one family; but most northern villages are now inhabited by families of several surnames,

and some of these families are relative newcomers. Until the Communist revolution, this situation would have been socially unacceptable in the south.

Since ancestor worship, or to be more accurate, the reverence of ancestors, was so fundamental an institution of family life, it was natural that the maintenance of ancestral graves was an important charge on the living members of the family. Public cemeteries were not established in China. Every family buried its dead on some part of its own property, in the fields that had nourished its members during their lifetime. Important families set aside large areas for this purpose, with ceremonial gates, sculpture, and groves of fine trees. The supreme example can still be seen at the Ming imperial tombs near Peking (illustrated on page 29). The sacred area there extends for miles, and the tombs are concealed under vast artificial hills. A minor landowning family kept a corner of some field, shaded with a few trees, on which earthen mounds were raised to cover graves. In the south, graves were cut out of hillsides; paved or tiled shallow curved ledges were built before them, on which the family could place the offerings that were made to the dead at certain seasons. There are a great many variations in the style of graves and tombs throughout China. Much productive land was taken up by cemeteries. Since the establishment of the present regime, a strong campaign has been waged to concentrate these tombs in public cemeteries that are located on land of marginal value.

It is very rare to find a private cemetery that has been in use for more than two or two and a half centuries, even though the family may have owned the land for much longer than that. It is said that when a new dynasty came to power all graves and tombs were leveled, either to provide more room for farming or because the new regime was considered a

A Han dynasty terra cotta depicts a father (center) holding his three-day-old son in accordance with ancient ritual, while an archer shoots arrows skyward to protect the child against evil.

new start, and therefore ancestors who had served the fallen regime should no longer be so conspicuously remembered. The fact that tombs in all parts of China are of relatively recent date may be a result of this custom, for the last dynasty, the Manchu, came to power little more than three centuries ago. Those who owned no country property—city dwellers and the very poor—buried their dead on wasteland just outside city walls. At some cities, such as Chungking, the necropolis extended for miles on all sides. The rich owned their plots. The very poor could find free land on the river bank, which was subject to flood in summer; it must be supposed that few of their humble interments survived the summer floods.

The inconvenience and difficulty in extending the boundaries of a city girt about with the army of the dead was great. Wherever hills or mountains stood near a city or farming area, the slopes were used for private cemeteries. In theory all wasteland belonged to the state, but there was no objection to private

families setting up their cemeteries on hill slopes, which, being rather rocky and often shaded with trees, were useless for cultivation and at the same time pleasant as a location for tombs. Unfortunately, in the north China plain, for hundreds of miles, there are no hills at all.

The Chinese paid great attention to the siting of tombs. This was determined by the pseudo science of geomancy. The natural configuration of the landscape, the direction of streams, the aspect of hills, woods, and slopes, were held to be either auspicious or malign. Tombs well sited for lucky influences to prevail ensured not only the happiness of the dead but the prosperity of their descendants. It is said, perhaps correctly, that the compass was invented to make it possible to site tombs with greater accuracy. The south-facing aspect is the most desirable. This is the yang, or sunward, direction and is associated with strength, endurance, and the positive qualities of all nature. The north is yin, the sunless side. This was unlucky, and no house was ever built to

MR. AND MRS. WEN C. FONG COLLECTION

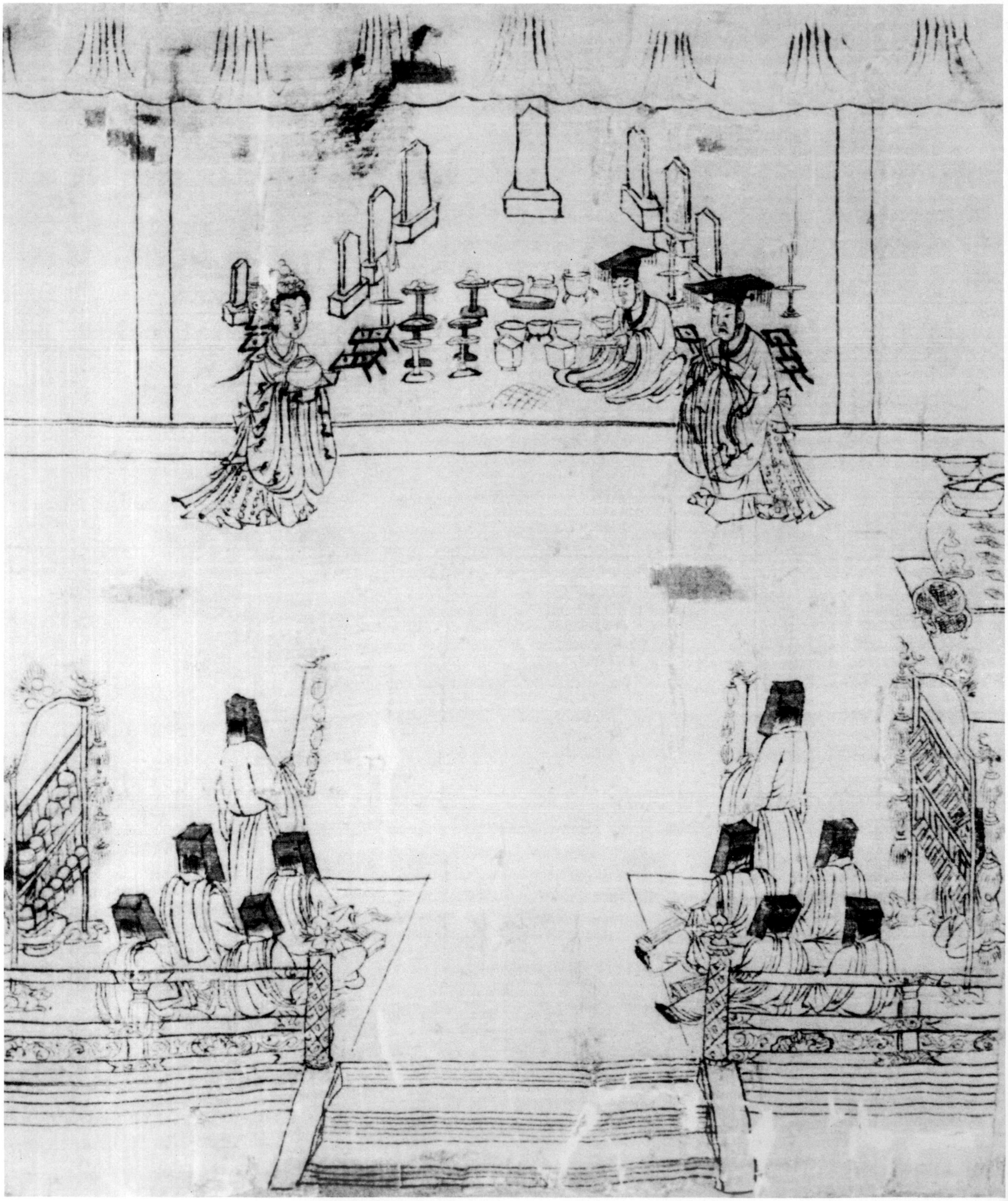

face north. A perfect example of this belief is afforded by the palace of Peking, which has to the north an artificial hill called Ching Shan, or Prospect Hill, which was built to ward off evil influences coming from the unlucky direction. On its northern slope there is only one building, a large hall where the coffin and corpse of an emperor awaiting interment were kept until the auspicious day for his funeral arrived.

It was an age-old custom for the family, and sometimes guests who might be far from home, to go up to the graves of the ancestors at the spring festival in March or early April, when the air is clear and sunny. (The festival was called Ch'ing Ming, which means "pure brightness.") An elaborate picnic was held on the grass in front of the graves. Before each dish was served, it was placed for a moment on the altar stone that stood before the tomb of the chief ancestor; sometimes it was presented to other, more recent, ancestors as well. A member of the family, often a teenage daughter, then made obeisance, or kowtow, before the tomb and removed the dish, which was then served to the assembled family and its guests. The little ceremony symbolized the providing of sustenance to the ancestral spirits by their descendants. Such customs varied from region to region, but the observance of Ch'ing Ming was universal in China. A great many of these ancient customs are now in disuse; the present regime, although not actually forbidding the veneration of ancestors, regards the elaborate ceremonies and private cemeteries that are associated with their veneration as feudal.

At the mid-autumn festival a more elaborate ceremony was held in the home. Before an altar set with food, the head of the family read out the names of every ancestor or deceased member of the family, in genealogical order, from slips of paper on which these had been written in red ink. The slip was then placed for a moment on the altar, to receive the food-offering, as it were; then it was burned in a brazier. Even in a family of moderate fortune the number of names to be read was very great, and the ceremony could last for several hours. This rite was performed in the courtyard of the house, in front of the main hall, and the altar faced south, the yang direction. These rites were probably confined to families of landlords or merchants; the poor and ordinary peasants had neither the means nor the literacy to perform them.

In both Chinese and Western literature, the Chinese family has always been described as being of the extended or great family type, in which many relatives and collaterals inhabit the same house, under the control of a patriarch and male and female elders. This was the ideal, and certainly it was the reality among a restricted circle of the rich. But it can never have been true of the mass of the poor. Their cottages were not large enough to house more than the immediate family. Other relatives might live close by in the village, but they lived in separate establishments. Still the obligations of kinship, even distant kinship, remained the same for rich and poor alike. A wealthy man or official had to aid and often support a large number of relatives, some of whom did nothing at all, while others gave help in various ways, acting often as agents or messengers. He could not discharge them; they were his family and had a claim upon any wealth he earned, which he himself could not dispose of at will. The burden they imposed on the very important man was enormous, and it was one of the main causes of corruption in official life. The great man had constantly to refill his coffers, which a horde of relatives and retainers constantly depleted.

No family escaped kinship demands. If its farm was too small to provide a livelihood for

all the sons, some of them would go off to towns to engage in a trade or work as artisans. They were expected to remit some money home. When they lost their employment or fell sick, they in turn expected to return home and be supported till they found work or recovered. There was no other form of social assistance. The state did nothing for the sick or the unemployed; they were for the family to sustain. No religious foundations existed devoted to the help of the needy: there were no orphanages, hospitals, or almshouses. Ancestor worship was rooted in the family and had no wider range. Buddhism did not inspire concern for the needy; it considers the world an "illusion" from which man may escape through knowledge. A payment was even involved before one could seek refuge by becoming a monk in a Buddhist monastery. These were the conditions of life that made the family all-important and the kinship ties so close in China. A man with no family was flotsam on a hostile sea.

From such solitaries, people from "broken families," as the old Chinese term had it, men who had no property, no home, no surviving kin, were recruited naturally the most des-

perate and violent criminals—the bandits who haunted the mountains and robbed travelers and, often enough, the ruthless leaders of rebellion. The family provided the only constant social discipline, the only welfare and relief, the only true focus for loyalty and virtue. The state claimed to be the family *in excelsis*, the all-embracing institution presided over by the father-emperor; but in practice it could fullfil this function only to a very limited degree for its close supporters, official retainers, military officers, and civil servants. The fortunes of this group rose or fell with the dynasty. They were not always treated with mercy, but in general they lived by and from the emperor the way a rich man's kinfolk lived by and from him. Without a central government they had no career and no future. Thus the scholar-officials were almost always loyal to the dynasty, even to the last. When it had really fallen, they hastened to submit to its successor.

It has been pointed out that the Chinese preoccupation with the rights and duties of the family, rather than of the community as a whole, retarded the growth of the economy, especially in the early stage of the development of capitalism. Because business was a

94

family affair, outsiders were not admitted, being considered untrustworthy. The capital was the family capital. No share capital was raised, for why should strangers share the profit or incur the losses for which the family owners were responsible? So joint stock companies had no place in the Chinese economy. Attempts to start them in imitation of Western models were rarely successful. This is one reason why the overthrow of the capitalist system, which had developed to some extent in China, met with so little resistance and evokes so few regrets. It was alien, run mainly by foreigners or by their imitators, a class of newly rich merchants who had no roots in the country and received little respect from their countrymen.

Family business was perhaps less adventurous than capitalist enterprise has been. A family's entire fortune could be lost by an investment that brought in no return or one that required the expenditure of great sums before any return could be expected. Mining, shipping on a large scale, and similar enterprises were too risky for one family to undertake. In the nineteenth century, when the state tried to enter these enterprises, it was badly served. Civil servants were totally inexperienced in business management, and businessmen who were enlisted for state enterprise from the merchant class tended to see their employment as an opportunity for personal enrichment and for the advancement of their own relatives to posts of influence where wealth could be acquired.

Merchant capital was a precarious possession in China. There was no system of insurance; fire, sack of a city, flood, or any calamity, natural or man-made, could wipe out a merchant's fortune overnight. Socially, the merchant class was placed below the peasantry. The government, usually rather hostile to commerce, did little to protect merchants and much to lighten their pockets. Even in the nineteenth century the merchants who were chosen by the government to monopolize foreign trade at Canton were very often ruined by government exactions. They were blamed for troubles with foreigners. Their activities might bring great profit for a short time, but seemed certain to ruin their families in the end. Naturally, merchants sought to put their savings into land in order to improve their status and to stabilize their fortunes. Under several dynasties this was forbidden by law, but the law was constantly evaded.

The economic consequence of the Chinese family system had many ramifications. The system fostered social stability, but hindered economic development beyond a certain point. Because mineral development was neglected, technology, a field in which the Chinese were no less gifted than any other people, had little chance for development. The shoulder harness for horses, the water mill, improved gears, gunpowder, the compass, paper, and printing were invented by the Chinese. Except for the last two, which served the tastes and interests of the scholar-gentry, these inventions were not fully exploited.

The Chinese family system had a profound effect on society. In conjunction with the state, which was patterned on it, it kept China in balance for many centuries, free from major social dislocations. Dynastic change became merely a political upset that did not touch the family system; on the contrary, it usually strengthened it, weeding out undesirable anomalies, such as the expansion of great landholdings.

Chinese literature, especially the great novels of the period from the sixteenth to the eighteenth centuries, which have the family system as one of their main themes, shows very plainly that the system did not always work in accordance with theory. Theory made the

*Seven members of a prosperous Ming dynasty family are shown
wearing richly brocaded robes and posing for a group portrait.*

senior male member, the father or grandfather, the patriarch, with unchallenged power
over his relatives and descendants. In practice
the senior female member of the family, the
grandmother or even great-grandmother, was
more powerful within the household. The
head of the family did indeed rule the outside
interests of the whole group. He made the
business decisions, planned investment and
the purchase or sale of land, and chose the
careers of the younger members. But inside
the house he deferred to his wife or mother.
She ran the household—engaged, dismissed,
or punished servants, took charge of accounts,
and arranged leases for any part of the property. Her social influence was paramount, and
it was usually conservative.

Over the younger women of the family the
matriarch held exclusive authority. Marriages
were her business, and it was rare, indeed, for
one to be arranged by the men without her
consent. In rich and official families the
women were educated, although not to the
high standard of classical learning that studying for the civil service examination imposed
on men. Women's taste ran to popular fiction,
Buddhist or Taoist literature, and the arts.
Religion had its strongest hold among the
women, who did not, as a rule, study the
Confucian classics deeply. Men were often
agnostic; women usually strongly Buddhist.
Mao Tse-tung has referred to the attachment
his mother had for Buddhism—a situation
that was normal in all educated families. As a
result, religion in the home was dominated by
the views of the women. Buddhist monks
were called in to perform ceremonies and conduct rites, in which the men for the most part
did not believe.

These upper-class customs were reflected to
a degree among the peasants and the poor.
Poorly educated men were often enough as
superstitious as their wives, and the peasant

wife, with no servants, no education, and little
money, had small scope for her authority
within the home. But like the upper-class
woman, the peasant woman ran the household. Her domination was mainly expressed
through command over her daughter-in-law.
Concubinage, widely practiced by the rich,
was economically impossible for the poor, and
in consequence large households were not
found in peasant society. Still the standards
that were set by the scholar-gentry were those
the peasant aimed at and hoped to emulate if
he grew rich enough to sustain them.

The Communist reformers found repugnant the domination of these standards, which
they called feudal. Since their advent to power
they have done their best to eliminate them
and to remove their economic foundation.
The nationalization of the land and its distribution into co-operative farms grouped in
communes has entirely destroyed the position
of the landlord-gentry, a position they had
held for some two thousand years. A former
landlord can now lay claim only to whatever
"work points" he earns on the co-operative
farm and to the share of the co-operative's income represented by the small portion of his
land that was left to him at the first land reform—a portion big enough for only one man
to work. He is reduced to the same position as
any other peasant farmer. Some educational
advantages have lingered among landlord
families because they were literate before the
revolution. However, their literacy counts for
very little, for members of landlord families
are excluded from the managing committees
of co-operatives and communes. (Although
they are legally eligible, they are never, in fact,
elected.) Therefore a great many former landlords have probably left the land for the cities,
where they are better able to profit from the
fact that they are educated.

The new government abolished legal con-

cubinage. The extended family in its large mansion has almost disappeared for economic reasons as well as because of political and social pressures. Although private house property in urban centers has not been abolished, most families cannot afford to own and use a mansion. Either it is sold to the government or rented. Everyone is under strong social and economic pressure to work. Members of a large family can no longer count on the wealth of its head to support them, nor upon his social and political influence to find them jobs. The motives for living in large kin groups have diminished or disappeared. The modern Chinese family is usually the immediate family —parents and children—but often an old parent who cannot work is part of the household. This was, of course, the reality of peasant society in earlier times; the Communist movement in very many ways represents a transference of peasant custom and society to the whole nation. Nowhere is this seen more clearly than in the changing character of the family.

Contemporary Chinese sociologists argue that this change is really due more to the modernization of society than to the political character of the Communist regime. They point out that in medieval Europe also, the great family was the norm among the nobility and gentry; it began to die out in the sixteenth century and was nearly obsolete by the end of the eighteenth century for economic rather than political reasons. Suitable, they claim, for a feudal society and economy, it became obsolete and obstructive when the capitalist system developed.

In a broad sense the modern Chinese sociologists are probably correct in this assessment of the decline of the extended family system. Its decay was already visible under the republic. The great cost of education at modern universities in China or overseas was already seri-

ously eroding the status of the gentry in the countryside. Confucian classical education was relatively cheap and easily available at local schools maintained by the clan, but after the fall of the last dynasty, in 1912, it was no longer the gateway to office, and thus to wealth and power. The lesser gentry could not even afford to send all their sons to the new local university, let alone overseas. As a result, power and office increasingly passed to the sons of wealthy merchants in the coastal cities, who could easily bear the costs of modern education. The rise of the Soong family, a merchant clan from Shanghai, is an outstanding example of the change in the traditional power structure that took place before the Communist revolution. The heavy taxation and the other exactions of the military governors who ruled the provinces during the years of the republic were another direct cause of the decline of the gentry. Life on the land was ceasing to be profitable, comfortable, or even safe. The gentry withdrew to the cities and sought new occupations. This tended to undermine and destroy the old family system.

It is most improbable that the traditional system will ever be revived. Modern industry and technology, and the professions that they create, will increasingly absorb the educated class, which itself is growing in size with the expansion of universal education. The peasants now work collectively, which removes many of the incentives for close family connection and kinship group-activity. Industrial workers rarely concern themselves with relatives more distant than their own parents and children. The Chinese family system was an institution perfectly adapted to a stable agricultural society. It is manifestly not well-adapted to a dynamic and rapidly industrializing society. That society will certainly generate its own problems, but they will not be those of the old family system.

99

The Second Sex

According to an old Chinese proverb, the most beautiful and talented daughter is not as desirable as a deformed son. Preference for boys was so open, in fact, that in upper-class families a cherished son was occasionally given a girl's name during his childhood in the belief that evil spirits, thinking the child a girl—and therefore less valuable—would pass him by. The birth of a male heir was considered a matter of utmost urgency and was sought by every possible magical, medical, and spiritual means. The birth of a daughter was greeted with considerably less enthusiasm, and peasant fathers, who were unwilling or unable to support yet another female, sometimes drowned newborn girls.

The practice of infanticide, though never common, increased during times of economic duress, when widespread unemployment made sons a burden as well. During these periods of famine, however, a grown daughter could be placed as a cook, musician, or concubine in the home of a wealthy official. While still a child she might be purchased by a far-sighted financier and raised in his household to be wed to one of his sons or—in cases where a son was expected but as yet unborn—retained as a "daughter-in-law in anticipation."

No matter what her circumstances, a woman could look forward to a life of subjugation—to her father and eldest brother in her childhood, to her husband and his mother after her marriage, and to her own sons upon her husband's death. (Her only opportunity for self-assertion came through her sons' marriages, when she too became a mother-in-law.) Once married, she was known only by two surnames, her husband's and her father's, and regardless of her age or status, she was generally addressed as "aunt" or "grandmother." She could be divorced if barren, chronically ill, or neglectful of her father-in-law, and she was expected to live a life of perfect submissiveness as outlined in a T'ang dynasty manual: "A chaste woman must not go out often . . . and must work very hard. If asked to come, she must come at once; if asked to go, she must go quickly. If she fails . . . reproach and beat her. . . ."

The painting opposite, attributed to a fourteenth-century artist, shows the sixth-century Emperor Hou Chu seated before a landscape screen, composing a poem. To inspire him a concubine plays the lute, while three servants look on. 101

SMITHSONIAN INSTITUTION, FREER GALLERY OF ART

FOGG ART MUSEUM, HARVARD UNIVERSITY, FRANCIS H. BURR FUND PURCHASE

LADIES OF THE COURT

Feminine obesity—in imitation of the ponderous Yang Kuei-fei, concubine to Emperor Ming Huang (A.D. 685–762)—came briefly into vogue during the T'ang dynasty; but the fashion soon gave way to a more durable concept of feminine beauty, one which emphasized pale skin, a moon face, and a boyishly slim figure. The classic Chinese beauty clad herself in the *cheong-sam*, a loose-fitting gown with overlong sleeves, and bound her feet from childhood, believing that her efforts to walk on deformed "lily feet" produced an alluring sway. Socialites and singing girls alike shared a taste for head ornaments, powders, pearls, and feathers.

T'ang dynasty tomb figures, above right, represent opposite ideals of feminine beauty: one fragile, the other portly. At far left is another T'ang figure clad in a gown called a cheong-sam. *The drawing at center shows ladies of a Sung dynasty court adjusting their coiffures.*

CONCUBINES AND COURTESANS

"Be moderate in all seven passions," a Confucian maxim urges. Despite tales of decadent self-indulgence, the Chinese generally observed that dictum. Sexual passions were discussed openly and satisfied without shame. Wealthy officials maintained concubines, and—according to Marco Polo—the less affluent enjoyed the attentions of a "multitude of sinful women," who lay waiting "in richly ornamented apartments" or, more frequently, in taverns, aboard small sampans, and in wayside huts. Amid such licentiousness, officials' wives were permitted to take "complementary husbands." The pampered lives of imperial concubines fostered tales like that of one indulged beauty whose favorite pastime was tearing up expensive silk. Perhaps the most famous of all concubines was Yang Kuei-fei; horsemen brought litchi nuts to her daily from a thousand miles away.

In a detail from a seventeenth-century painting at left, a couple embraces in a comfortably furnished garden pavilion. At center is a pampered Han dynasty courtesan reclining seductively beneath a canopy. At right, Ts'ui Ying-ying, the famous heroine of a Yüan dynasty drama, Romance of the West Chamber, *is shown with her lover, while her maid, a counterpart of the Spanish duenna, acts as a chaperone for the happy proceedings.*

CHILD'S PLAY

Under China's extended family system, in which several generations lived under the same roof, the offspring of any family member was considered the proud possession of all his relations. In this hierarchal commune the older children took care of their younger siblings. All of them played together in the compound or the streets, and generally received only mild reproof for misdeeds.

Often forced to amuse themselves in cramped courtyards with the few crude toys that were available to them, Chinese children developed simple group games such as "shuttlecock," "jack stones," "cat's-cradle," and "fox and geese." The playing of these games ended when the children reached the age of seven. After that age, in accordance with classic prescription, boys and girls were no longer permitted to play together, nor to "occupy the same mat or eat together."

Reminiscent of the work of the Flemish master Pieter Bruegel, this detail, from a Sung dynasty miniature called One Hundred Children at Play, *shows a group of small fry (upper right) playing "tease the crane," while others, with false mustaches, pretend to be grown-up jugglers and acrobats. Still others—some riding hobbyhorses—play soldier.*

THE WOMAN'S ROLE

"Rearing the silkworm and working cloth are the most important of the employments of the female," proclaimed the Confucian essayist Lu Chao. "Preparing and serving up the food for the household and setting in order the sacrifices follow next, each of which must be attended to; after them, study and learning can fill up the time." Generally, after sewing, cooking, caring for the old and young, and handling a variety of social obligations, Chinese women found little time remaining. Those with spare time—these were mostly women from the wealthiest households—happily passed up cerebral pursuits for hours spent conversing, embroidering, playing mah-jongg, and, among some, smoking opium.

Two details from a twelfth-century scroll show women preparing newly woven silk by pounding the cloth with pestles and then ironing it. The painting, which has been attributed to Emperor Hui Tsung, is copied from an older work.

AMAZONS

Many of China's legendary heroines and remarkable historical figures are of peasant origin, and Chinese lore abounds with tales of warrior-maidens and crusading damsels, such as the T'ang dynasty "Joan of Arc" who built a citadel at Lei-chou to protect herself and her followers from marauders. Among the most remarkable were General Mu Lan—who served his emperor with distinction on the battlefield for twelve years before revealing to his employer and his army that he was in fact Miss Hua Mu Lan —and the unscrupulous Wu Chao, who rose from child-concubine to empress of all China through a series of Machiavellian palace intrigues.

The elaborate coiffures, plucked eyebrows, heavily made-up faces, fragile figures, and voluminous brocade gowns associated with Chinese womanhood actually were the accouterments of only a small minority. Few of the delicate, deliberately crippled, "lily-footed" courtesans could have withstood a single day—let alone a lifetime—in the rice paddies, where sturdy peasant women in ragged clothes worked from dawn to dusk beside their husbands.

Terra-cotta figures, dating from the seventh century, show women playing polo. T'ang dynasty women, unlike those of later times, were allowed to participate in rigorous outdoor games.

5 The Three Ways

A sixth-century gilt bronze sculpture shows Kuan-yin, the Buddhist goddess of mercy, holding a lotus, the symbol of purity and of fruitfulness, in her hand.

The place assigned to religion in the lives of the people and in the minds of their rulers has been one of the most distinctive aspects of Chinese civilization. Alone, perhaps, among the peoples of the world, the ancient Chinese made no images of their high deities, contenting themselves with jade symbols of varying shape. They alone were willing in later ages to accept three differing religious systems at the same time, according to each a measure of belief and harmonizing quite inconsistent theologies with the saying, "three ways to one goal." When considering the nature and development of religious beliefs in China, it is necessary to discard most of the preconceived ideas about religion that Western man has absorbed through the Judaeo-Christian tradition. In the Chinese world the rites of organized religion were at an early period separated from ethical teaching, which became increasingly indifferent to the supernatural and ended in outright agnosticism. Religion branched out, developing separate forms, with very different practices and beliefs adopted by the masses and by the educated class. Alien influences were late in coming and slow in operation; Buddhism, the one significant foreign religion that did affect China, was much transformed by Chinese ways of thought.

There is some resemblance to the history of religion in other parts of the world. In China, as in the ancient world of Greece and Rome, there is a sharp break between the early age of purely native religion and the later age that saw the introduction and spread of a universal religion. In the West this religion was Christianity; in China it was Buddhism. In the West the triumph of Christianity was complete; all other creeds faded out, and the modern scholar of Greek or Latin civilization is not in any way tempted to believe in the ancient gods. In China the ancient gods lived on, in coexistence with foreign creeds. The philosophy of later China owes little or nothing to Buddhist thought. The religious history of Europe would have been very close to that of China if educated Europeans had remained Stoics or Epicureans, giving only grudging recognition to the religion of the masses—Christianity—and not permitting it to influence education or accepting it as the highest moral teaching.

The earliest record of Chinese religious practice and belief is contained in the oracle bone inscriptions of the Shang period. A Shang king would make his request for guidance to the royal ancestors; their reply was interpreted by the oracle from cracks formed on the bone. These inscriptions reveal that the royal ancestors were thought of as protective spirits, with power to forewarn their descendants and aid them in distress. Another early document that demonstrates this belief is the prayer offered to the royal ancestors by the duke of Chou early in the Chou dynasty. The duke appeals to his ancestors to spare the life of his elder brother, King Wu, and take his own instead, as he is less worthy and less important to the dynasty. The royal ancestors thus appear as even more important than or at least equally significant as the supreme deity, t'ien, "heaven." It would appear that the royal dynasty believed its first ancestor to have been Heaven itself.

Much of what is known about the belief and character of the ancient religion is conjectural. Documents are few and monuments do not exist. Except for temples devoted to ancestor worship, there are no temples dating from this early age, and indeed, no evidence that any ever existed. In the Chou period, in the first millennium B.C., records begin to mention more gods. One was the god of the Yellow River, who was styled by a title that has been translated as "count," the same title that was used in the feudal hierarchy. This rather suggests that feudal titles may have had

religious origins. Human sacrifices were performed to the divine Count of the Yellow River. A girl was chosen to be his bride and then set adrift in a boat on the swift and dangerous current. The belief in river gods in the form of dragons survives in popular religion. Although human sacrifice was discontinued in ancient times, the idea continues that the river god claims as his own any man who falls into the stream. Boatmen are often afraid to rescue such unfortunates, believing that the god, cheated of his sacrifice, would claim them as a substitute. It may well be that Chairman Mao Tse-tung is deliberately trying to break down this ancient superstition with his much-publicized swims in the Yangtze.

In time many other local deities are recorded, deities of mountains and lakes. There is one thing they all have in common: no image of them was made or worshiped. The ancient jade symbols did stand for the great gods, but did not depict them. They are geometrical or have the form of some instrument presumably used in the rites. A round jade disk with a hole in the center was the symbol of Heaven; it was probably intended as a picture of the sky and the sun. A hollow square-shaped jade tube, perhaps originally a phallic symbol, is known to have represented the earth god. In later times both Heaven and Earth were symbolized by a plain wooden or lacquer tablet on which was inscribed the name of the appropriate deity. The same practice was employed in ancestor worship, the only religious representation being the name on a tablet. Ancient Chinese religion had this abstract quality to a marked degree: relationship with the supernatural was through one's ancestors, not through acts of personal worship of a great deity. Since the ancient Chinese were not accustomed to represent their gods in human form, the art of sculpture did not develop at an early date; when it did finally develop, in pre-Buddhist times, it had a secular character.

If the religion of the ruling class in the far past remains obscure to modern scholarship, the religion of the people is hardly recorded at all. It is clear that they had no part in the feudal rites of ancestor worship; they probably worshiped the gods of rivers and mountains. The only form of unorthodox, or popular, religion that is known to have had a wide currency in the feudal period was the Shamanist cult. Shamanist priests or priestesses, called Wu, were recruited among people who had the capacity to enter into a trance and to prophesy in that condition. They could not, of course, form an hereditary priesthood. They seem to have been numerous, respected, perhaps feared, and certainly influential. Confucian historians and writers did not appreciate this type of religious activity, and one consequence of their prejudice is that little has been recorded of the Wu and their practices. There is good reason to believe that such cults have survived in popular religion down to the present day, especially in south China.

From the fifth to the third centuries B.C., from the waning of the feudal period to the foundation of the unified empire, widespread changes in social conditions were reflected in religious innovations, or perhaps in the spread and recognition of cults that had long been active, if obscure. Ancestor worship ceased to be a special prerogative of the feudal nobility and became the general practice of the people. Local magical cults, especially those of the eastern seacoast, spread through the united empire in both Ch'in and Han times, and obtained the patronage of emperors and other powerful men. Before long these local cults began to influence and to be influenced by the quietist philosophy of Taoism, which used allegories and accounts of supernatural occurrences to illustrate its teaching. Perhaps, as

some scholars think, Taoism was the ethical refinement of an ancient nature worship rather than an independent philosophy unattached to any religious system. Just as Confucianism was an ethical outgrowth of the ancient ancestor worship, substituting moral duties for the performance of traditional rites, so ancient Taoism may have been the refined doctrine of a simple worship of the powers of nature.

In the Han period Taoism became increasingly identified with the magical cults, which seem to have originated mainly on the eastern seaboard. Ideas that later became widespread in medieval Europe originated with these cults. Belief in the Philosopher's Stone, by which dross metal could be converted into gold, and in the alchemist's doctrine that it is possible to discover the *elixir vitae*, or drug of immortality, are both of Chinese origin. Already in Ch'in times the Emperor Shih Huang Ti had sent an expedition to the Isles of the Immortals in quest of this drug. Later the Han dynasty Emperor Wu (156–87 B.C.) was equally fascinated by the drug and attempted to send emissaries to the Immortals to obtain it. More worldly wise than Shih Huang Ti, he had his envoys watched. When he discovered that they had neither embarked for the Isles nor met any Immortals on the mainland, he put them to death.

These failures do not seem to have checked the growth of the magical cults. Its practitioners maintained a regular school, and perhaps more than one, at which their arts were taught. How much the adepts themselves believed can hardly be ascertained, but popular support for their doctrines was very real. Taoist beliefs spread, too, to the well-educated classes. Some of the Han bas-reliefs that depict religious scenes are clearly inspired by the magical cults. These reliefs decorated the tombs of influential and wealthy men. This is not the only piece of evidence indicating that the educated

A Ming dynasty carving of white jade shows a portly Mother Earth riding upon a mythological deerlike animal.

Han gentry were not so Confucian as the historians would like to believe. The scenes portrayed on these tombs show nobles living a life of luxury and enjoyment, hunting, feasting, visiting in smart chariots, and watching theatricals or acrobatic entertainments. The life of the mind is not very conspicuously illustrated, and the motifs of Han art are far more earthy than those of later periods. Han gentlemen lived like sporting country squires and had no reluctance to display this manner of life in their tomb decorations, doubtless believing that the soul would enjoy in the future life the pleasures that man had enjoyed on earth.

A comparative uniformity of religious belief among all social classes seems to have characterized the Han period. At the close of the period this uniformity was disrupted by two factors. The first was the outbreak of revolt among peasants who were followers of popular religious movements. The second was the introduction of Buddhism. The revolutionary religious societies, one called the Red Eyebrows and the second the Yellow Turbans, arose in times of deep distress that resulted from famine and administrative inefficiency. Both, inspired by a doctrine of the magical cults, preached invulnerability to wounds and immortality for the faithful. The Yellow Turbans, the more formidable of the great peasant risings, were actually led by a priest of one of the magical cults, a man who claimed to have found a magic cure for an epidemic that was prevalent at the time. The Yellow Turban movement directly contributed to the fall of the Han empire.

In later times, largely as a result of these uprisings, it became a fixed belief among the ruling class that popular religious movements were potentially dangerous, if not actually subversive—and this was indeed very often true. Apocalyptic creeds readily appealed to men who were near despair from starvation and misgovernment. Almost all the great peasant risings were based on such circumstances. The pattern continued down to modern times, among both the T'ai P'ing rebels of the mid-nineteenth century, who adopted a variant form of Christianity, and the Boxers of the 1900 rebellion, who preached invulnerability to their followers. Much of the hostility to Christianity displayed over the centuries by the Chinese ruling class stemmed from this situation.

The coming of Buddhism is the second factor distinguishing the religion of the post-Han period from that of earlier times. Buddhism reached China along the trade routes to India and Central Asia, which Han conquests had opened up in the first century B.C. Soon monks as well as merchants traveled these roads. The consequences of Buddhism's arrival were profound, but they were slow in developing. Not until the second century A.D. did the Chinese government take official notice of the religion, which then began to receive court patronage. After being received by the merchant class and by others who came into contact with travelers along the great caravan routes, Buddhism was accepted in court and educated circles. Only very slowly did it spread downward through the mass of the people.

Shamanist magic was thought to give man power over the gods. An unknown Ming artist depicted a shaman seated under a tree and exorcising demons.

115

The famous Buddhist pilgrim Hsüan Tsang, who set out from China for India in A.D. *629, is shown returning sixteen years later, laden with Buddhist scrolls and with sacred relics.*

Unlike Christianity, which arose within the Roman empire, Buddhism was an alien religion whose early missionaries were foreigners, Indians. There is a very wide difference between Chinese and any Indian language, a difference made more acute by the fact that Chinese is written with ideograms and the Indian languages with an alphabet. Many obstacles had to be overcome before Buddhist teaching could be translated and disseminated.

By the sixth century, however, Buddhism was widespread in China—in the north, where Tatar dynasties reigned, and in the south, which was controlled by Chinese regimes. Buddhism was patronized by rulers in both parts of the country. One southern emperor, Wu Ti, was so devoted an adherent that he renounced the throne three times to become a monk; twice he had to be ransomed by great payments to monasteries before he was released for imperial duties. On the third occasion his conduct sparked a rebellion that dethroned him. Around this time some of the finest Buddhist art was executed, largely sculpture carved in the walls of monastery grottoes; its situation has fortunately helped preserve much of it. Buddhism brought about a profound revolution in art, partly by emphasizing sculpture in the round and partly by providing new motifs and inspiration. Art became, and for a while remained, predominantly religious.

Great though the influence of Buddhism was on art, it was not able to equal the impact of Confucianism on philosophy, history, and literature. The Chinese remained Confucians in government and education. At the period when Buddhism reached its apogee in China its limitations appear most clearly. It was not a social religion, and the Chinese people have always had a very strong humanist outlook. One part of Chinese nature was little touched by Buddhism, remaining concerned with the ordering of the world and its people, which

the true Buddhist considered "illusion." Since Buddhism made no effort to enter the fields of government, family life, or community activity, these remained dominated by Confucian thinking. There arose that peculiarly Chinese phenomenon, the ability to hold two opposing theologies at the same time on the grounds that both might be partly right. In any case, to the Chinese practice was much more important than theory.

To be consistent, a Confucian, believing in the duty of sons to parents and in the duty of parents to beget sons to continue the race and the ancestral sacrifices, could not believe that the soul of man migrated at death to another being, man or beast, retaining no connection whatever with the earthly parents of the previous existence. Equally, a true Buddhist could not believe in ancestor worship or in the duties of filial piety. Why should a man revere a physical ancestor whose spirit was now transmigrated into some quite different being, perhaps even a nonhuman. The begetting of children was not a proper concern of the Buddhist. Children would be the temporary habitations of souls transmigrated from no one could know where or what, owing only their physical form to their parents. The duty of the Buddhist was to gain through knowledge a higher incarnation, until ultimately he achieved nirvana, the absence of striving and reunion with the infinite, with Buddha. These ideals were far indeed from the Confucian scholar's secular and ethical outlook.

Taoism presented yet another category of belief with its pantheon of gods, many of them from the ancient Chinese world. Confucianism made very slight obeisance to the ancient gods, in whom Confucians had largely lost belief. Taoism, on the other hand, organized its gods into a hierarchy in charge of the celestial and terrestrial functions of nature, just as if they were officials in charge of ministries

and provinces. The river dragons regulated or
failed to regulate the flow of the great streams.
They demanded their due respect and worship,
their temples, and their priests. Mountain
gods ruled the high peaks and received similar
deference. This pattern was followed with all
the phenomena of nature. The Jade Emperor, a celestial monarch modeled on the
emperor on earth, presided over all nature in
remote majesty.

This was the outer doctrine, but Taoism
also preached to the more learned and enlightened an inner teaching that instructed devotees
in the lore and exercises by which the drug of
immortality could be obtained and gold made
from dross. The old philosophic teaching of
Taoism lingered also. This concentrated on
the way in which the sage might find identity
with Tao, with nature, and thereby transcend
the vicissitudes of human existence. Philosophic Taoism made physical immortality a
side effect of identity with Tao rather than an
end in itself.

Belief in these Taoist doctrines was inconsistent with both Buddhism and Confucianism. Physical immortality was an irrelevance
to Buddhism, an undesirable possibility to the
Confucian. An immortal might have millions
of offspring in due time, but he could not be
anyone's ancestor in heaven. This was a shock-
ing and destructive notion to the ordered
world of Confucian thought. Fortunately, it
presented a purely theoretical problem; the
alleged Immortals proclaimed by Taoists were
rarely accepted as such by Confucian critics.

The formative period of religion in China
extended to the close of the seventh century
A.D. From the fifth to the seventh centuries the
Chinese developed several new schools of
Buddhism that were unknown in India; there
the Buddhist religion was already succumbing
to a revival of Hinduism. The most famous and
influential of the new Chinese schools was the

In this Sung dynasty painting, Buddhist holy men demonstrate the mysterious power of their sacred scriptures to a group of Taoists.

Ch'an, which is well known to the West under the Japanese form of this word, Zen. Ch'an was undoubtedly influenced by Taoist thought. Like Taoism, it discards the need for book learning and derides formal teaching. Enlightenment must come as a sudden revelation, the product of long meditation, withdrawal from the concerns of the world, and concentration on self-knowledge. Ever since the feudal age these ideas have served as a counterweight in Chinese thinking to the formality and the logic of Confucian doctrine. When the lifelong Confucian scholar and official was at last permitted to retire, he would become a Ch'an monk or a Taoist hermit, withdrawing to some mountain retreat to devote his old age to contemplation, painting, and poetry. The Chinese did not find any violent inconsistency in the "three ways," for they could all be directed to the "one goal," the attainment of wisdom, peace, and tranquillity of spirit. Ch'an had a great following in China. Later the school reached Japan, where it was equally widespread. In modern times it has had a strong appeal for Western scholars and artists.

By the early tenth century A.D., at the end of the T'ang dynasty, Buddhism, except for Ch'an Buddhism, was past its prime. It had become worldly and overly wealthy. The monasteries were great landlords, the monks were more interested in politics than in religion, and even Buddhist art was becoming secular in spirit. A T'ang scholar-critic remarked that sculptors and painters made the Bodhisattvas look like dancing girls, so that every dancing girl thought she should be a Bodhisattva. Han Yü, a famous Confucian scholar and official of the ninth century, bitterly attacked the superstitions that contemporary Buddhism was encouraging and wrote a memorial to the emperor complaining of the reception of a holy relic, a bone of Buddha. His complaint (which appears on page 199 in the anthology of Chi-

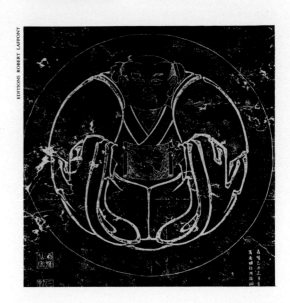

nese literature) is one of the gems of Chinese prose, but it seems to have made no impression upon the Buddhist-minded emperor, except to provoke him to disgrace and exile Han Yü. One of the late T'ang emperors, inspired by the wealth of the monasteries rather than by any positive aversion to Buddhism, instituted a widespread persecution of the religion. Monasteries were sequestrated. Monks and nuns were forced to return to secular life and to marry each other, since their renunciation of family ties was offensive to Confucian ideas and, incidentally, reduced the number of tax-payers.

This persecution by the Emperor Wu Tsung in A.D. 845 was directed at first against another alien religion, Persian Manichaeism, which had made some progress in the T'ang period. When the prohibition against Manichaeism was extended to other alien creeds, not only Buddhism suffered; Nestorian Christianity also felt the effects. Nestorianism, which had been introduced by monks from Syria, then part of the Byzantine empire, in the early seventh century A.D., became popular and influential in T'ang China. A monument that still exists in the T'ang capital at Ch'ang-an records the restoration of the city's church in the eighth century and lists among the benefactors several imperial princes.

Buddhism seems to have recovered ground swiftly when Wu Tsung was succeeded by emperors less opposed to it—and uninterested in despoiling a religion that had already lost much of its worldly wealth. But Nestorianism and Manichaeism, both much more recent arrivals in China, did not recover from the persecution. In the tenth century a visiting Syrian Nestorian monk reports that the churches were abandoned and in ruins, and the faithful diminished and dispersed. Perhaps even the memory of Nestorian enterprise in China would have perished had not the Ch'ang-an

monument survived to be noticed by Christian missionaries in a later age.

Manichaeism had originally been introduced by Persian visitors to China; in the early T'ang period more Persians, refugees from the Persian Sassanid empire, recently conquered by the Arab Moslems, established themselves in Ch'ang-an, and despite some persecution, were permitted to practice their Zoroastrian religion. It never seems to have spread beyond their narrow circle, however. The refugee community, which included the heir to the Persian throne, was gradually absorbed into the ruling Chinese upper class.

Another alien religion, Islam, did establish a foothold in China during the T'ang period, and gradually extended its influence in later centuries. Islam was introduced in the north by Uigur mercenary troops in the late seventh or early eighth century A.D. Almost at the same time the Arab traders who frequented the ports of Canton and of Ch'uan-chou in Fukien brought their religion to southern China. One of the two earliest mosques surviving in China was constructed some time later in Canton. (The second was built in Ch'ang-an, the T'ang capital.) The practice of the religion was for long confined to aliens, whether soldiers or merchants. For this reason the introduction of Islam is hardly noticed by the Chinese historians. Perhaps because it attracted so little attention and seemed a foreign custom, it was permitted to exist and extend its influence slowly.

The Moslem community has always been regarded as alien. Today Moslems are officially classed as a national minority. This permits the Chinese Communist government to countenance the practice of Islam as a custom of a minority people, but does not permit the preaching of the religion to non-Moslem Chinese. The Moslem community is widespread in China. It is found in every province, but

The Chinese had the unique capacity to embrace more than one religion simultaneously. A perfect illustration of that ability can be seen in this stone rubbing of a figure with the head of a Buddha and the characteristic robes of a Confucian scholar.

OVERLEAF: *A detail from a Taoist fresco,* The Lord of the Southern Dipper, *shows Taoist luminaries. The haloed Empress of Heaven is at left; at center is her consort, the Jade Emperor, and beside him is Lao Tzŭ, the philosopher-teacher of Taoism.*
ROYAL ONTARIO MUSEUM; WALTER CURTIN, COURTESY *Life*

A sixteenth-century porcelain bowl is inscribed with a good luck formula in Persian, the language spoken by the Moslems of China.

large numbers of Moslems appear only in the northwest and southwest, in the provinces of Shensi, Kansu, and Yünnan. This reflects the fact that most of the first Moslems in China were mercenary soldiers recruited from Central Asia and later settled in border areas. The original Moslem community in Canton has survived, but its numbers are small. In later centuries the Moslems increased their strength by buying up the children of famine refugees and rearing them as Moslems. This practice gradually introduced much Chinese blood into what was originally a foreign community. Yet even to this day, especially in Yünnan and the northwest, Moslems have characteristic Armenoid features, sharp noses and long oval faces, which mark their distant Central Asian origin. In almost all other respects they are wholly Chinese, and even their mosques are built in Chinese architectural style.

Moslems were also identified by the rather restricted range of occupations in which they engaged. Transport, especially land transport by mule and camel caravan, was almost a Moslem monopoly. They were famous for their excellent restaurants, and at the other end of the scale, dominated the small cookshop and itinerant food-vendor trade. They were also favored as butchers. These trades were Moslem largely because Moslem restaurants and butcher shops were reliable and hygienic. The Islamic rites connected with the slaughter of animals ensured that the beast be cleanly killed and that no meat be taken from an animal that had died of disease or old age.

Strangely enough, Moslems were also the principal curio and art merchants. As this trade involves the buying and selling of Buddhist and Taoist works of art—graven images that are strictly forbidden to Moslems—it is curious that Moslems should have become so prominently associated with it. One reason for their involvement is that works of art are easily

transportable merchandise, and the Moslems controlled transport. Naturally they preferred to obtain and transport objects that would fetch high prices. The second reason is that many, if not most, Buddhist and Taoist sculptures and paintings offered on the curio market were originally stolen from monasteries and temples or sold by indigent and impious monks. Moslems would have little fear or reluctance to buy up stolen holy objects of religions that they regard as idolatrous.

In the Sung period, A.D. 960–1126, a community of Jews became established at the Sung capital of K'ai-feng in Honan province. The community remained in K'ai-feng for some eight hundred years, until its dispersal and disappearance in the late nineteenth century. It is hardly noticed by the traditional historians, but some literary record of it has been discovered. The accounts given of the few and impoverished survivors by early missionaries leave no doubt that the community flourished for a very long time, with its synagogue and with some scholars who could read the Hebrew scriptures. It is not clear why it should have declined at so late a date after having survived many catastrophic events, such as the capture of the city of K'ai-feng by barbarian invaders. Although the K'ai-feng Jews were, doubtless, originally immigrants from western Asia, they became almost entirely indistinguishable from their pure Chinese neighbors, except in religion. There is no evidence that these Jews were at any period persecuted for their religion or discriminated against on account of their race. Probably very few Chinese were aware of their existence, and still fewer aware of their connection with the Jewish people and religion in other parts of the world.

With the exception of Buddhism, all these foreign religions were transitory phenomenons in China and made but limited impact. These facts must be remembered in assessing the later influence of Christianity as preached in China by Catholics and Protestants. The Chinese were not unaccustomed to alien religions, which came and in due course went. The court favored some for a time, but court favor is fickle. Those that had a secure base in a sizeable foreign community that slowly assimilated with the Chinese people tended to survive. Those that were primarily based on small or restricted groups of foreign residents tended to wither away as these groups lost power and influence.

In the late sixteenth and early seventeenth centuries, after the Portuguese discovery of the Indian Ocean sea route, some Catholic missionaries came to China. They were, of course, quite unaware of their Nestorian predecessors and their ultimate fate. They saw in China a vast mission field, ripe for wholesale conversion. There was no dominant religion hostile to Christianity, such as Islam in the Middle East or even Hinduism in India. The educated class, Confucian scholars, were imagined as similar to the Stoic philosophers of the late Roman empire, men trained in moral philosophy, which was not repugnant to Christian doctrine. The uneducated masses followed pagan creeds and polytheistic cults very similar to those that the Church had fought and conquered in the Roman world. No Catholic missionary could doubt that a similar triumph awaited the Church in China. The victory of the Christians in late Roman times had been secured and perpetuated by converting the emperor himself. What was needed in China was a Chinese "Constantine."

One of the first missionaries to the Chinese, Saint Francis Xavier, died on a small island off the coast without ever setting foot on the mainland. But in 1601 Matteo Ricci reached Peking and established himself there as a respected, if foreign, scholar. The early Jesuits had every advantage for their work. They were

When the declining T'ang dynasty lost control over Sinkiang in the eighth century A.D., *Moslems moved into the region and assumed control of the Western trade routes. Moslem communities have survived in some east coast cities and in northwestern China, where the pagodalike mosque (above) is located.*

123

*A detail of a Nestorian wall paint-
ing, discovered along the silk route in
Sinkiang, depicts worshipers holding
palms on the first Palm Sunday.*

men of wide learning, high intelligence, and
deep dedication. They came to China with no
expectation of ever leaving the country. In order to make the teaching of Christianity acceptable to the scholar class, the missionaries
exerted every effort to make themselves into
Chinese scholars. They learned the language,
studied the classics, and practiced Chinese
calligraphy and painting, at which some of
them attained real proficiency. Their efforts
made some impression. For the first time in
many centuries Chinese scholars found foreigners who were able and apparently eager to
learn about Chinese civilization and able to
contribute something of value to it.

The Jesuits were good mathematicians and
astronomers. They could correct errors that
had crept into the Chinese calendar and devise
and make astronomical instruments—some of
which survive in the observatories of Peking
and Nanking. The Jesuits were also good
engineers, and their skill in casting cannon
was an improvement on contemporary Chinese practice. The work may not have been a
very Christian contribution, but as the Ming
dynasty was at this time encountering the
internal and external troubles that were soon
to bring about its fall, it was much appreciated. After the dynasty was finally overthrown
in 1644, and an almost fugitive court held remote areas of the southwest, the Jesuits received their long-sought reward. The last
Ming empress was converted, and her son and
heir would have been brought up, it was
hoped, to be a Christian. But it was too late.
The Chinese "Constantine" did not live to
reign. His dynasty was driven from its last
strongholds, and the Manchu conqueror
reigned in its stead.

The Jesuits were undeterred by a setback of
this kind, which the Church has often encountered and survived. They started again in
Peking with the new Manchu rulers, and a

J. B. DU HALDE, *Description géographique . . . de la Chine . . . .*, PARIS, 1735

first had some hope. The young Emperor K'ang Hsi was an enlightened and energetic sovereign, who reduced the whole empire to obedience. He was infinitely more desirable as a convert than the last fugitive Ming princes. K'ang Hsi seemed to appreciate the scholarship and character of the Jesuits. He was not converted, but he was tolerant, and during his reign Christian teaching made considerable progress, not only among the humble but also in educated circles.

Then an unfortunate quarrel between Jesuits and Dominicans marred Christian prospects. The Jesuits tolerated a number of old Chinese customs as not necessarily antagonistic to Christianity. They permitted reverence to ancestors. They allowed the discharge of firecrackers at the celebration of the Mass, for in China this was a religious custom. Dominicans denounced these practices as pagan and improper. They appealed to the pope, who forbade the Jesuits to continue their tolerant attitude. In 1715 the Emperor K'ang Hsi became aware that a foreign ruler—a "barbarian chief" in his view, his Holiness the Pope in Christian eyes—was interfering in the affairs of the Chinese empire. Incensed at what he deemed an unwarranted and impertinent invasion of his imperial prerogatives, he put an abrupt stop to all Christian teaching, expelled most of the missionaries, retaining only a few whose skills and services were useful to him.

The attack on the pagan world of China through the imperial court had failed, and it was never to get a second chance. Throughout the eighteenth century some Catholic missionaries were permitted to work in Peking and elsewhere, but under strict limitations. They acquired a certain following, but were unable to make large-scale conversions. Catholicism was another small foreign sect, tolerated to some degree, but without influence.

Three centuries after Ricci first preached in Peking, the Catholic population of China did not exceed two millions, out of a total population of some five or six hundred millions.

It was not until the nineteenth century that Protestants entered the field. When Protestant missionaries did arrive, it was difficult for them to obtain permission to work in the empire; the prohibition imposed on Catholics applied also to them. However, when China was defeated in the Opium War of 1840, the terms of peace imposed by the Treaty of Nanking opened the empire to Protestant missionaries, who could travel, preach, and reside where they wished. It seemed as if force had accomplished what scholarship had failed to do. But the circumstances of the Protestant entry were prejudicial. It was not forgotten that the Protestant missionaries owed these rights to military victory, and they were resented and resisted by many Chinese.

In the middle of the nineteenth century the T'ai P'ing Rebellion, led by a man who had drawn inspiration from Protestant tracts, swept south China and for a short time threatened to drive the Manchu dynasty from the throne. Hung Hsiu-ch'üan, the "Heavenly King," was a religious prophet as well as a rebel leader, believing himself to be in direct relation with God. Because the T'ai P'ing movement, strongly influenced by his teaching, was a kind of Christianity, Protestant missionaries were at first inclined to welcome it; but they drew back when they found that its leader claimed the status of a prophet, making new revelations that ran contrary to many of their own doctrines. In rejecting the movement they may have given away the only serious possibility that ever existed for any form of Christianity to gain a dominant position in China. The T'ai P'ing movement was crushed by the Manchu dynasty, with considerable assistance from Britain and France. The Chinese

Three Jesuit missionaries in China are shown in a French engraving. Matteo Ricci, at left, points to a cross; Ferdinand Verbiest, at right, to an armillary sphere. At center is Adam Schall, dressed in a Chinese costume.

A seventeenth-century English portrait shows a Chinese convert to Christianity holding a crucifix in his hand.

ruling class was more convinced than ever that Christian teaching was a form of subversion. The masses were disillusioned by the failure of the Christian powers to support those who might be thought to be their friends.

For almost one hundred years after the T'ai P'ing movement, the Protestant missionary endeavor continued in China, but made only limited headway. Often it provoked a fierce and violent resistance, as in the Boxer movement of 1900. Those converted were largely from the young, educated class, who had attended mission schools to study foreign languages and acquire the new Western learning. Many of these converts did not remain Christians; many other Chinese attended such schools, but were not converted. The following of the Protestant religions tended to be drawn from two main groups: young men of the less well-to-do literate class, often of merchant origin (as was the Soong family, so influential in the Nationalist regime), and people from country towns where a mission had been established. Catholic missionaries tended to concentrate on certain villages where a majority of the population might be converted. The Protestants scattered their efforts more widely and had much less effect among the peasants. Centers, whether rural or urban, in which Protestant Christians were a large minority were very rare indeed.

Many missionaries had hoped that once the reactionary Manchu dynasty was dethroned, the new republic would be far more open to their evangel than the empire had been. This hope was frustrated. Under the republic very powerful anti-Christian movements, strongly tinged with xenophobia and reflecting the general nationalist surge of opinion, made mission work in the interior more difficult and precarious than it had been under the hostile, but cowed emperors. The missionaries saw the need to make their appeal more national

and less patently that of a foreign creed. An increasing number of mission stations were turned over to Chinese pastors or clergy. This development was accelerated by the second World War. Much of China was then occupied by Japanese invaders, who interned or drove out all missionaries of allied Western nationality—British, American, and Dutch Protestants, and French Catholics. This greatly reduced the numbers of Protestant missionaries in the field; among Catholics, Spanish or Italian missionaries were substituted for the French. At the end of the war the process went into reverse. Those whom the Japanese had permitted were now excluded as former enemies. At the time the Communists came to power, after the civil war of 1946–1949, few missionaries remained in many parts of China, except in large cities.

Communist policy soon eliminated all those who were left. The Protestants for the most part withdrew, leaving the churches to the Chinese Christians in the belief that this was the wisest course to follow. The Catholic missionaries were deported, often after being imprisoned. The disappearance of foreign missionaries after so long a presence in the country marks a significant change in the fortunes of the Christian Churches of China. They now had to stand alone and to convince the new regime that they had no ties with foreign powers. This meant the end of all foreign financial help. The response of the Protestants has been to unify hitherto diverse sects into one Chinese Protestant Church. As many of the divergencies and differences among the sects were founded on historical events in Western Christendom, wholly remote from China, the reaction of the Chinese Protestants was natural and, perhaps, sensible. But as a result, doctrinal questions and differences that are still seen as important in Western Protestant Christianity are now slurred or completely

ignored by the Christians of China.

The Catholic Church had more difficulty in adjusting to the requirements of the new regime. Catholics owe obedience to Rome, and Rome was for many years quite uncompromisingly opposed to Communism. And the Communists in China were equally hostile to the Catholic Church. Those bishops and clergy who continued to obey Rome were deprived of their power, and often imprisoned. The lower clergy, who, under the pressure of the congregations, tried to keep the churches open and say Mass, were forced to accept the authority of the state and to recognize a Chinnese Catholic Association as their immediate superior. Thus the Church has been forced into schism. It is not heretical, for Catholics are permitted to observe orthodox doctrine as laid down by Rome, but they are not permitted to give allegiance to the pope or to receive financial aid from Rome.

The future of the Christian Churches in China is a matter of importance and concern to Christians elsewhere and to many Western people who are not active Christians. But it must be remembered that in China Christians were only a very small percentage of the population. Christianity was the smallest of the foreign religions of China. The Catholic and Protestant moieties, each with approximately two million adherents, were seen by ordinary Chinese as two distinct religions. It is improbable that the Christian communities will decline very rapidly or disappear; but it is equally unlikely that they will expand. Their significance in China lay mainly in their role as mediators of the new Western learning and of the ways and fashions of Western civilizations. Not only is this role now denied to them, but it would be extremely risky for them to try to resume it. In an atmosphere where religious belief, so long regarded as unsophisticated, is now under still greater disfavor, it is not easy for the Churches to gain new adherents. There is little to induce people to become converts, but it is possible that the Churches will hold on to their sincere and lifelong members.

The Chinese are not a religious people. The bent of their minds has always been humanist, and this characteristic can be observed in the earliest period. Men and their ways, their fate, and their history mattered more than did the gods and their powers. In no other country, until very modern times, has the educated class, which was also the governing class, been openly agnostic, even atheist. This has been the outlook of China for the past eight or nine hundred years, at least since the early and middle Sung period. Chu Hsi, the great Sung philosopher and reshaper of Confucian ethics, said that "there is no man in Heaven judging sin." His opinion, fundamentally antideist, has been accepted and shared by the educated classes in China ever since. This underlying fact goes some way to explain why the educated Chinese could and did accept Marxism with fewer qualms than could Western men, trained from childhood to believe in God.

6   The Early Empire

(200 B.C. *to* A.D. 600)

In a detail from a Han dynasty tile, two bearded gentlemen of the leisure class—wearing long robes and headdresses—engage in conversation.

The consolidation of China into an empire under the rule of a single sovereign had constituted a revolution as deep and far-reaching as the twentieth-century revolution by which that empire was overthrown and from which the Chinese People's Republic emerged as the final victor. The Ch'in-Han revolution of the third century B.C. destroyed China's feudal system. It overthrew the power of the aristocracy and substituted a much more open society in which men of talent could rise from lowly origins, and high birth would no longer guarantee lasting wealth and influence. The revolution also expanded the frontiers of China until they approximated those of the present republic. Only the far southwest, the provinces of Yünnan and Kueichou, remained outside the empire. As a consequence of this expansion, Chinese armies advanced into the deserts of Central Asia as far as the Caspian Sea and opened for the first time a safe, if long and arduous, communication route with Greece and Rome, as well as with India and Persia. All this was not achieved at once, but each change proceeded logically from the conditions produced by the previous one.

The destruction of feudalism resulted in the development of a new system of land tenure, which produced the landlord-tenant relationship and made possible the sale of land, the introduction of a money economy, and the rise of new social classes. The consolidation of the whole country into a unified empire gave China the strength and resources to expand and conquer weak barbarian neighbors, fight off nomad invaders, and advance into Central Asia to outflank those nomads. The occupation of Sinkiang, and of territories even farther afield, opened western and southern Asia to the Chinese and gave them a glimpse of Europe also. Finally, the Han empire, lasting for four hundred years, from 202 B.C. to A.D. 220, established a tradition of unity that, although interrupted, proved durable for the Chinese state.

At the beginning of the new Han dynasty the traditions of feudal separatism were still strong. The old royal families had perished, but the reign of the dynasty's founder was troubled by the ambitions of his own generals. The emperor disposed of them all and made a law by which only members of his own imperial family, the Liu, could hold a fief. These fiefs were small, scattered among the provinces, and before long made heritable by division among all the sons of the lord. This rapidly reduced them to the size of estates and to political impotence.

The swift growth of imperial power was impeded by the ruined condition of the country after nearly three hundred years of ever more destructive wars. It is reported that when the new Han emperor ascended the throne, he could not find horses of the same color to draw his state chariot, a pound of gold was required to buy one hundred twenty pounds of rice, and horses of any kind were so scarce that even the highest officials had to use oxen for transport. All this gradually changed under the wise and competent rule of the early Han emperors. Before two generations had passed, the contemporary historian Ssŭ-ma Ch'ien was able to record that abundance prevailed. Gentlemen scorned to ride mares; the granaries overflowed with tax grain. Ssŭ-ma's own life showed it was possible to travel the length and breadth of China in security.

It is true that Ssŭ-ma paints this happy picture in order to denigrate the reign of his sovereign, the Emperor Wu Ti, whom he disliked. This new master of the Chinese world came to the throne as a young man in 140 B.C. He had a long and famous reign of fifty-three years, lasting until 87 B.C. This period was one of the great formative ages of Chinese history. The emperor took his title, "Wu," which means "martial," from his successful wars in Central Asia, south China, Korea, and Manchuria, and from his great achievement in defeating the Hsiung-nu nomads (believed by some historians to be the ancestors of the Huns, who centuries later were to invade the Roman empire). These wars were fought and won by the emperor's generals; the real work of the emperor was in formulating internal and external policy, a task at which he showed great imagination, flexibility, and freedom from prejudice. Apart from the defense of the empire against the nomads, the main problem facing the emperor was economic—the question of how to organize a money economy. Along with this went another problem—establishing a philosophical structure that would sanctify the institutions of the unified empire.

Because free coining of money had traditionally been permitted, those fortunate landowners who found copper mines on their properties flooded the empire with their mintings and became, as was said, "richer than princes." When the government stopped this, illicit coining at once became a major industry. The emperor tried several ingenious devices to solve the problem, but none worked. Finally, with considerable courage and in open defiance of the prejudices of his court, he put the whole question under the care of a merchant, Sang Hung-yang, a member of a socially despised class, who found a satisfactory policy, one that would now be seen as commonsense, but then was novel. Coining was made a state monopoly, and the value of coins ceased to be fixed by arbitrary decree, but was allowed to rise and fall in accordance with market movements.

The emperor's concern with economic questions, and his trust in men like the merchant Sang Hung-yang, were offensive to the Confucian scholars and historians. They constantly criticized the economic measures, be-

Ssŭ-ma Ch'ien, China's greatest historian, held the hereditary office of court astrologer. Despite certain reverses in his career—one of which resulted in his castration at the emperor's command—he ended his days in imperial favor as a minister of state.

lieving that such matters were not for the government to manage. But the critics were unable to show that the government measures were ineffective; Ssŭ-ma Ch'ien, an honest historian, records grudgingly that the emperor's policy filled the granaries and restored the economy.

If Emperor Wu paid little attention to Confucian views on the economy, he did patronize the Confucian school of philosophy in other ways. Education was organized on Confucian lines and entrusted to Confucian scholars. The rites of the state religion of Heaven and Earth were formed; supposedly they were modeled on rituals of the most ancient era, but in all probability they were elaborated from vague traditions to suit the needs of the new empire. Personally, the Emperor Wu was addicted to the magical cults and favored their adepts, who promised him the drug of immortality. But he was not blindly confiding; he expected results, and when no elixir was forthcoming, he executed the magician who had promised it to him. Active and tireless, the emperor toured his dominions even in advanced age. His reign was not disturbed by internal rebellion, sure proof that it was at least tolerable to the mass of the people.

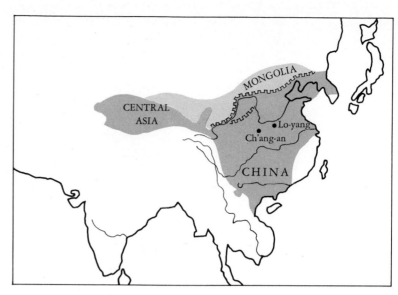

Internal reform and administration were successful; foreign policy and war had a more checkered pattern. The complete defeat and disintegration of the nomad power of the Hsiung-nu were not achieved until the reign of Wu Ti's successor. But it was the Emperor Wu who first sent out missions to explore the far west. Later he followed these with military expeditions that penetrated to the lands beyond the Hindu Kush. He permanently incorporated the southern provinces of Fukien and Kuangtung into the empire, and made conquests in what is now North Vietnam and North Korea. Chinese culture, introduced into these distant lands by his military campaigns, outlasted direct Chinese rule and remained the basic culture of Vietnam and of Korea. The Emperor Wu defined the limits of the Chinese world and shaped its internal structure along lines that survived until the early twentieth century.

The two emperors who succeeded Wu were also able men, if less flamboyant. They continued his work. China was run by a civil service recruited by recommendation; those promoted to office had to be educated men of good character, loyal and industrious. It was unwise for a great officeholder to recommend or appoint men who had not at least some of these qualities, for he was held responsible for their failures. So long as the sovereign remained an active participant in government, alert for weaknesses, ready to innovate, and firm in justice, the system worked remarkably well. Crises resulting from the failure of imperial progeny or from the succession of a minor were handled with skill and dispatch by very able ministers.

After three generations, the ruling house showed signs of debility. The families of the empresses repeatedly shook the court with plots and conspiracies, which brought about the extermination of the conspiring consort

family. In A.D. 9, however, one of the most powerful consort families, the Wang, achieved what all had attempted, and usurped the throne. Wang Mang, "the Usurper," enjoyed a reign of sixteen years. Internal troubles then shook his power. There was a great flood of the Yellow River. Widespread risings, led by members of the fallen imperial family of Liu, broke out, and Wang Mang was overthrown and slain. After several years of civil war, the Han dynasty was restored by the Emperor Kuang Wu Ti, scion of one of the numerous minor collateral branches of the old imperial family. The new Han dynasty—like the old—lasted almost exactly two hundred years, from A.D. 25 to 220.

The history of the Later Han dynasty, as it is called, fits the pattern of the dynastic cycle far better than does the history of any other dynasty. The founder reigned peacefully, with justice and firmness, for many years. His immediate successors were able and industrious men. The empire expanded, prosperity increased, and so did the accumulation of wealth and lands in the hands of the great families. It was during the Later Han period that the Chinese fully consolidated their hold over Central Asia and came into closer touch with Persia, India, and the Roman empire. A high standard of luxury and civilization was widespread, as can be seen from bas-reliefs and tomb furnishings, many of which were discovered in remote parts of the empire. Literature and art responded to the stimulus, and a great work of historical scholarship, the *History of the Former Han Dynasty*, was compiled. But a subtle corruption was at work; the power of the consort families emerged once more as a threat to the imperial system. Society, although no longer feudal, was still aristocratic in the sense that the governing literate class was small, wealthy, and locally influential. The great families came to overshadow the imperial house.

The early Han emperors expanded their domain deep into Central Asia, inaugurating Chinese contact with the West. From their capital—first Ch'ang-an and later Lo-yang—most of the Han emperors exerted effective control over this sprawling empire. Around the year A.D. 121 Chinese armies crossed the Great Wall to conquer the steppeland of Mongolia.

*The first emperor of the Later Han dynasty, Kuang
Wu, restored peace to China after years of disorder.
A Ming dynasty painting shows him, accompanied
by a group of attendants, fording a mountain stream.*

To counter this sinister and dangerous
menace, the emperors turned to a new source
of support, the eunuchs. By their nature these
men could not produce families who would
acquire an undue influence. Eunuchs came of
humble origin; their fortune was wholly dependent on imperial favor. They could be
trusted, or so thought the later emperors of
the Han dynasty.

Eunuchs may not be able to leave posterity,
but they could acquire wealth and bequeath it
to their relatives. As their influence increased,
men sought their favor, which the eunuchs
sold for money. The eunuchs grew greedy,
and their authority challenged that of the established civil service, the preserve of the Confucian scholar. A conflict between these two
classes arose in the reigns of Shun Ti (A.D. 126–
144) and his successor Huan Ti (A.D. 146–
167). This period of forty years marks the
rapid decline of the dynasty and foreshadows
the sanguinary troubles that were to bring it
to an end. The eunuchs had aided the emperor
to get rid of one of the most influential of the
consort families, the Liang family, whose matriarch had dominated the court for half a century and had ruled the empire in all but name
for twenty years. On the death of the Emperor
Huan the eunuchs put on the throne a young
boy, known to history as the Emperor Ling Ti.
He was completely in their hands and became
the blind instrument of their ambitions.

As long as he lived, the eunuchs remained
supreme. They terrified the youthful emperor
with stories of conspiracy and obtained his
authority to exterminate the leaders and many
thousands of members of the association of
scholars, the Confucian civil servants' counter-
force to the power of the eunuchs. This massacre disrupted the civil service, which the
eunuchs then filled with their agents. They
obtained the right to adopt children and to
leave them their vast estates. This nullified

Wu Ti, the founder of the Southern Liang dynasty (A.D. 502–557), *took the reign title of "Martial Emperor," but his main interests were scholarship and Buddhism. Three times he left the throne to become a monk.*

the main advantage that the throne had derived from eunuch support.

The corruption of the administration became more and more oppressive. An epidemic swept through the empire, and a leader of the magical cults arose, with a magical cure for it. He gathered thousands of followers among the peasants, and before long, they rose in rebellion. His followers, called the Yellow Turbans, swept up and down the provinces for years in one of the greatest and most famous Chinese peasant rebellions. The imperial army was only moderately successful in combating the rebels, but in the process it acquired far-reaching authority in the countryside. With their booty, army commanders purchased the favor of court eunuchs. The emperor was kept in complete ignorance of what was going on. When Confucian officials heroically tried to enlighten him, the eunuchs were at hand to accuse them of being secret supporters of the association of scholars, which the emperor had been trained to hold in horror. The officials were at once sent to execution. In A.D. 189 the Emperor Ling died, leaving no adult heir; the eunuchs decided to put on the throne a boy who was not the nearest heir and not the son of the empress.

They had, however, overlooked the fact that the brother of the empress was the commander in chief of the army. In answer to the empress' appeal, he summoned the provincial generals to the capital and planned to exterminate the eunuchs. But he was lured into the palace by them and cut down in the great court of the Hall of Audience. When the commander in chief failed to return, his colleagues, waiting outside the palace walls, demanded news of him. For answer the eunuchs threw his severed head over the wall. Thereupon the commanders gave the order to their troops to assault and carry the palace, which they did, massacring every eunuch except for a handful who

had dragged the empress and the two young princes into hasty flight through an unguarded back gate.

The next day they were found by soldiers of the ambitious and brutal commander Tung Cho, who now seized the capital and palace, and installed as emperor the same boy the eunuchs had chosen. The empress, against whom Tung Cho had a grudge, was imprisoned and soon slain along with her son, who might have been an inconvenient rallying point for rival commanders. Thus began the purely nominal reign of the last Han emperor, Hsien Ti, who for nearly thirty years was the prisoner, sport, or tool of rival military commanders. These, aided by the still-active Yellow Turbans, tore the empire to pieces, in the process destroying its administration. They brought about its division into three rival kingdoms, the strongest of which, Wei, controlled the powerless Han court. Finally Emperor Hsien Ti was dethroned, and the king of Wei claimed the empire.

His rivals denied him recognition, and a war or series of wars continued for years among the kingdoms of Wei in the north, founded by the famous and infamous General Ts'ao Ts'ao, Wu in the southeast, and Shu in the far west, ruled by Liu Pei, a soldier of fortune who claimed, possibly truly, to be the scion of a collateral branch of the imperial family.

The Three Kingdoms period, from A.D. 220 to 265, is one of the very few for which the traditional historians are uncertain where legitimacy lay, if it lay anywhere at all. In all other periods of division the Chinese historians are sure that this or that contender is the real emperor; but in the Three Kingdoms era they have found it impossible to make such a judgment. This is why it alone is known by a collective term, "Three Kingdoms," and not by the name of a single dynasty. The political in-

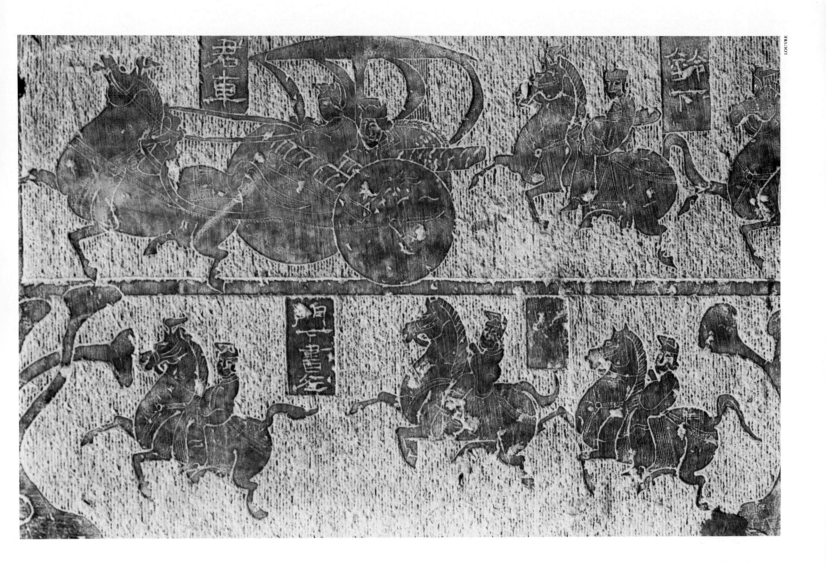

stability that marked this age shows that the experiment of dividing China was fruitless, and the division proved to be brief. After forty-five years of constant warfare, the three kingdoms were once more united in a new central empire, under a new dynasty, which had usurped the throne of the northern kingdom, Wei, and then conquered the other two.

The Tsin dynasty, which came to power in A.D. 265, should have rebuilt the old Han empire. It might have done so had not a new factor intervened—a foreign invasion. During the long, confused military struggle that had followed the death of Emperor Ling Ti in A.D. 189, the defense of the northern frontier had not been the responsibility of any leader, for all had been preoccupied by the struggle for internal power. New nomad nations had formed beyond the Great Wall, replacing the Hsiung-nu, some of whom had migrated westward. The most formidable of these nations,

already noticed in late Han times, was that of the Hsien-pi. The Tsin empire ignored this danger. After the death of the warrior-founder, his sons disputed among themselves, engaged in civil wars, and began to enlist the Hsien-pi as mercenary troops. Fifty-one years after the Tsin reunion of the empire the storm broke. In A.D. 316 the Hsien-pi, realizing their opportunity, swept into China in strength, captured the capital, Lo-yang, destroyed it, and drove on to the Yangtze River. That obstacle and the general unsuitability of the wet rice lands for nomad cavalry made it possible for a prince of the fugitive Tsin house to establish himself in Nanking and regain control of the Yangtze valley. But the north, then the most populous and richest part of China, was lost. Hundreds of years were to pass before the empire was once more united.

This period, known to the Chinese as the Northern and Southern Empires, has some-

A Han tomb relief shows a procession of horsemen riding behind a solid-wheeled chariot, in which a dignitary sits. The relief, like most of the bas-reliefs that were made during the period, is probably a copy of a painting.

135

times been compared to the Dark Ages of Europe, which followed the barbarian invasions of the Roman empire in the fourth and fifth centuries. There are certain resemblances in the two historical situations that have been over-emphasized, while the basic differences have been too often overlooked. In China, as in Rome, a great empire fell into confusion and was invaded by barbarians who seized half of it. Imperial power was confined to the southern half of China and to the eastern half of the Roman empire. At around the same time, in both parts of the world, new universal religions became established and dominant, Christianity and Buddhism.

Up to this point the comparison is striking, but it is invalid to take it any further. In China there was no true Dark Age. Literacy was never lost, history continued to be recorded as fully as before, and new styles developed in literature. It was a turbulent age, but a cultivated one. Moreover, the period of uncontrolled barbarian invasion was relatively short in China and it was limited in extent. The Hsien-pi never penetrated south of the Yangtze. The southern Chinese empire had no enemies of dangerous strength behind it, as the Eastern Roman empire had with the Persians and later the Arabs. The northern part of China, the region under barbarian rule, was the most populous and richest region of the empire, unlike those Roman regions that had been conquered by barbarians. In China the conquerors soon found themselves outnumbered by their Chinese subjects, and were forced to co-operate with them to retain power. The period of ravage and violence was relatively brief. It endured for only seventy years, during which the northern provinces were the scene of constant struggle between various nomad tribes that set up ephemeral regimes that lasted only a few years and occupied only a small part of the area. In A.D. 386 a new bar-

barian tribe, the T'o-pa, descended on China, destroyed the Hsien-pi kingdoms, and attempted to conquer the south, but failed. Having united the north under one rule, the T'o-pa held it for more than one hundred fifty years in comparative peace.

Their dynasty, the Wei, as it was styled in China, favored Buddhism and encouraged the production of Buddhist art. Some of the greatest Buddhist cave sculpture dates from the Wei period. The regime was very soon far from being barbarous. Chinese literature and scholarship flourished at court, and Chinese scholars served in the ministries. The government was modeled on that of the old Han empire, with some modifications to suit the needs of the T'o-pa military aristocracy, who in time intermarried with the Chinese and produced a mixed ruling class.

The Chinese empire in the south was less stable politically. The Tsin held power until A.D. 420, just over a century after their loss of the north. They were followed by four short dynasties, only two of which ruled for more than half a century, and all of which fell into confusion and civil war once the strong founder of the dynasty died. Power was shared by a small aristocracy of great landowners, the leaders of powerful clans, which had migrated when Lo-yang fell to the Hsien-pi and which had become established in the rich under-populated provinces of central and southern China. South China was then the least developed part of the country; it greatly benefited from the establishment of the imperial government in Nanking, which became a great and luxurious city. Colonization spread along the valleys of the rivers that flow into the Yangtze from the south.

In north China, under barbarian rule, the Chinese population probably already exceeded twenty millions, and the barbarian invaders were a small minority. No new nations, formed by the merging of barbarian and native populations, appeared, as happened in the former western provinces of the Roman world. As a result of this and of the other factors cited, the division of China was a passing phase, while the partition of Europe has remained to the present time. Within a generation or two, the nomadic invaders had lost their own language, which has left few traces in Chinese. Surnames of barbarian origin remained conspicuous in the aristocracy for some centuries; in later times they all but disappeared. For nearly a century before reunion was achieved, there was little difference between the empires of north and south. Their union was prevented more by the weakness of the two regimes, neither strong enough to conquer the other, than by antipathy between the populations.

The society of China did not undergo as profound a transformation as that which the Teutonic invasions and the spread of Christianity combined to effect in Europe ("the triumph of barbarism and religion," as Gibbon puts it); but in China the long period of division and weak central rule had important consequences. In the Han period, especially the early Han, the structure of Chinese society was more open than it had ever been before. Serfdom had disappeared, replaced by a peasant class that rented or owned its land, and the wealthy class was now made up of career men, without aristocratic background, and of the descendants of such men. Education counted for much and wealth for a great deal, but blue blood for very little. In addition to education and wealth, the aspirant for office needed the recommendation of a powerful man, who need not be a relative. Much of this freedom disappeared by the end of the age of partition.

With weak and short dynasties on the throne, the attractiveness of an official career was much diminished for civilians. Ever since the confused times at the end of the Han dy-

MUSEE CERNUSCHI,
PARIS-LUC JOUBERT

A helmeted warrior, dating from Later Han times, is shown with his arm raised ready to hurl a spear. The terra-cotta tomb figure was probably originally buried holding a spear in his hand.

A Buddha, probably from the eighth century, is shown with the urna, *symbol of enlightenment, on his brow.*

nasty, it had been the military profession that led to power. A young man of ability sought to attach himself to a successful commander and rise in his service. One day, with luck, he might become a great commander himself; perhaps even the throne would not be beyond reach. Some men of this stamp did, in fact, attain supreme power. Even if the new military leaders never managed to reach the throne, they established themselves and their families with large landed estates, exercised great influence, and monopolized high command. A new aristocracy emerged, not founded on feudal privilege, but securely based on military power, and only marginally dependent on imperial favor.

The history of the southern empire revolved around the rivalries, alliances, and treasons of this group. They dominated the scene no matter which family occupied the throne. The imperial family would not be there for long, perhaps two generations; then a new turn of the wheel would bring supreme fortune to another military clan. The forms of the old empire still survived. The leading military aristocrats dominated the government in all respects; they occupied the highest civil posts, and were ministers as well as generals. The lower officials played the same role, both civil and military, and were the clients of the great families. The client relationship was essential to any career. Young men with the right connections and patronage could hold senior posts, to which in a more regular system they could not have aspired for years.

Chinese historians, faithfully adhering to the dynastic framework, try to represent these short-lived regimes, which were in fact only military dictatorships, as regular dynasties invested with the mystic virtue of the Mandate of Heaven. But after the Tsin the four successor regimes reigned respectively for 59, 23, 55, and 32 years. It can be seen that this involved, in effect, just the reigns of their founding fathers, plus a few troubled years under the rule of some weak inheritor.

Inevitably, the prestige of the sovereign suffered from these brief incumbencies. In Han times imperial prestige was such that even a foolish and improvident ruler could live out his reign without question until he died of natural causes. Now any man of influence and power could aspire to become emperor; no family need expect to hold the throne for more than a lifetime. Later this legacy of instability was to present a serious problem to the rulers of the new united empire.

When the Wei declined and north China was divided between rival dynasties, the conditions that had long prevailed in the south became familiar in the north also. Military families, all closely interrelated and all connected either with the fallen Wei or their successors, disputed the throne. It hardly mattered whether they were of Chinese or Tatar patrilineage. Yang Chien, founder of the Sui dynasty, was Chinese on his father's side, but Tatar on his mother's. The Li, founders of the T'ang dynasty, were also Chinese by patrilineal descent, but on the maternal side were closely related to a great Tatar family, the Tu Ku, and intermarried with others who were descended from the Wei Tatar imperial house.

The north, after the decay of the Wei dynasty around A.D. 540, had been governed successively by two short-lived dynasties, which had imperfect control over the whole region. The second of these was overthrown by Yang Chien, who was a relative by marriage of the sovereign he dethroned. Eight years later, in A.D. 589, Yang Chien invaded the southern empire, ruled by a feeble dynasty, and easily destroyed it. China was once more united under one regime, the new Sui dynasty. This sequel to the story of the division of China reveals most clearly the difference in

This temple, known as the Gallery of the Thousand Buddhas, is in Kansu province in northwestern China. Its images of Buddha were laboriously carved out of the precipitous mountainside early in the sixth century, when Buddhism enjoyed imperial favor.

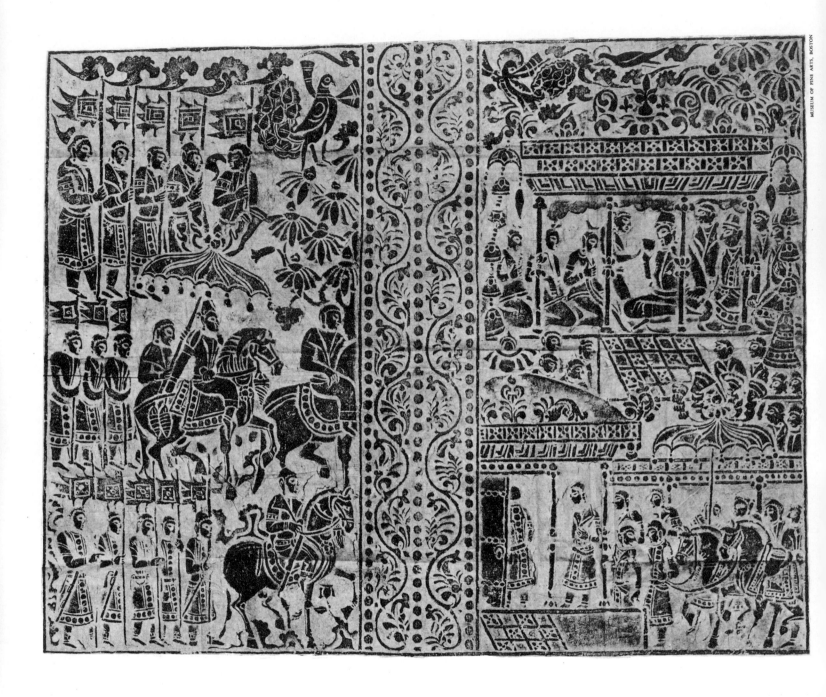

situation between China and the former Roman world. In the same period that Yang Chien of the Sui made a nearly painless and rapid conquest of the whole of China, the Eastern Roman Emperor Justinian was laboring in vain to restore Roman rule in Italy, without even hoping to recover Gaul, Spain, Britain, or western Germany. The heritage of the Han empire proved stronger than that of Rome.

There seemed at first no great reason to expect that the Sui dynasty, which had begun with Yang Chien's reunification of China, would prove to be any more durable than its predecessors in north or south China. It still depended on the support of the great military aristocrats, both in war and peace. These men would never give their allegiance to a weak or unsuccessful ruler. Unless Yang Chien's son and successor commanded their respect, they would soon dethrone him. Emperor Yang Ti, son of Yang Chien, was not a weak man, but he was inordinately ambitious and vain. Believing that he had the mission to restore the full glory of the old Han empire, he embarked on invasions of the north Korean kingdom of Koguryŏ, which occupied not only north Korea but also most of what is now south Manchuria. This region had been a Han frontier colony, but was lost in the troubles that followed the fall of the Han dynasty. Emperor Yang demanded the submission of the king of

Koguryŏ, who refused it; thereupon the emperor twice invaded the northern kingdom. Both invasions were disastrously repelled, partly by the severity of the Korean winter and partly by the obstinacy with which the Koreans defended their walled cities, cities that the Chinese needed to capture in order to winter in.

The historians unreservedly condemn Emperor Yang for folly and ambition in persisting with this policy, which even after his defeats he planned to continue. Their view rather overlooks the reasons that probably motivated the emperor. There had been a considerable movement of refugees and taxpaying peasants from China into Koguryŏ, caused by distress in the northern provinces and by high taxation. Also, the emperor needed to employ the armies of the military aristocrats, who now were not required to defend the empire against its defunct rival in south China. Emperor Yang may well have thought they were better employed in arduous campaigns in Korea than in raising revolts against his own rule.

His extravagance was another charge laid against him by the historians, and here, too, although the charge was well founded, not all the expenditure was wasted on pomp and ceremony. The emperor rebuilt the capital and palace of Lo-yang, and set up a new capital in Yang-chou, just north of the Yangtze in what had been southern territory. Although Yang was a northerner, he loved the south and learned to speak "the language of Wu"—the dialect of the east Yangtze delta. To connect the two capitals, he constructed the Grand Canal, a vast waterway still in use, linking the Yangtze and the Yellow rivers. He has been accused of wasting great sums on this project merely to permit himself easy and comfortable boat journeys from Lo-yang to Yang-chou. But this biased view ignores the very real economic value of the Grand Canal

for transporting the produce of the south to the north: southern rice was needed to maintain the emperor's armies and to feed the population of the capital. It was also considered advisable to improve commerce between the two halves of China.

It is probably true that the resources of the empire were not adequate to undertake such large public works and at the same time engage in foreign wars with large armies in an inhospitable region to which all supplies had to be transported by land. After the second invasion of Korea, in A.D. 612 to 613, Emperor Yang, undismayed, called for new levies to resume the war. At this point the military aristocracy refused to comply. The emperor was urged by his wisest counselors to call off the war; Korea, a poor country, they said, was not worth the effort. The emperor would listen to no one and persisted in issuing decrees raising more troops.

The effect was fatal. The troops were indeed raised, but they only swelled the ranks of the rebellions that broke out on all sides. These were led by members of the military aristocracy, the great clans of mixed Chinese and Tatar descent. In the south some of the old Chinese imperial clans raised their heads, and for a time established "dynasties" in the Yangtze valley. But the main center of the complex civil war, in which nearly a dozen competitors sought to seize the throne, was in the north. The south took no active part in this struggle, and its dynasts seem to have hoped that the northern part of the empire would break up into several states, leaving them in peace.

Emperor Yang had withdrawn to Yang-chou, where he resided in luxury, ignoring the troubles except when he issued decrees condemning the rebels. He was unable to oppose them; his armies had melted away. But his vanity was intact, and he seems to have

The Grand Canal, shown here flowing through a town near Shanghai, extends a thousand miles, linking central and northern China. The completion of one part of it early in the seventh century was celebrated by a water festival in which the Emperor Yang Ti traveled along the canal in a dragon boat, accompanied by thousands of other vessels.

been quite unable to understand how swiftly his power was waning. Rebellions had already eliminated Sui rule over most of the northern provinces before the ultimate victors, the T'ang, took the field. Li Yüan, head of the T'ang family, was governor of the territory that is now the province of Shansi, a region well defended by mountains and strategically placed north of the Yellow River. He was not energetic or ambitious, but his second son, Li Shih-min, had these qualities, and others as well. He persuaded his father to revolt. He did this in part by using a current prophecy that a Li family would inherit the throne, a prophecy that Li Shih-min said had made the emperor morbidly suspicious of all named Li. He also contrived to get his father implicated in the grave crime of violating imperial concubines, who were at a hunting palace situated within Li Yüan's jurisdiction. Caught in this trap, Li Yüan had no choice but to rebel.

He had no need to fear defeat; his son, Li Shih-min, then sixteen, proved to be a military genius, who, unlike his competitors, could select objectives of real importance, ignoring

tempting prizes that would not contribute to ultimate victory. His first act was to seize the western capital Ch'ang-an, once the Han capital, situated in the strong and easily defended region called Shensi. This was the "Land within the Passes," which in antiquity had been the homeland of the conquering Ch'in dynasty and the center of the Han empire. In possession of it, the new dynasty could be proclaimed and could function in a recognized metropolitan center. While rival would-be emperors contended among themselves for the eastern plains, Li Shih-min left them to their strife. He consolidated the northwest and blockaded the capital, Lo-yang. At last one of his leading rivals was persuaded to come to Lo-yang's relief. He was decisively defeated in a crucial battle fought at the point where the road from the eastern plains to Lo-yang begins to enter the hill country of west Honan. Lo-yang surrendered; the eastern plains were exposed to T'ang invasion and soon subdued.

At Yang-chou Emperor Yang at last realized his peril. One day, gazing in the mirror, he remarked to his attendants, "such a beautiful head, who would dare to cut it off?" The answer came soon. The commander of his own guard, also a member of the great military aristocracy, and connected with the former ruling house of Northern Ch'i, decided that the Sui were finished, and that the imperial treasure in Yang-chou would enable him to enter the competition for the throne with some hope of success. He occupied the palace, slew Emperor Yang and all other members of the Sui family he could find, looted and burned Yang-chou, and moved off to the northern battlefields.

Although there can be little doubt that every other contender would have eliminated the Sui in much the same way, they would have perhaps shown more respect for good form. The assassin was universally condemned, found no support, and was soon himself defeated and slain. The supremacy of the T'ang was speedily confirmed by the surrender or rapid defeat of the southern aspirants to power.

Li Shih-min, who later reigned as the Emperor T'ai Tsung, was not only the architect of his family's fortune, but, when on the throne, showed great ability as a statesman. He devised and put into force measures that slowly undermined the authority and influence of the military aristocracy and that replaced it with a civil service divorced from military power. These changes took time, and the T'ang dynasty was to be menaced by more than one crisis before they took effect. But they did take effect, for the T'ang had the good fortune to produce a remarkable series of rulers who for one hundred fifty years controlled China with more power and effectiveness than had been known at any time since the reign of the Han Emperor Wu—and perhaps more than had been known even in his time.

One of the most striking developments in this early period of the reunited empire was the passivity of the south in the face of so many violent revolutions. Had the south felt itself to be a nation different from the north and enslaved by conquest of the northern Sui, this would have been the time to revolt. But the chance was hardly taken. Some few old families attempted to revive their fallen fortunes, but they met with little solid support. The contest for the empire was not a war between north and south to impose a shaky unity. It was an internal conflict in the north, with the objective of restoring an empire covering the whole country. This situation very clearly illustrates the fact that the Chinese people as a whole did not feel themselves divided into two or more nations by the long period of partition. The popular feeling was for unity, and this feeling quickly rallied around the party that proved best able to achieve and maintain an imperial restoration.

Modern Communist historians, who seek to stress the involvement of the people in the great events of history and to minimize the role of kings and rulers, consider that the T'ang owed their victory to their skillful use of popular discontent and of the risings against the oppressive government of Emperor Yang. Yet they do not explain why the Li family, rather than any one of its numerous rivals, should have been able to mobilize this discontent to further its own ambitions; nor do they pay any attention to the interesting fact that so long a period of disunion, and so short a reunion as the Sui dynasty, had not implanted in north or south a feeling of alienation from the other half of China. Since they regard all early periods as under an equal feudal oppression, they are not able to perceive or admit the special role of the military aristocracy at this time, or how it differed from the Han leadership and from the leadership that arose in the later T'ang period. New classes within the feudal pattern simply must not exist. Marx has not recognized them.

145

7   The Spirit of Invention

This Han tomb model is the earliest-known representation of a hand crank. The crank, used to turn the winnowing fan built into the wall at left, stands idle, as does the rotary mill at lower right. The miller is operating a tilt hammer to hull grain.

WILLIAM ROCKHILL NELSON GALLERY OF ART

In the past Western Sinologists were not inclined to give the Chinese much credit for scientific discovery or the development of technology. As a result of the gap that exists between Chinese technological achievements and those of the Western world, the Sinologists rather readily assumed that the thinking of Europeans was responsible for the discovery of fundamental theories and for their practical application. Any inventions the Chinese may have made were arrived at accidentally, a result of mistaken theories that had nothing to do with true scientific inquiry.

New knowledge of the Chinese past has led to a revision of these ideas. Archeology and the study of texts that are not included in the traditional collections of literary sources have shown that the Chinese are responsible for the four primary inventions on which so much modern technology rests: the magnetic compass, paper, printing, and gunpowder.

It is now realized that outside the Confucian tradition, with its values that ignored, or actually impeded, scientific development, there existed another strand of thought that was directly interested in the phenomenal world and in man's mastery of his environment. The study of the surviving text of the school of Mo Tzŭ, one of the philosophers of the Warring States period, has shown many indications of attempts to formulate theories about the phenomenal world, theories that are protoscientific. Measurement and observation were stressed, and efforts were made to differentiate categories and qualities. These efforts took the form of paradoxes, such as "a white horse is not a horse." The aim here was to point out that whiteness is not an essential characteristic of horses, nor are all white objects horses. There is a similar paradox concerning the passage of an arrow in flight ("There are times when a flying arrow is neither in motion nor at rest."), which seeks to examine the nature of motion. The Mohists might have developed these ideas into a more comprehensive system had their school survived the persecutions of the Ch'in dynasty.

In the Han period, some part of early Mohist thought was taken up by the Taoists, who incorporated it within a tradition that was directed more toward alchemy than toward physics. Study of the Taoist texts reveals the same mixture of magical theorizing and empirical investigation of the properties of various substances that is found in Western medieval pseudo sciences. From this combination the true sciences emerged in the West in later times. Taoist attempts to concoct the drug of immortality were often fatal to the experimenter. Mercury and lead, and other toxic materials, were compounded to make the drug; and frequent resort to this potion did, indeed, lead to immortality—but not on earth. The search for a method of turning dross metals into gold did not end in success; but along the blind alleys of the quest the Chinese learned many things that later were given practical, technical application. Behind the discovery of a valuable technique or a new fact was some Taoist theory, often a wrong theory, but one that nonetheless served as a guide to action and inquiry.

Taoism gave a great significance to the theory of *feng shui*, literally "wind and water," a pseudo science that is usually called geomancy in the Western world. The run of the country, the relationship between streams and hills, valleys and bluffs, were believed to be lucky or unlucky; the siting of graves and dwellings, the orientation of cities and streets, were decided by the principles of geomancy. To orient correctly it was necessary to determine the true points of the compass. At a very early date the Chinese had discovered the lodestone and devised a technique for using its properties to determine directions.

The stone was carved into the shape of a spoon with a curving handle; when the base of the spoon was balanced on a smooth surface, the handle would point to the south. This was definitely known in the Han period, around 100 B.C., and some references strongly suggest that it was probably known more than a century before that time. The Han dynasty magician Luan Ta proved his skill to the Emperor Wu Ti by making chessmen of lodestone, which "attacked" opponents made of iron. (This same Luan Ta won renown by evoking the ghost of the emperor's favorite concubine in a darkened room. To make it seem as though the ghost was appearing, he probably relied on the technique of shadow projection, which he may have invented.)

A chain of development from Han times led to the invention of the magnetic compass. The compass is first described in quite positive terms in the year A.D. 1044; but a large number of references in works dating from the end of the Han dynasty onward make it more than probable that the magnetic needle had been known long before. On the other hand, the application of the compass to navigation does not appear to be earlier than the tenth or eleventh centuries A.D. This late use of the magnetic needle for what seems to the modern mind its most essential purpose is to be explained by the history of its origin in geomancy. The geomancers used their wisdom as part of their art and concealed their technical knowledge behind the veil of magic. They had found a way of determining the "four directions" with accuracy and had already discovered that magnetic north is not true north, although they did not, of course, know the reason why.

By Sung times the Chinese were aware that the magnetic needle could either be suspended on a thread of silk or floated in a dish of water. They preferred the latter method for many

A stamp showing a model of a lodestone compass

centuries, and the compass that reached the West via Arab intermediaries was made of a piece of steel shaped like a fish and floating in a bowl of water. The head of the fish acted as the pointer. It appears from Sung dynasty texts that lodestone spoons were still used for finding direction, especially by troops traveling across difficult country and in foggy weather. In that period, which was one of great commercial expansion, Chinese merchant ships normally used the compass when making voyages out of sight of land—to Japan, Indonesia, Malaya, the Philippines. It was long incorrectly believed that the Arabs first used the compass for navigation. Actually the Chinese themselves were the first to use it in this way. Fukien province, a famous source of Taoist geomancers, was also a maritime region that then, as now, bred a population accustomed to the sea and traditionally skilled in navigation.

It has often been overlooked that in order to make a useful magnetic needle, one that will retain magnetism for more than a very short period, fine quality hard steel is necessary; such steel was manufactured in China from the fifth century A.D. The stimulus for this development was not directly connected with scientific inquiry; rather it was a result of the effort to perfect weapons in an age when the men in power were soldiers who directed their subjects' skill and resources to conform with their own interests. Long before, the Chinese had learned to build their pottery kilns on hillsides in order to increase the height and draft, and thus obtain higher temperatures. This technique was as necessary to the making of high-grade steel as it was to the development of porcelain. The supersession of the lodestone by the magnetic steel needle was not possible until circumstances had brought hard steel into use for other purposes. It was the production of hard-steel weapons that made the magnetic needle possible.

According to tradition, paper, the writing brush, and ink were invented late in the third century B.C. by Mêng T'ien, the commander in chief in the wars that liquidated the feudal kingdoms and established the Chinese empire. Archeology shows, however, that the brush and ink are earlier than that; they were used on a unique silk manuscript discovered in Hunan in the ancient kingdom of Ch'u and dating from some decades before the time of Mêng T'ien. Perhaps writing on silk with ink and brush, rather than incising strips of wood or bamboo with a stylus, was a Ch'u invention; and it is possible that Mêng T'ien was responsible for bringing the art to north China after the conquest of Ch'u. The tradition is also wrong about the invention of paper, which occurred long after the time of Mêng T'ien; its inventor was Ts'ai Lun, who lived around A.D. 105.

It has been pointed out that the invention of paper in China at this early date was in some respects a misfortune, for printing was not really evolved until almost eight hundred years later and did not become widespread until the tenth and eleventh centuries. As a result, the Chinese were using paper for hand-copied texts for a very long time, and paper is much more perishable than parchment, bamboo strips, or silk. The loss of early literature resulting from the Ch'in proscription of books was made greater by the normal hazards of life to which paper books were subjected. Once printing had replaced hand copying, Chinese literature had a much higher survival rate, for many copies were printed of each work.

Printing was not a sudden and complete development. It has a long history, beginning with ink rubbings made from stone inscriptions. The art of stone rubbing, which still flourishes, arose in the Han or post-Han times after the invention of paper, without which it

would hardly have been possible. In time it was realized that a similar effect could be produced by stamping a sheet of paper with an inked block of wood, carved with a charm, a Buddhist sutra, or a picture. By T'ang times, if not earlier, this was the established method of reproducing Buddhist prayers and charms. The first-known book so printed, a Buddhist tract, with a single, separately carved block for each page, dates from A.D 868. By the end of the T'ang period this new way of reproducing books—in many copies—was so well known and esteemed that the classics themselves were printed. In A.D. 1045 movable type was introduced in the form of separately carved characters made of clay. Metal type came in later periods. It is clear that the invention of printing depended on the invention of paper; the use of paper for stone rubbings led to wood block printing and to movable type.

Gunpowder, first employed in war in the tenth century, after the end of the T'ang period, developed from the experiments of Tao-

ists searching for the Philosopher's Stone. Explosive powder had probably been developed by Taoist experimenters in the T'ang era. At first it was used only in magical ceremonies. Doubtless related to this is its continuing use at festivities as a "lucky" adjunct to scare away evil influences. The Lunar New Year at Hong Kong is greeted by a deafening barrage of enormous firecracker chains.

It seems that explosive grenades were employed for the first time in the tenth century by the infantry in encounters with Tatar cavalry. After the fall of the T'ang dynasty in A.D. 906, the Chinese lacked easy access to horse-breeding areas, which were in the hands of their enemies, and consequently were hard-put to maintain large cavalry forces as the T'ang had done. The use of explosive grenades was an effort to overcome the Tatar cavalry; the grenades were probably intended to scare the horses as much as to wound or kill them. The development of the cannon, or barrel gun, seems to have come about a century later. It

The spoon-shaped lodestone, opposite, forerunner of the modern compass, was used for both divination and navigation by the ancient Chinese, who observed that the spoon handle swung south when the spoon was placed on a polished bronze surface. In the upper righthand corner of the Han dynasty bas-relief, above, is a crouching figure who appears to be studying a similar lodestone compass. The major portion of the relief shows jugglers, acrobats, and musicians performing.

149

The process of papermaking, invented in the second century A.D., has remained practically unaltered. At left, workers are shown hanging up sheets of paper to dry; below is a shop with rolls of paper for sale; large sheets are stored on a rack at the rear.

was used, perhaps for the first time, in A.D. 1123.

It was formerly believed in the West that China had always been a pacific nation, unskilled in the art of war. This idea was propagated by Confucian scholars and historians, who were men of peace, neither interested in nor informed about the skills of the soldiers. The fact that after the unification of the empire all Chinese wars were either against the northern "barbarians" or civil wars made war inglorious. Nevertheless, wars occurred in many periods. The practical-minded Chinese who waged them were fertile in expedients and in the invention of new weapons.

It is not possible to say just when the crossbow came into use; but it must be attributed to the period of the Warring States. It may well have been an invention of the northern kingdoms, perhaps of the kingdom of Chao, which had to defend a long frontier facing the nomadic Hu. In the ages before gunpowder was invented, the crossbow was the best weapon against the cavalry. Its bolt, with a greater penetrating power than the arrow, was effective against the light-armored horsemen of the nomads. In Han times the crossbow became standard equipment for the Chinese armies; its use was no doubt responsible for the successes of the Han dynasty in many wars against the Hsiung-nu nomads. In early Han times the powerful crossbow could not be strung except by elite warriors called strong men, who had to lie on their backs, put their feet on the arms of the bow, and pull the string back to the cocking position. While performing this task these "strong men" had to be protected by a hollow square formation. Clearly this was a cumbersome practice that made an army's movements slow and greatly exposed it to attack.

At some time during the Han period, perhaps in the first century B.C., a cocking piece of bronze was invented, which enabled the cross-

bowman to wind back the bow string himself whenever he shot a bolt. This greatly increased the rapidity of fire and the mobility of the force. One such cocking piece was identified recently in the museum at the ancient Greek city of Taxila in Pakistan; it must be a relic of the Later Han intervention in that region early in the second century A.D. The crossbow long remained a Chinese monopoly. It did not reach western Europe until the twelfth century; there it was first used in Italy, having probably been introduced from the Levant.

The Chinese can now perhaps be credited with another vital military invention, the stirrup, whose use was not confined to warfare. Two steles have recently been found with bas-reliefs showing saddled horses and clear representations of short stirrups. The steles are dated A.D. 300 and 301. From depictions of horsemen on Han bas-reliefs it is evident that stirrups were not known a century or two earlier, in Han times; nor were they used by the nomad enemies of the Chinese, natural horsemen who seem to have found no need for such aids to mounting or secure riding. But the Chinese were not natural horsemen; they were a people of the agricultural plains and the hills. The Chinese word for stirrup, *teng*, is the same as the Chinese verb for "to mount." The original purpose of the short stirrup was to serve as an aid in mounting the horse; it is too short to be used when in the saddle.

The development of a longer stirrup that enabled the rider to keep his seat securely when at the gallop or in a charge came soon after. Chinese tomb figures of clay, also dating from the fourth century A.D., portray fully armored horsemen mounted on horses equipped with stirrups. The stirrup was a necessary adjunct to the equipment of the heavy-armored cavalryman. Wearing a considerable weight of chain or laminated armor (armor

composed of small plates sewn onto a thick undercoat) and carrying a spear and a large shield, he probably could not mount his horse or sustain himself in the saddle during the shock of a charge without the stirrup. Fourth- and fifth-century warriors are shown mounted on horses that wear defensive armor on the breast, indicating that they were trained to charge head on. The knight in armor, who several centuries later dominated European feudal society, was therefore a Chinese product. The Tun-huang cave frescoes of T'ang times depict many of these heavy-armed cavalrymen, who were the regular troops of the T'ang empire.

The idea of the heavy-armored horseman seems to have reached Byzantium in the seventh or eighth centuries, at the same time as did the stirrup. From there it spread to western Europe. Byzantine ivories of the sixth century do not show the stirrup in use; but an ivory Byzantine casket of the eleventh century, now in the cathedral at Troyes in France, shows mounted warriors with stirrups and hunters without them. It would seem that in the West, as in early China, the stirrup was probably considered primarily a part of the cavalryman's equipment; mounted men not wearing heavy armor did not think they needed them.

Another Chinese invention was the shoulder collar for horses. It greatly increased the animal's power to draw wagons or carts because it avoided the strangling effect of the earlier neck collar. The invention probably dates from the Han era or shortly thereafter and appears in China about six centuries before it does in the West. The wheelbarrow also appeared very early in China, but took almost a thousand years to reach Europe. The Chinese barrow was different in construction from its European counterpart, and perhaps superior to it. The wheel is large and is placed in the center of the frame, the load being carried in baskets

As early as the Han dynasty the Chinese were making inks out of lampblack and a gummy binding substance. In later times powder, made from rhinoceros horn, crushed pearls, or spices, was added to the mixture. This Ch'ing dynasty print shows workers pressing carbon into flat cakes, which were dissolved in water to make ink.

This Buddhist wood block print, dating from the tenth century,
was presented to a shrine by a worshiper as a votive offering.

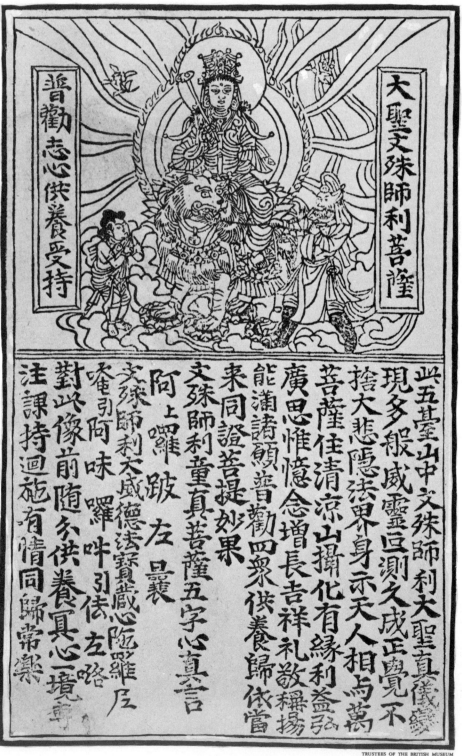

or boxes on either side. A strap running across the pusher's shoulders and secured to the ends of the wheelbarrow's handles helps maintain balance. The pusher does not have to bear a very heavy weight on his arms, and his strength is mostly deployed in pushing the barrow. The large central wheel is able to negotiate rough surfaces fairly easily, and the barrow can be used for transporting passengers as well as goods.

Even in recent times it was common to fit barrows with side seats, like an Irish jaunting car, and two passengers—usually women—could be carried on each side. As late as the 1920's most girls still had bound feet, even those who worked in cotton mills in big cities. They could not walk to work, and so they commonly rode on barrows. In south China, where there were few wide roads, and carts were not used, people were often transported in barrows across flat or undulating country. In hilly regions litters were used. The form of the Chinese barrow was set by the conditions of its use, which were normally travel of several miles along paved or cobbled paths. When the circumstances were suitable, barrow men would sometimes hoist a small sail and let the wind help their load along.

Such common appliances as stirrups, wheelbarrows, and weapons must have been so familiar that they escaped much literary notice; they are better known from pictorial representations or clay sculptures than they are from any written source. But literary records survive describing machinery for weaving, milling, and casting metals. These records are usually of a fairly late date, from Ming or even Ch'ing times, but many of the inventions they describe are very old. Canal locks were devised in China in the eleventh century, several centuries before they came into use in the West. This development was probably a by-product of the extensive drainage and reclamation of swamp lands that was undertaken by the Sung dynasty, perhaps as a result of the heavy increase of population that occurred in the Sung period. In the fourteenth century water power was employed to drive silk spinning mills; at an earlier date it had already been used to drive blowing engines in metallurgical works. Piston bellows may have been in use in pre-Han times, and the chain pump was known in the Han period.

In many inland parts of China there is no easy access to supplies of salt. From Han times onward, salt was a government monopoly. In the western province of Ssǔch'uan, at a town called Tzu Liu Ching ("The Self-Flowing Wells"), there are brine wells that the Chinese have exploited since Han times. The development of the salt industry required the mastery of the art of deep drilling, which was effected entirely with iron-tipped bamboo drills. The Chinese used natural gas tapped from other wells at Tzu Liu Ching as fuel for evaporating the brine. The piping was also of bamboo, since brine corrodes metal pipes.

It has long been known and accepted that the first example of deep drilling anywhere in the world appears in the salt industry of Ssǔch'uan. The methods employed were later copied in Europe and America, and were in use until very recent times. Yet it took more than a thousand years before they were utilized to drill artesian wells in Europe.

Although the Chinese had very early invented elaborate and ingenious techniques for extracting and evaporating brine in Ssǔch'uan, they did not, until very recently, solve the problem of transporting so heavy a material as salt in inland regions, where boats could not be used and where the terrain was too hilly for wheelbarrows. Since the mountain provinces of Kueichou and Yünnan produce no salt, their salt supply came from Tzu Liu Ching. It was transported in large lumps that were strapped onto a frame; the frame in turn was strapped to a man's back with bands that passed under his arms. The porter could not rid himself of this load without the help of another man. In order to rest, he carried a stick with a flat crosspiece. He could place it under the load and then lean back for a time, with the weight supported by the stick. But he could not sit down and hope to rise again; the load was too heavy. If he slipped and fell, he could not get up. His fellows could not help him rise, for they dared not stoop, lest they too fall. In cold weather, when the paths across high and steep mountains were often icy, porters who slipped and fell were left to die of exposure. Except for the long lines of salt porters, who could give no help, travelers were few. A few decades ago, in one morning after a night of frost and snow, four dead salt porters were observed by the author on a road near Tsun-i in Kueichou, where Mao Tse-tung was around the same time elected Chairman of the Chinese Communist Party.

Glass was not a Chinese invention; it had been made in the Near East for a very long time before any imports reached China. Because glass beads are easily passed on and are attractive and novel, their importation to China had doubtless developed several centuries before the Han conquests opened the so-called Silk Road to western Asia. Once the Chinese were familiar with glass, they experimented and evolved a manufacturing process different from that used in the West. The Han naturalist and scholar Wang Ch'ung (A.D. 27–97) wrote a famous treatise containing the first description, or even mention, of the use of a burning glass to "bring down fire." The use of glass for spectacles was long attributed to the Chinese, but it is, in fact, probably of Middle Eastern or European origin. There is no record that spectacles were used in China before the late fourteenth century, after an ex-

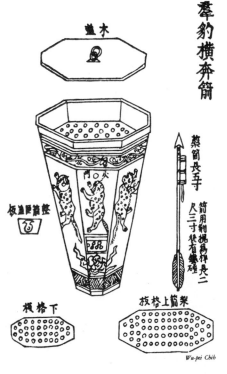

Wu-pei Chih

One use of gunpowder was to propel arrows. These noisy weapons were launched from decorated boxes, like the one above, and powered by a powder-filled capsule strapped to the shaft.

153

Short stirrups, used by the Chinese when mounting a horse, soon gave way to long stirrups, such as those shown in this T'ang dynasty relief. Long stirrups enabled a rider to maintain his seat easily, even while galloping.

tensive period of contact with Persia and the Arab lands.

The history of coinage of China shows a long, independent development, reaching back to the earliest recorded period. In the tenth century B.C. a kind of bronze coin was used, shaped like a knife; the shape has survived in modern times as one of the shop signs of the knifegrinder, although the form of modern Chinese knives is quite unlike that of the ancient Shang knives. Later the shape of coins resembled a spade. It was not until the Warring States or the Han period that round coins with a hole in the middle, through which they could be strung on cords, became standard; this type lasted until modern times. In remote parts of the mountainous western provinces strings of "cash," as the coins had been called by Western residents, could still be found in use as recently as 1938. It is believed that the Chinese never minted silver or gold coins until modern times, although some references in literature suggest that the short-lived Ch'in dynasty (221–207 B.C.) may have done so. If they did, no trace of them has yet been found in archeological digs. The Chinese preferred as a medium of exchange small ingots of gold and silver of a standard weight; as early as

the eighth century B.C., such ingots, carrying an official stamp, were in use in the kingdom of Ch'u.

It would seem strange that a people so addicted to trade, and a government in control of so large an empire, should not have found the minting of silver and gold advantageous. The omission was not because the Chinese never had the idea, as the early bronze coinage and later copper "cash" proves. Perhaps the illicit coining that plagued the Han government when copper "cash" was introduced prejudiced the Chinese against minting the more valuable metals. Until the late nineteenth century, the liang, or Chinese ounce of silver, remained the standard medium of exchange for large-scale transactions, and gold ingots did not circulate freely.

However, the Chinese did make one financial innovation, paper money, centuries before this method of exchange was adopted in the Western world. In the T'ang period, bankers and money shops in Ssŭch'uan province began to issue what may be called drafts, payable at the capital, Ch'ang-an. As a result, they could remit sums of money over great distances, obviating the risk of loss or theft by bandits. In 1024, early in the Sung dynasty, paper money was issued with government approval and backing. In the Sung period commerce was expanding, and for the first time in Chinese history revenues from taxes on commodities and from excise taxes exceeded land revenues, which were traditionally collected in grain. The use of paper money does not seem to have outlived the Sung; it was probably discontinued as a consequence of the vast dislocation of society caused by the Mongol conquest.

In the Sung period, from the tenth to the thirteenth centuries, a very large number of Chinese technological innovations became important to the economy. The population of

China exceeded one hundred million. Population growth and the loss of the northern provinces were factors that caused the Southern Sung regime to depend increasingly on revenue from commerce and industry. Overseas trade was expanded as a result of the advance in shipbuilding technique and the use of the maritime compass, which made communications by sea better and more reliable. Among these innovations was the expanded use of paddle boats, propelled by men working a treadmill to turn two paddle wheels. These had been known in the T'ang period, but they were used only as pleasure boats on the lakes of the imperial palace; now they were utilized commercially on rivers and estuaries. Silk spinning and porcelain manufacture were organized in factories, which fulfilled large orders, including those that came from overseas as a result of a flourishing export trade. Sung export porcelain has been found in plenty in the Arab lands and along the east African coast. It did not reach Europe until two centuries after it reached the Near East.

The origin of silk spinning is so ancient that no date for it can be given; but porcelain, true porcelain as opposed to hard-glazed pottery, which dates at least from Han times, was manufactured before the T'ang period. The patronage of the early Sung emperors advanced porcelain technology until it attained a perfection that, in the view of many collectors and connoisseurs, has never been equaled, although in later periods new styles and a more elaborate and colorful decoration were developed. During the Sung period there were a number of centers of porcelain production in both north and south China. In A.D. 1004 the emperor reorganized the imperial kilns in Kiangsi province near the hill of Kao-ling, or Kaolin; this center was called Ching-te-chen. It became, and has remained, the main center of Chinese porcelain manufacture because the

Kao-ling region contains immense deposits of clay. Indeed, the name "kaolin" has been given to the fine white clay from which porcelain is made.

The Sung period is also the age in which the Chinese abandoned the ancient custom of sitting on floor mats and adopted raised furniture, a change based on the development of the chair. The chair decides the style of all other furniture. Tables must be relatively high, so that the knees of someone sitting in a chair can fit beneath the tabletop; cupboards can be high, because the user will normally be standing, rather than sitting on the floor. Lamps must be high to give light to someone seated in a chair. Many other details of decoration—the placing of ornaments and pictures, and even the style of the rooms themselves—were modified by the adoption of the chair.

It began in the Later Han period, when the Emperor Ling Ti, under whose reign the empire began to disintegrate, took a fancy to what the Chinese had long called *hu ch'uang*, or "barbarian beds." These were a kind of large, folding camp stool, not long enough to be used as a real bed, and they had been known in prehistoric times in Europe and western Asia Minor. The Chinese called them

An astronomical clock tower, built at K'ai-feng in the eleventh century under imperial orders, relied on a highly sophisticated combination of water-driven gears (seen at right center in the cutaway diagram above) to rotate an armillary sphere (under the thatched roof) and a celestial globe (located within the tower on the second floor). Additional gears turned the five horizontal discs at left center, bringing a series of figures into view in the apertures along one wall of the tower. These jacks announced the time with placard, drum, or gong.

JOSEPH NEEDHAM, *Science and Civilization in China*, CAMBRIDGE UNIVERSITY PRESS

155

By the third century B.C. *the Chinese in Ssŭch'uan province had sunk brine wells to great depths using only iron-tipped drills and simple overhead rigs like that above.*

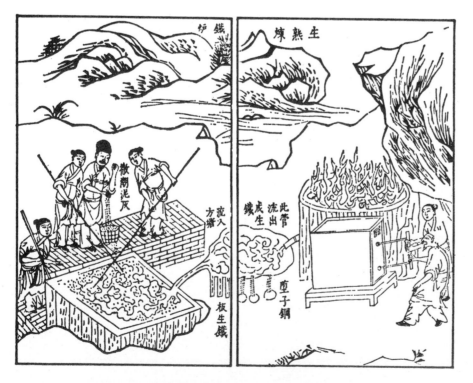

Iron ore was smelted in blast furnaces (right) fanned by double-action piston bellows; the ore was tapped (center) and then combined with silica (left) to make wrought iron.

beds because they were raised above the floor, as Chinese beds were, and barbarian because they came from the Hu, the northern barbarians. But the word *Hu* also applied to the peoples northwest of China, who were reached by the silk route across Central Asia; there can be no doubt that the original barbarian beds were, in fact, similar to the European camp stool.

The camp-stool type of chair continued to be popular in China for a long period after Han times, mainly as part of the equipment of officers on campaign. It was especially practical in open country, particularly in south China, where the ground was often wet. By the sixth century the camp stool had become domestic; it was first used in gardens, and then in houses, but as an informal piece of furniture, not normally placed in reception rooms. It continued to be used in this way in the T'ang period; but toward the middle of the ninth century clear indications appear of the first frame chairs with backs. These did not fold. They, too, were at first used out of doors, in gardens and on terraces.

Literary evidence from early in the Sung era confirms the fact that at this time the chair habit spread to the whole upper class, and that the old camp stool was now given a back to become a true folding chair. With the adoption of the frame chair came the abandonment of the floor mat and its replacement by either carpets or tiled floors. A famous twelfth-century scroll, *Ch'ing Ming Shang Ho T'u,* or *Life along the River on the Eve of the Ch'ing Ming Festival* (one version of it is reproduced almost in full on pages 266 to 279), shows the whole population of K'ai-feng celebrating the spring festival of Ch'ing Ming; without exception, rich and poor are seen sitting on benches and chairs in their homes and in wayside teahouses along the riverbank. Both fixed frame chairs and folding chairs are depicted—and both

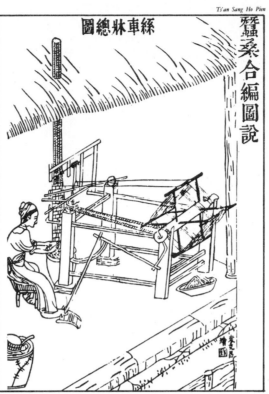

研硃

絲車總圖

蠶桑合編圖說

水碓

Laborers produce vermilion pigment in the shallow iron trough at rear by grinding cinnabar with a disc-shaped suspended millstone.

A single foot-treadle powers this silk reeling machine, which threads fibers through a series of guides and onto a large reel (right).

Trip hammers, which were used to hull rice and pulverize minerals, are repeatedly lifted by lugs along the shaft of this waterwheel.

踏車

車輪舸圖

南方獨推車圖

Shaded by a thatched roof, two workers operate a chain pump, whose square paddles lift water to irrigate the rice-paddies at rear.

Four side wheels—driven by treadmills within the hull—propel this paddle-wheel warship, whose sides are emblazoned with demon heads.

Unlike its Western counterpart, the Chinese wheelbarrow is designed sensibly to center the full weight of the load over the wheel.

The folding camp stool was the proto-type for the fixed frame chair and also for the fixed frame stool, on which the women in the painting at right are sitting. The fixed frame chair had become a familiar sight in Chinese households by the twelfth century; by approximately the same time the game of double-six, a version of backgammon being played by the seated women, had also become popular.

types have continued in use to this day.

The rapid technological advance under the Sung dynasty, and the failure of Chinese civilization to carry this advance forward with the same impetus in the subsequent periods, raises a great question about Chinese technology and science, and about the development of the economy as a whole. By the twelfth and thirteenth centuries China seemed to have approached or reached the point that is today called take off—when a preindustrial society is ready to turn to large-scale industry and commerce, and in consequence elaborate a technology that would swiftly lead to the use of power-driven machinery, relegating handicraft to a secondary place. It has been suggested that China's technology and advanced handicraft were no less developed than were Europe's on the eve of the Industrial Revolution. China might have anticipated the West by about five hundred years.

It can be argued that the Mongol invasions put the clock back. They did indeed devastate much of north China. But the south, the old Southern Sung domain, was not so severely ravaged, and by the time of the Mongol invasion it had already become the wealthiest and

probably the most populous part of China. It is a huge area, and it could certainly have sustained a major economic and technological revolution. A simple mechanical interpretation—retardation by the devastation of a foreign invasion—is not sufficient to explain the failure to advance. Modern Chinese writers, and many Western scholars of varying political standpoints, agree that China's lack of further advance in technology and industrialization was caused by the social and political system. The roots of the retardation lay in the dominance of the scholar gentry—with its literary culture and its economic base in a peasant-landlord agricultural system—and in the autocracy of the Ming and Ch'ing monarchs, who imposed the scholar's values upon society more firmly than the T'ang or Sung rulers had done.

This explanation is probably correct so far as it goes, but it does not explain why an impasse existed in China and not in the West. European society had been dominated as much as Chinese society, or even more, by a feudal and postfeudal landlord class. In most parts of Europe the absolutism of monarchs such as Louis XIV was no less than that of such Chinese emperors as Yung Lo or K'ang Hsi. The one factor not common to both societies is the distribution of political power, which was fragmented in the many nation-states of Europe, and monolithic in the centralized empire of China. This may have an indirect connection with the differing development of Europe and China. The existence in Europe of city-states, many of them seaports, politically independent of the great monarchies, gave the merchant class opportunities for power and initiative that they would not have enjoyed in firmly governed empires, and which they never acquired in China.

The domination of landlord gentry in their roles as scholars and officials would not in itself be enough to retard technology in China had there been a powerful, politically secure class of merchants able to exploit technology for their own profit and advantage. This class was potentially present in the great port cities of Canton and Hang-chou and in the cities of the lower Yangtze valley; but it could not free itself from the political domination of the landlord-gentry officials. Nor could it emancipate itself from a cultural tradition that despised and decried commerce, treated scientific inquiry as Taoist chicanery, and technology as a fit study only for craftsmen, men who might be employed by the ruling class, but who were considered the lowest of the four classes of society: scholar, farmer, merchant, and artisan. It is worth pointing out that as soon as Western pressure in the nineteenth century created in Treaty Ports, such as Shanghai, conditions under which merchant capital could prosper free from official oppression, Chinese merchants very rapidly advanced into the field of modern capitalism and opened their minds and hearts to the teachings of science and technology.

The first airplane flight in Asia, which is commemorated in the painting above, had special meaning for the Chinese, whose third-century B.C. invention, the kite, was the precursor of the biplane.

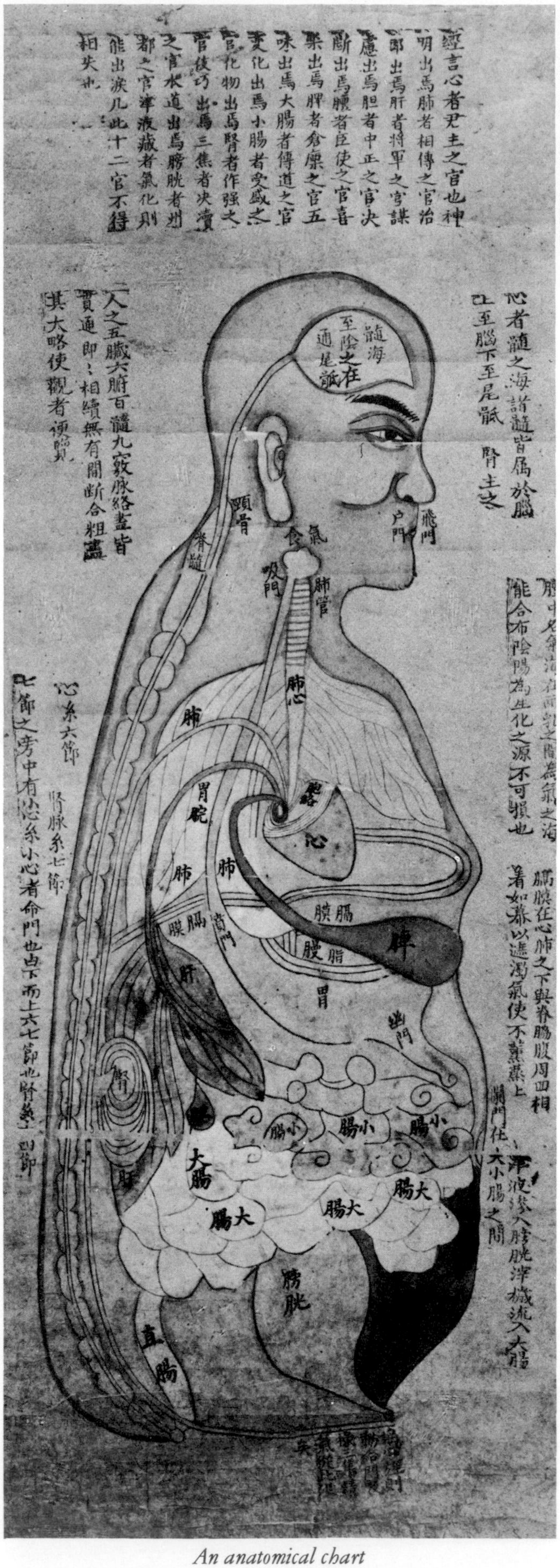

An anatomical chart

PHYSICIAN
AND PHARMACIST

In the course of their search for the elixir of immortality, Taoist alchemists discovered dozens of potions that prolonged—or were presumed to prolong—life. It is not surprising, therefore, that one of China's first medical treatises was a pharmacopoeia, a compilation of those discoveries listing 365 different drugs. By Han times Chinese physicians could diagnose such diseases as gout and cirrhosis of the liver, although they had almost no knowledge of anatomy. Indeed, Chinese history records only two dissections before the sixteenth century, and early Chinese anatomical charts, such as the Ming dynasty diagram at left, are incomplete and inaccurate. Certain obstacles stood in the way of studying anatomy; Chinese women preferred to remain fully clothed in the doctor's presence, and they indicated the site of their discomfort on medicine dolls, like the one shown at far right.

The Chinese stressed preventive medicine, recognizing the importance of proper dress, diet, and exercise. They believed that good health was dependent upon maintaining the proper balance of yin and yang elements in the body. Disease resulted from an imbalance between the moist, weak, feminine elements and the dry, strong, masculine ones. Convinced that each organ produced a separate pulse that could be detected at a given point on the body, the Chinese made pulse reading, or sphygmology, their chief diagnostic tool. Having determined the seat of a patient's trouble, the doctor then inserted thin needles into the patient's body at predetermined points, which were supposedly linked to the internal organ that was causing the trouble. (The bronze figure at near right bears a group of these points at locations that might have some effect on a contracted right leg.) Although this process, known as acupuncture, has no proven medical value, it continues to be practiced by China's traditional doctors, who even today outnumber the practitioners of Western-style medicine by about ten to one.

Bronze acupuncture figure   *Ivory diagnostic doll*

8 The Golden Age

(A.D. 600 *to* 1260)

A larger than life-sized portrait shows the great T'ang dynasty Emperor T'ai Tsung in an imperial robe of yellow silk embroidered with dragons.

The reunion and reconstruction of the empire by the Sui dynasty (A.D. 590–618) and its successor, the T'ang, is the turning point in the history of China; it determined the future nature of the society and the political framework within which China was to develop. What happened in China at this time could have been paralleled in the West if the sixth-century Byzantine Emperor Justinian had fulfilled his ambition to reconquer all of the former Roman empire and hand it on to his successors intact, enabling Rome to continue down to modern times as a great imperial state. It is easy to see that such a development would have profoundly altered the whole course of European history and civilization. In China, unlike Europe, a centralized empire throve, and tendencies toward separatism withered. New nations, arising from the mixture of natives and barbarian invaders, never had the chance to evolve.

The Chinese people welcomed the country's reunification. The idea became axiomatic that divergence could only mean anarchy, and that peace and prosperity could only flourish when there was unity. Centuries later, after the revolution of 1912, the Chinese republicans rejected out of hand any idea of a federal republic of states on the American model—although they were in so many other matters strongly influenced by the United States. One of the underlying reasons for this attitude was the widespread belief that all forms of local autonomy were signs of weakness and would lead to disorder and the partition of the country. This view is still universal in China among both Communists and Nationalists.

Under the T'ang dynasty (A.D. 618–906) several important consequences flowed from this outlook and from the fact that China was firmly controlled by a central imperial power. Warfare no longer brought glory and prestige to the military caste, for now it could only

162

mean civil war or frontier defense. The army became primarily the "army of the frontier," and is often so described in T'ang and later literature. The rest of the armed forces consisted mainly of the palace guards, prestigious formations that were more likely to be involved in *coups d'état* than in hostilities against the national enemies. Generally, provincial troops were few, and the provinces were ruled by civil servants. So long as the provinces were well governed, there was no need for large garrisons. This was the ideal; and for long periods, especially during the first one hundred fifty years of the T'ang dynasty, the ideal was largely realized.

Since military service outside the palace guards generally meant long years on a bleak northern frontier, far from court, it was not very attractive to the scions of the great aristocratic houses. Men of the aristocratic class, who had dominated the short and insecure dynasties of the period of division, had been at the center of the political world, and they were not about to surrender their power. The T'ang emperors, themselves originating from this class, understood all too well what dangers their fellow aristocrats, some of them their close relatives, presented to the imperial government. In the course of the seventh century the emperors systematically weakened and destroyed this class, and deprived it of its power and influence. Prominent men had traditionally served as both soldiers and statesmen; in the T'ang period, and still more in the Sung (A.D. 960–1279), the separation of the two professions became sharp and complete. Until the middle T'ang period, Chinese society, dominated by martial aristocrats, had many resemblances to the medieval society that would emerge in the West; however, with the rise of the scholar-bureaucrat, the resemblances diminish.

The rise of the scholar-bureaucrats—later named Mandarins by Europeans—was a profoundly important result of the reunion of the empire. The early T'ang rulers deliberately fostered their rise as a safeguard against the great power of the military aristocracy. Under the T'ang the method for choosing bureaucrats was standardized, with an examination system evolved from earlier methods of selecting suitable candidates for official posts. Candidates had to pass a written examination on officially chosen texts and subjects. This was carefully supervised, and success in it was rewarded with a degree that determined the rank and career open to officials in the bureaucratic hierarchy. This system grew steadily under the T'ang. For a time an alternate method of picking officials, through the recommendation of men in high office, survived, but gradually this was replaced completely by the examination system, which endured throughout Chinese history as the normal method of recruiting the civil service. The Chinese were the inventors of examinations as we now understand them. Ironically, the present regime in China has attempted to abolish them.

The new scholar-bureaucrats were derived from poorer and more obscure families than the military aristocrats, whom they steadily displaced in office. The scholars had no great local influence, for they did not command military forces or have the wealth and authority to raise them. They depended for their careers on the government, which could promote, transfer, or dismiss them at will. Economically they depended on relatively small landholdings rather than on emoluments received for public service. As they served in the capital or in provinces far from their homes, they could not themselves manage their estates. These were left to the care of less-talented members of the family. The scholar-official drew income from the family estate and added to it whatever other wealth he acquired, so

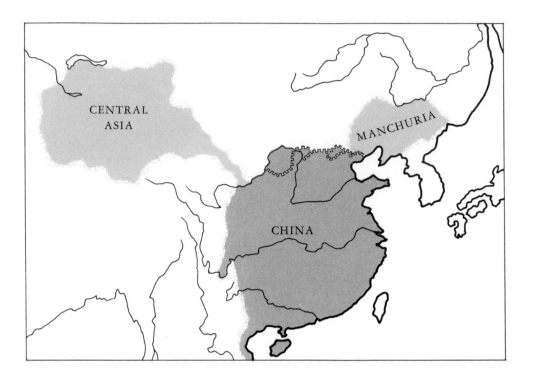

Territorial expansion during the T'ang dynasty (A.D. 618–906) extended China's borders beyond the Great Wall to include Manchuria in the northeast and Central Asia in the west. After the fall of the T'ang, China broke up into several kingdoms; it was reunified by the Northern Sung dynasty (960–1126). Sung rulers emphasized native traditions rather than the reconquest of frontier lands; and Sung territory was limited to regions inhabited primarily by Chinese. The T'ang domain is shown by light shading; the Sung by dark.

that his children and those of his kinfolk could be supported while they, in turn, followed the arduous course of study needed to enter the civil service. The Chinese ruling class that developed in the T'ang period had a very different social background and life experience from the land-based gentry of Europe.

The T'ang dynasty had the fortune to produce within a brief interval three outstanding personalities: T'ai Tsung, the Empress Wu, and Ming Huang. Interestingly, not one of these was the direct heir. The first of the three, the Emperor T'ai Tsung, was the second son of Li Yüan, the rather uninspiring founder of the dynasty. At the age of sixteen the future emperor urged his father into rebellion; the youth commanded the rebel armies and led them to total victory. He eliminated his elder brother, who had conspired against him, and succeeded to the throne of their father, who had abdicated in his favor. T'ai Tsung was perhaps the greatest of all Chinese emperors. His military ability was outstanding, but his competence as a civil ruler surpassed it. Almost all the great reforms of the T'ang dynasty sprang from his initiatives: the examination system, reformed land tenure, the establishment of a professional army increasingly free from aristocratic control. He was also a historian and a scholar of wide knowledge; and

his calligraphy is so much admired that it still serves as a model for school children.

T'ai Tsung failed in only one respect—his choice of a successor. After being forced to degrade his eldest son, an eccentric, unbalanced youth who had conspired against him, he chose as heir another son, who was a submissive and dutiful weakling. When T'ai Tsung died, one of his many concubines, Wu Chao, seduced the young emperor. She eliminated the new empress, her rival, and obtained the title for herself. For more than fifty years she ruled China, first as consort of the weak Emperor Kao Tsung and then in her own name. When the emperor died, she judged, rightfully, that their sons were incompetent; she soon pushed them aside and ascended the throne herself. She was the only woman in Chinese history to hold the official title of "monarch."

In her ruthless and carefully schemed rise to power, the Empress Wu had to rid herself of critics who were outraged by her gross violation of traditional procedure and of the rules of morality. (Technically she was guilty of incest.) These critics were, for the most part, members of the great military aristocracy. She destroyed them. In their place she promoted "obscure men, but those who had talents"— as the official historians grudgingly admit. In order to further her own ambitions she sponsored an important and necessary social change: the rise of the lower gentry and of men still lower on the social scale—provided they were able, and loyal to her. As these men had no hope of a career, or even of survival if they deserted her, she could be sure of their loyalty.

Nevertheless, when she was old and in bad health, the very men she had raised from nothing dethroned her. They broke into the palace by night, slew the court favorites to whom they had strong objection, and proclaimed the restoration of her feeble son, the Emperor Chung Tsung. The old lady rose from her bed, came out, and roundly abused the rebels as a foolish and ungrateful pack of traitors; then she turned her back on them and went back to bed. The empress was forced to abdicate; but within a few years the new emperor, Chung Tsung, was murdered by his ambitious wife. After a brief period of palace intrigues, the situation was settled by the Empress Wu's grandson, Hsüan Tsung, who is generally known by his sobriquet Ming Huang, the "Brilliant Emperor."

He, too, was not an oldest son, but his father had chosen him as heir. For once the Confucian ideal of brotherly love prevailed. Ming Huang's five brothers, including his older brothers, lived out their lives in perfect friendship and loyalty to him. He reigned from A.D. 712 to 756. Able, and for many years attentive to the duties of the monarch, Ming Huang is best known as a patron of the arts. At his court Li Po and Tu Fu, the great poets of the T'ang dynasty, held office; the first form of the novel appeared; artists of durable influence painted; and Chinese drama had its beginnings. (Ming Huang has ever since been the patron spirit of actors.)

The empire was administered by a very competent civil service, which was sufficiently in control of all facets of Chinese life to take detailed enumerations of the population. Western scholars long believed that these figures were merely estimates of taxpayers; perhaps the scholars were incredulous of the level of government efficiency that China attained so much earlier than did their own countries. But actual census returns have been discovered; these show that not only the head of the family but his dependent young children were listed. The census of A.D. 754, the most complete of four censuses taken between 640 and 754, gives the population as 52,880,

OSVALD SIRÉN, *A History of Early Chinese Art*

488. China contained 321 prefectural cities, 1,538 subprefectures, and 16,829 unwalled market towns. In A.D. 726 the population figure is 41,419,712. This implies a rise of about ten millions in just under thirty years. The period was one of unexampled peace and prosperity, which may explain the great increase in the population. Also, the efficiency of compiling returns may have improved. Even if the figures are not as accurate as their detail suggests, it is certain that the T'ang empire was then the most populous state in the world. (At that time its population was only a fraction of that contained in almost the same area today.)

The capital, Ch'ang-an, the modern Sian in Shensi, had a population exceeding one million, a figure probably surpassing that of Constantinople, its only significant rival. The city today occupies only a small part of the T'ang enclosure, which stretches for miles around

The much-restored Wild Goose Pagoda, a Buddhist shrine begun in the year 652, is one of the two buildings surviving from T'ang dynasty Ch'ang-an.

Khitan Mongols, who united most of Mongolia and in 936 conquered part of north China, assimilated Chinese culture, but retained many Mongol traditions—among them a love for hunting. Above, Khitans hunt with birds of prey.

it. Scholars can recognize the exact limits of the enclosure from surviving landmarks, which are mentioned in T'ang literature. The location of Ch'ang-an presented one drawback, which was already causing difficulty in the reign of Ming Huang. Although it was situated in the fertile Wei valley, it lacked a sufficiently large arable hinterland, and the problem of bringing grain to the capital was serious. The communications from Honan province, the nearest great grain-producing region, were mainly by way of the Yellow River and its Wei tributary. But the Yellow River runs through hill country and is barred by dangerous rapids, including the famous San-men, or Three Gates Gorge. The transport of grain barges up the river was, therefore, laborious, costly, and wasteful. Transport by cart was also slow and uneconomical.

The army presented the T'ang emperors with another problem. Early in the period T'ai Tsung had formed a professional army stationed on the frontiers; his aim was to solve the problem of political instability caused by the presence throughout China of ambitious military men. But the professional army also had its dangers. It tended to recruit from the tribes beyond the frontier, just as the Romans had done in Germany, and the British were to do on the northwest frontier of the Indian empire. Barbarian soldiers of fortune rose high in the ranks and attained positions of command. When they visited the capital to receive honors and rewards, they could see for themselves that the empire was rich, luxurious, unwarlike, and dependent on their loyalty for its protection. There was little to oppose a frontier general who wanted to lead his troops in a swift march on the capital. It was perhaps inevitable that toward the end of Ming Huang's reign a general should appear who succumbed to this temptation.

As a result, the last years of the reign of Ming Huang were darkened by disasters. These years have become famous in Chinese literature because of the romantic but tragic love story of the emperor and his concubine, Yang Kuei-fei. In the following generation the poet Po Chü-i was to give this story its enduring form in one of the few Chinese poems of epic quality. Innumerable plays have embellished the details of the love affair and dwelt on its tragic outcome. According to the traditional story, An Lu-shan, a gross and cruel frontier general of barbarian origin, was the villain who brought about the downfall of Ming Huang and the death of Yang Kuei-fei. An Lu-shan was the buffoon and the favorite of the frivolous court and of Yang Kuei-fei, its mistress. He secretly resented and despised the soft manners of the silken courtiers. Any suspicions about his trustworthiness that reached the emperor's ears were dissipated by the persuasions of Yang Kuei-fei. Resolving to overthrow the emperor, An Lu-shan returned to his command, raised his forces, and swiftly marched on Ch'ang-an, driving the court into panic-stricken flight. During its flight, mutinous imperial guards insisted on the execution of the beautiful Yang Kuei-fei, threatening to slay the emperor and go over to the rebels if she were not surrendered to them. So, "She of the moth eyebrows perished before their horses." In Po Chü-i's poem this tragic conclusion of the traditional story is called the "everlasting wrong."

The tale is substantially historical, but there are points that the poet slurred over. Yang Kuei-fei had been the concubine of one of the emperor's own sons, and Ming Huang himself had been over sixty at the time he took her into his harem. When An Lu-shan took Ch'-ang-an, the emperor was an old man of seventy-two, and Yang Kuei-fei was in her forties. It is all too likely that she influenced his failing judgment and distracted his attention from his duty. An Lu-shan was a shrewd and able general, who seems to have laid his plans with care and foresight. But in the end his plans failed. The emperor escaped to the western province of Ssŭch'uan, which was almost inaccessible to invaders (in the second World War the Nationalists held it against Japan), and officials loyal to the dynasty slowly beat back the rebellion, aided by dissension among the rebels. In the end Ch'ang-an was recovered and the rebellion was crushed; but Ming Huang abdicated and remained in retirement in Ssŭch'uan.

Under his successors the central government suffered grievously. Provinces occupied by the rebels had to be reconquered, and the generals who accomplished this task retained some power. As a consequence of the pacification, a system of military governorships was set up, and the emperor had to tolerate the governors' authority. In the later T'ang period, from about 760 to 906, the struggle between the court and the military governors was the dominant political concern. For more than a century the imperial government managed to maintain itself, aided by the civil service, but China was no longer unified, as it had been in the seventh century and first half of the eighth.

The second half of the T'ang period has sometimes been described as a sad decline from the glories of the era that preceded the rebellion of An Lu-shan, and in one sense this is true. But literature, art, and technology continued to flourish, and the court was by no means so powerless or so poor as the traditional historians often imply. By skillful policy the emperors were able to play off the too-independent provincial governors against each other. The court could not abolish the system of military governorships; but it could make sure that the governorships were not turned into hereditary fiefs, and that officers of the emperor's choice were appointed to vacancies. These appointments often resulted in civil war between local rivals for the office; but the court was quite content to sit back and see them weaken each other. A chronic, and in the end more serious, problem for the government came as a result of the short lives of the later emperors. The frequent change of ruler encouraged court intrigue and gave increasing power to the eunuchs.

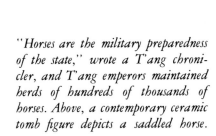

AVERY BRUNDAGE COLLECTION

"Horses are the military preparedness of the state," wrote a T'ang chronicler, and T'ang emperors maintained herds of hundreds of thousands of horses. Above, a contemporary ceramic tomb figure depicts a saddled horse.

167

涇陽不肯守孤城

單騎權為見雲行

扣馬力遠郭晞步

芟手任葛羅擎吐

蕃迴紇心咸服元

It was in this age that some very important technical and social advances were made. The earliest printed book dates from the ninth century. Porcelain making became common, and porcelain shards have been found far outside China, in the now-deserted city of Samarra in Iraq, proving that there was an active export trade. In the ninth century a tax was first put on tea, showing that this beverage had become a popular drink. In earlier times tea had been thought of as a medicine. The development of the custom of tea drinking, which involves boiling water, and the growing use of porcelain for dishes and bowls, are considered important factors in the increase that later took place in China's population. Boiled water decreased the risk of infection from a polluted supply; porcelain could be washed clean so

that it did not harbor decaying food particles. Tea drinking also reduced the consumption of alcohol, which, to judge from the Chinese poetry, had been considerable before the late T'ang period. In China teahouses, which do not normally serve alcohol, are still called winehouses, for the winehouse was the ancestor of the teahouse.

The rebellion that finally ruined the T'ang empire began with a mutiny of the frontier army of the south. In A.D. 868 the southern frontier army was mainly composed of northern men. The lax control the court exerted in this distant region had led to great arrears in their pay. They mutinied and then started to march northward to their home provinces. The court ignored this remote danger, leaving the problem to the governors of the lightly

Details from a scroll, attributed to an unknown Sung dynasty master, depict the story of a T'ang general, Kuo Tzŭ-i, who is shown (opposite at left) receiving homage from Uigur chieftains, while his groom and the officers of his army (above) look on. The Uigurs, a Turkish tribe, had invaded China and sacked Lo-yang. A few years after the sack, Kuo entered a Uigur encampment unarmed and persuaded the Uigurs to make peace and join the Chinese in fighting other tribal incursions.

garrisoned southern provinces. These men were less concerned with meeting the mutinous army in battle than with seeing it pass into the provinces of their neighbors.

After seven years of desultory plundering and wandering, the rebels obtained an energetic leader in the person of Huang Ch'ao. He was a new phenomenon in Chinese history, the first but not the last of the rebel leaders drawn from among the educated malcontents who had failed to pass the civil service examination. Huang Ch'ao led his followers north, but finding opposition stiff, turned south in A.D. 879 and swept through Kuangtung to capture a very rich prize, the great trading city of Canton. With his army increasing in size, he again turned north. In 881 he advanced swiftly, almost unopposed by the pro-

vincial governors, and captured Ch'ang-an, forcing the court to flee to the safety of Ssǔch'uan, as had Ming Huang.

This conquest destroyed the cohesion of the empire and plunged it into anarchy. A few years later Huang Ch'ao was slain, but by then no real restoration of the T'ang dynasty was possible. The court returned to Ch'ang-an, a city left half desolate by the occupation forces. There the government became the puppet of rival military commanders—much as the last Han emperor had been, and as centuries later, the early republican government was to be. These generals—some of them "pardoned" ex-rebels and others nominally loyal—fought each other for control of rich provinces and used the last shreds of imperial authority to sanction their depredations. In 904 one of

A copy of a T'ang dynasty scroll shows the Emperor Ming Huang, on horseback, watching his famous and rather hefty concubine, Yang Kuei-fei, mount a gaily caparisoned horse. Assisting the lady in her ascension are a groom, two maids-in-waiting, a supervising official, and a footstool. The original picture may have been commissioned by Ming Huang, a considerable patron of the arts, and it was probably painted by one of his court painters, Han Kan, who was well known for his portrayals of horses.

171

very little fighting. By A.D. 975 all the southern kingdoms had submitted. Their rulers were not put to death, as defeated rivals for imperial power usually were; they were allowed to live in peace and dignity at the new capital, K'ai-feng in Honan. There can be no doubt that the main reason this almost peaceful reunion of the empire was possible was that it corresponded with the wishes and ideals of the scholar class and was in no way inimical to the simpler aspirations of the peasantry.

Reunion of those parts of the empire inhabited and governed by Chinese was not a very difficult problem, for in them the forces of traditional Confucian thought were still strong. But the Sung had no success in reconquering those outlying areas that had been ceded to foreign tribes or that had broken away from the empire when the T'ang dynasty fell. North of the Great Wall, and in the northeast in what is now Manchuria, the Khitan tribes, who had been under strong Chinese influence since T'ang times, arose as a new power. The Khitans set up a kingdom called Liao (from the Liao River in southern Manchuria), and for the first time in Chinese history made Peking a capital, naming it the secondary capital of their dynasty. They were the first strong power to arise in Manchuria, a region suitable for agriculture and capable of supporting a large population.

The Sung never ruled in the northwest either. Much of Kansu province and the adjacent region of Inner Mongolia formed the kingdom of Hsi-hsia; this was ruled by a dynasty of Tibetan-Tangut origin and inhabited largely by peoples of the same stock. Hsi-hsia developed its own ideographic script, which

farm
the s
T
elim
for
mon
peas
Befo
posa
migl
need
as fo
one
Mor
allov
too,
the
labo
A
of la
that
requ
prov
aime
inequ
duce
not
profi
Othe
were
syste
whic
A
a hor
prese
curin
Inne
norm
on th
clearl
a suf
pire.
most

still defies full interpretation. The utter destruction of the kingdom by the Mongol invasion early in the thirteenth century buried its culture and did much to reduce the region to a near desert. But in Sung times Hsi-hsia was a flourishing kingdom. It barred China from using the old land route to west Asia, which, as a result, lost much of its commercial importance.

Being confined to purely Chinese territories, the Sung developed a more narrowly national outlook than the T'ang. Their contact with the West was secondhand, through Arab merchants. Their interests in foreign affairs were relatively small; their preoccupation with Chinese civilization and traditions was intense. It is in the Sung period that archaism in art first appears—a clear sign of national sophistication, if not decadence. The

Sung began to collect ancient bronzes and copy them. Their methods of government were markedly more humane than those of their predecessors. Sung officials who fell from court favor were not put to death, but were sent to remote country districts as magistrates. With a turn of the political wheel, they could regain power and rank.

A political system arose that tolerated some opposition, even if such toleration was not officially admitted. Two schools of thought emerged. The conservatives stuck firmly to their ancient doctrines, which opposed all innovations; the innovators sought to introduce new laws that they considered necessary to deal with new situations. Despite their differences, both parties were bound by common ideas and ties. Under a series of monarchs, who were well intentioned but not brilliant, the government veered from one side to the other. The emperors were the arbiters, and to a great extent seem to have based their actions on the arguments of their counselors rather than on the persuasion of intriguing courtiers or feminine favorites.

The strength of the innovators' party lay in the fact that China's situation had changed. There were no longer pressing problems within the country. Internal peace was well maintained, and no great rebellions seriously threatened the power of the Sung dynasty. (This makes the Sung a remarkable exception in China's history.) The civil service was efficient and much more powerful than ever before, for it had no military competition to contend with. But danger came from beyond the frontiers, from foreign foes. The empire no longer controlled the vital passes leading from the steppelands. The threat of invasion ensured the loyalty of an army, which was wholly employed in guarding a weak and difficult frontier. What was needed, argued the innovators, was a tax structure that would be able to bear the New Laws were Wang An-shih, the propagator of the measures, and his opponent, Ssŭ-ma Kuang, the leader of the conservative scholars and a famous historian. The main period in which the laws were in force was during the eighteen-year reign of the Emperor Shên Tsung, from A.D. 1068 to 1086. The laws continued to be enforced after Wang An-shih resigned from office in 1076; but in 1086, the year in which both he and Shên Tsung died, his great opponent Ssŭ-ma Kuang came to power and persuaded the empress regent to repeal them in the name of the young Emperor Chê Tsung. In 1093, when the emperor came of age, he recalled innovator ministers to power and put the New Laws into force again, under a disciple of Wang An-shih named Ts'ai Ching. In and out of office, Ts'ai Ching was able to maintain the new system until the Chin Tatars overran north China in 1126. The New Laws were in operation for a little more than fifty years.

During that period the Sung government took two censuses. The first, in A.D. 1083, counted 17,211,713 families, estimated at 90,000,000 persons. The second, forty-one years later, in the year 1124, gave a return of 20,882,258 families, estimated at 100,000,000 persons. Conservative critics had claimed that the New Laws were oppressive to the peasantry and would cause a great rebellion, such as the one led by An Lu-shan, which had ruined the T'ang dynasty. No rebellion took place; and the considerable rise in the population in forty years argues increased prosperity rather than great distress.

The total effect of the New Laws is hard to evaluate. Their application was not consistent even during the period when innovators had the imperial favor. It was their critics who wrote the history of the times, and not much survives that was written by the laws' supporters. It is apparent that the New Laws did not bring the disasters that the critics foretold; it is less certain that they produced the beneficial results that Wang An-shih had expected. It seems that the civil service, even taking into account its relatively high efficiency, was asked to perform intricate tasks that were beyond its capacity, particularly in an age with slow communications and almost no printing.

The execution of the New Laws required a sophistication in administration, which was probably beyond the capacities of the civil service, just as the critics of the laws claimed. Yet it is not easy to demonstrate that the critics were right. Sung government was the quintessence of bureaucracy; it was far more advanced than any other government of the time. While the Sung were debating complex land laws and related questions of abstruse Confucian metaphysics (for politics and philosophy went hand in hand), western Europe was just recovering from the Viking invasions.

The full application of the New Laws would have meant great governmental control over the economy and the daily life of China. This is, indeed, what the present regime imposes, aided by modern media of communication. Even with these aids, the regime's task is clearly very exacting, and it is not always successful. Wang, however, had no mass following to carry his ideas to the countryside, no means of directly explaining his purposes to those whom he hoped would gain from them. His program depended on the support of the reigning emperor. In Shên Tsung he found a serious-minded man, willing to try a great experiment that might solve the pressing problems of state. But the emperor was under constant pressure from eminent conservative critics, supporters of the orthodoxy, in which he, like every other educated man, had been brought up. In spite of these adverse forces, it is remarkable that the New Laws were enforced at all, and for so long a period. They

The Confucian Ideal

Unlike China's two other great systems of thought—Buddhism and Taoism—which were essentially contemplative and largely mystical, Confucianism was profoundly activist and so secularly oriented that it can scarcely be described as a religion. Eschewing the goals of mystic revelation and personal redemption shared by Buddhism and Taoism, Confucianism focused on the structure and the needs of society at large. As Confucius saw it, maintaining the harmonious functioning of the social order was—or ought to be—the supreme objective of any man's life. It was each citizen's sacred responsibility to live according to the *li*, or rules of courtesy, which ensured social harmony. Strict observance of those rules made any man a gentleman.

Every man was also under a moral, legal, and social obligation to practice *jên*, or "human heartedness," in his dealings with others. *Jên*— or "virtue of the soul," as it was also known—was the central concept of Confucianism. The word was written with a combination of the symbols for "man" and "two," indicating its connection with human interaction. *Jên* guided men's daily decisions. With it one always knew the rules of courtesy, the appropriate response to any situation; almost invariably this was the most generous and deferential response a man could make. It was through virtue that the state's equilibrium was preserved.

Although *jên* was supposed to be the regulatory force in daily affairs, it was the Tao, which literally means the "way," that dictated the overall pattern of society and the life of the individual. The Way meant the way the universe was run—a concept that gave Taoism its name. To Confucius the Tao was based on the perfect interaction of *jên* and *li*. Confucius optimistically asserted that all men would, through education, come to see and follow the Tao. His assertion proved false, even though the rules of courtesy that he enjoined on his followers as a technique for approaching the Tao were rigidly observed for millenniums.

The comfortable appointments of this gentleman-scholar's chamber suggest the affluence and the respect acquired by the Confucian elite. A servant pours wine for the scholar, whose portrait is displayed in front of another painting.

As proof of filial devotion, a young couple (top right) sponsors entertainments for the husband's elderly parents.

The equality and mutual respect that Confucianism engendered is seen in this intimate view of a husband and wife.

FILIAL OBLIGATION

The keystone of Confucian education was the doctrine of filial piety, which meant not only devotion to one's parents but deference to all types of authority at all levels—imperial as well as familial. Filial piety was the first and most central obligation for the Chinese; all other duties were an extension of it. Indoctrinated from childhood to be unquestioning in his deference to his parents and unwavering in his affection for them, a young man could readily be taught to see his relationship to the emperor—the father of the people—in the same way. Even the emperor himself, the Son of Heaven, was bound by the system, owing obedience to Heaven, which was considered *his* father.

Filial piety became the overriding principle of social interaction, finding its expression in the rules of courtesy. *Li* originally meant "to sacrifice"; in time it came to mean simply "ritual." As indicated by the illustrations above and opposite (all taken from the same Sung dynasty scroll), the ritual connected with filial piety was elaborate. Kowtowing, which usually involved bowing forward from a kneeling position until one's forehead touched the ground, became an accepted method of showing reverence not only toward one's parents or sovereign but toward elder brothers, senior business associates, and aged in-laws too. Confucius had applied the customs and rules of court etiquette, such as the kowtow, to all human relationships, in an attempt to institutionalize "right" behavior. These conventionalized methods of demonstrating affection and loyalty were designed to provide people with a set of gestures that reaffirmed good intentions; but eventually they lost much of their original significance and developed into routine and rather unctuous symbols of polite behavior.

Although both men have reached middle age, the man at right kowtows, greeting his elder brother in a garden.

An emperor and his retainers, high above the common people, gaze on a group that includes three old widows.

Seated on a dais, an emperor receives his kowtowing censor, whose job was to offer criticism to the ruler.

Courts meted out severe punishments for marital infidelity; at lower right an adulteress is seen being whipped.

RULE OF THE WISE

The custodianship of the Confucian state fell to a group of men whose prime qualification for high office was their education (or, more specifically, their knowledge of classical Chinese texts). Unlike their counterparts in other countries, where the possession of office was hereditary, or was even considered a divine right, Chinese officials were generally awarded their places in the country's enormous bureaucracy on the basis of their performance on a national civil service examination. Confucius was convinced that education was the key to wisdom and that wisdom ensured harmony—on the civil as well as personal level. His disciples held office, believing, as he did, that "they who first apprehend principles should instruct those who are slower to do so." In times of disorder or foreign conquest, however, many Confucian officials withdrew to private life until the emperor was able to demonstrate by good government that he enjoyed Heaven's Mandate.

連騎桓教谷口迴下車欲
進步遙停觀書擁牖睁

The
preac
was
interp
stress
the c
adhe
his fo
live
"the
accor
fuciu
dyna
to rer
erecte
hono
him.
ing,
did d
imag
over t
the la
ples t
and g
the ta

Following Confucius' death, his disciple Yüan Hsien gave up his official post and retired to a solitary hut. In a painting done when China was under Mongol rule and many officials left public life, Yüan is shown at far left receiving visitors, former colleagues who still held office.

187

Confucius' urging that government offices be filled on a competitive basis led to the establishment of rigorous civil service examinations. Below, hopeful young scholars are shown awaiting the posting of their examination results.

The Chinese Way

The Chinese have been taking notes for thousands of years, jotting down the grand and petty details of life and, in the process, collecting a massive chronicle of their civilization. The earliest writings date from the Shang dynasty: dedications inscribed on bronze vessels, questions to the gods inscribed by priests on bones and shells. The people of the Chou dynasty kept written records of gifts sent to foreign emissaries, of the king's edicts, and of the names of slaves. Rulers were urged to study the records of their predecessors in order to profit from their mistakes and triumphs. Meanwhile, their own actions, good and bad alike, were recorded by court historians for the judgment of posterity. Literary men were employed by nobles, who were themselves often devoted to writing poetry and studying history. As the historian H. G. Creel writes: "It is doubtful that any other people living in the world of 1000 B.C. had such regard for . . . history as did the Chinese." In the third century B.C., when the Ch'in dynasty emperor Shih Huang Ti ordered all histories of past dynasties to be destroyed (in an attempt to silence those who censured his regime), he earned the lasting hatred of the Chinese people.

The literature that survived the holocaust was restored by Han dynasty scholars, among whom the Confucians were most influential. Their interpretations came to dominate the ancient texts, known ever since as the Confucian classics: the *I Ching* (*Book of Changes*), the *Shu Ching* (*Book of Documents*), the *Shih Ching* (*Book of Odes*), the *Li Chi* (*Book of Rites*), and the *Ch'un Ch'iu* (*Spring and Autumn Annals*). In succeeding times no man was considered great unless he knew the classics and could write beautiful prose or poetry. Such respect for literature encouraged an immense amount of writing—of philosophical and historical tracts, of letters, memorials, and diaries. Individually, these writings offer a personal view of everyday life in China; collectively, they form a great literary tradition.

With an ancient and unflagging reverence for the written word, Chinese scholars produced copious authorized histories of each dynasty as well as numerous personal reminiscences. In the picture opposite, which is entitled A Quiet Life in a Wooded Glen, *a young servant brings his scholar-master a bundle of scrolls, which may come from the man's personal library.*

CHRONICLES

The story of China's beginning is peopled with the demons and heroes of mythology, for it was myth and legend that brought the mysteries of creation within man's understanding. When Chinese history began to be recorded, the theory emerged that events proceeded in a cycle of change, of growth and decay. The historian's duty was to record the facts objectively so that the reader could discern the cycle of change in operation and understand the causes of growth and decay. Ideally, each historical incident served to illustrate some universal moral principle.

According to legend, two prime forces, yin and yang, gave order to the universe; a demigod, not nature, halted the deluge; and the birth of Confucius was attended, not by mere midwives, but by goddesses.

THE CREATION

by scholars of the Han dynasty

Before heaven and earth had taken form all was vague and amorphous. Therefore it was called the Great Beginning. The Great Beginning produced emptiness and emptiness produced the universe. The universe produced material-force which had limits. . . . It was very easy for the pure, fine material to come together but extremely difficult for the heavy, turbid material to solidify. Therefore heaven was completed first and earth assumed shape after. The combined essences of heaven and earth became the yin and yang, the concentrated essences of the yin and yang became the four seasons, and the scattered essence of the four seasons became the myriad creatures of the world. After a long time the hot force of the accumulated yang produced fire and the essence of the fire force became the sun; the cold force of the accumulated yin became water and the essence of the water force became the moon. The essence of the excess force of the sun and moon became the stars and planets. Heaven received the sun, moon, and stars while earth received water and soil.

YU STOPS THE FLOOD

from the Book of Documents

The inundating waters seemed to assail the heavens, and in their vast extent embraced the mountains and overtopped the hills, so that people were bewildered and overwhelmed. I mounted my four conveyances (carts, boats, sledges, and spiked shoes), and all along the hills hewed down the woods, at the same time, along with Yi, showing the multitudes how to get flesh to eat. I opened passages for the streams throughout the nine provinces, and conducted them to the sea. I deepened the channels and canals, and conducted them to the streams, at the same time, along with Chi, sowing grain, and showing the multitudes how to procure the food of toil in addition to flesh meat. I urged them further to exchange what they had for what they had not, and to dispose of their accumulated stores. In this way all the people got grain to eat, and all the States began to come under good rule.

THE BIRTH OF CONFUCIUS

by Wang Chia (*died* A.D. 390)

The night Confucius was born two azure dragons came down from the heavens and coiled about Cheng-tsai's room. When she had given birth to Confucius as her dream had said, two goddesses appeared in the sky bearing fragrant dew with which they bathed her. The Emperor of Heaven came down and performed the Music of Heavenly Tranquillity, filling the rooms of the Yen family. A voice spoke, saying: "Heaven is moved and gives birth to this sage child. Therefore I have descended and celebrate it with music," and the sound of the pipes and bells was unlike any heard in this world. In addition there were five old men ranged about the court of Cheng-tsai's house who were the spirits of the five stars. Before Confucius was born there was a unicorn which spat up a jade document before some people in Confucius' village of Ch'üeh-li and on it was written: "In the decline of the Chou the descendant of the spirit of water shall be an uncrowned king. Therefore the two dragons encircled the room and the five stars fell in the courtyard." . . . A physiognomist examined Confucius and said: "This child is descended from King T'ang of the . . . [Shang] dynasty. He shall become an uncrowned king under the power of the agent water and, as the scion of kings, attain the highest reverence."

CROWNING A KING

from the Book of Documents

The following excerpt describes a coronation ritual that was celebrated early in the Chou dynasty.

In the fourth month, when the moon began to wane, the king [of Chou] . . . died.

The Grand-protector then ordered Chung Hwan and Nan-keung Maou to instruct Leu Keih, the prince of Ts'e, with two shield-and-spearmen and a hundred guards, to meet the prince Ch'aou outside the south gate, and conduct him to one of the wing apartments near to that where the king lay, there to be as chief mourner.

On the day Ting-maou (two days after the king's death), he ordered a record to be made. . . . On Kwei-yew, the seventh day after, as chief of the west and premier, he ordered the proper officers to provide the wood for all the requirements of the funeral.

The salvage men set out . . . the five kinds of gems, and the precious things of display. There were the red knife, the great lessons, the large convex symbol of gem, and the rounded and pointed maces,—all in the side space on the west; the large gem, the gems from the wild tribes of the east, the heavenly sounding stone, and the river plan,—all in the side-chamber on the east; the dancing habits of Yin, the large tortoise-shell, and the large drum. . . .

The [new] king [Ch'aou], in a hempen cap and a variously adorned skirt, ascended by the guests' steps, followed by the nobles and princes of States, in hempen caps and black ant-colored skirts. Having entered, they all took their places. The Grand-protector, the Grand-historiographer, and the minister of Religion were all in hempen caps and red skirts. The Grand-protector bore the great mace. The minister of Religion bore the cup, and the mace-cover. These two ascended by the eastern steps. The Grand-historiographer bore the testamentary charge. He ascended by the guests' steps, and advanced to the king with the record of the charge, saying, "Our great lord, leaning on the gem-adorned bench, declared his last charge, and commanded you to continue the observance of the lessons, and to take the rule of the empire of Chow [Chou], complying with the great laws, and securing the harmony of the empire, so as to respond to and display the bright instructions of Wen and Wu.

The king twice bowed low, and then arose, and said, "I am utterly insignificant and but a child; how can I be able to govern the four quarters of the empire with such a reverent awe of the dread majesty of Heaven?" He then received the cup and the mace-cover. Thrice he advanced with a cup of spirits; thrice he sacrificed; and thrice he put the cup down. The minister of Religion said, "It is accepted."

The Grand-protector received the cup, descended the steps, and washed his hands. He then took another cup, and in his hand a half mace, in order to make the responsive sacrifice. Having given the cup to an attending officer, he did obeisance. The king returned the obeisance. The Grand-protector then took back the cup, and sacrificed with it. He then just tasted the sacrificial spirits, returned to his place, gave the cup to the attendant, and did obeisance. The king returned the obeisance.

The Grand-protector descended from the hall, when the various articles were removed, and the princes all went out from the temple gate and waited.

Chronicles

THE FAULTS OF CH'IN
by Chia I (199–168 B.C.)

*The price of unity under the Ch'in empire was op-
pression, as a Han dynasty statesman writes; before
long the people rebelled against the Ch'in despots.*

Duke Hsiao of Ch'in, relying upon the
strength of the Han-ku Pass and basing himself in the area of Yung-chou, with his ministers held fast to his land and eyed the house
of Chou, for he cherished a desire to roll up
the empire like a mat, to bind into one the
whole world, to bag all the land within the
four seas; he had it in his heart to swallow up
everything in the eight directions. At this time
he was aided by Lord Shang who set up laws
for him, encouraged agriculture and weaving,
built up the instruments of war, contracted
military alliances and attacked the other feudal
lords. Thus the men of Ch'in were able with
ease to acquire territory east of the upper
reaches of the Yellow River. . . . [Eventually]
Ch'in gained mastery over the empire and
divided up the land as it saw fit. The powerful
states begged to submit to its sovereignty. . . .

Then followed kings Hsiao-wen and
Chuang-hsiang whose reigns were short and
uneventful. After this the First Emperor arose
to carry on the glorious achievements of six
generations. Cracking his long whip, he drove
the universe before him, swallowing up the
eastern and western Chou and overthrowing
the feudal lords. . . .

Thereupon he discarded the ways of the
former kings and burned the writings of the
hundred schools in order to make the people
ignorant. He destroyed the major fortifica-
tions of the states, assassinated their powerful
leaders, collected all the arms of the empire,
and had them brought to his capital at Hsien-
yang where the spears and arrowheads were

melted down to make twelve human statues,
all in order to weaken the people of the empire.
. . . He garrisoned the strategic points with
skilled generals and expert bowmen and stationed trusted ministers and well-trained soldiers to guard the land with arms and question
all who passed back and forth. When he had
thus pacified the empire, the First Emperor believed in his heart that with the strength of his
capital within the pass and his walls of metal
extending a thousand miles, he had established a rule that would be enjoyed by his
descendants for ten thousand generations.

For a while after the death of the First Emperor the memory of his might continued to
awe the common people. Yet Ch'en She, born
in a humble hut with tiny windows and wattle
door, a day laborer in the fields and a garrison
conscript . . . stepped from the ranks of the
common soldiers, rose up from the paths of
the fields and led a band of some hundred
poor, weary troops in revolt against the Ch'in.
They cut down trees to make their weapons,
raised their flags on garden poles, and the
whole world in answer gathered about them
like a great cloud, brought them provisions
and followed after them as shadows follow a
form. In the end the leaders of the entire east
rose up together and destroyed the house of
Ch'in. . . . Ch'in, beginning with an insignificant amount of territory, reached the power of
a great state and for a hundred years made all
the other great lords pay homage to it. Yet
after it had become master of the whole empire and established itself within the fastness
of the pass, a single commoner opposed it and
its ancestral temples toppled, its ruler died by
the hands of men, and it became the laughing-
stock of the world. Why? Because it failed to
rule with humanity and righteousness and to
realize that the power to attack and the power
to retain what one has thereby won are not the
same.

The First Emperor

THE EMPEROR'S FUNERAL

by Ssŭ-ma Ch'ien (145-*c*.80 B.C.)

Ssŭ-ma Ch'ien, called the father of history, describes the burial of Shih Huang Ti, unifier of the Chinese empire and the self-styled "First Emperor."

In the ninth moon the First Emperor was buried in Mount Li, which in the early days of his reign he had caused to be tunneled and prepared with that in view. . . . when he had consolidated the empire, he employed his soldiery, to the number of 700,000, to bore down to the Three Springs (that is, until water was reached), and there a foundation of bronze was laid and the sarcophagus placed thereon. Rare objects and costly jewels were collected from the palaces and from the various officials, and were carried thither and stored in vast quantities. Artificers were ordered to construct mechanical crossbows, which, if any one were to enter, would immediately discharge their arrows. With the aid of quicksilver, [representations of] rivers were made—the Yang-tsze, the Hoang-ho, and the great ocean—the metal being poured from one into the other by machinery. On the roof were delineated the constellations of the sky, on the floor the geographical divisions of the earth. Candles were made from the fat of the man-fish [walrus], calculated to last for a very long time.

The Second Emperor said, "It is not fitting that the concubines of my late father who are without children should leave him now"; and accordingly he ordered them to accompany the dead monarch to the next world, those who thus perished being many in number.

When the interment was completed, some one suggested that the workmen who had made the machinery and concealed the treasure knew the great value of the latter, and that the secret would leak out. Therefore, so soon as the ceremony was over, and the path giving access to the sarcophagus had been blocked up at its innermost end, the outside gate at the entrance to this path was let fall, and the mausoleum was effectually closed, so that not one of the workmen escaped. Trees and grass were then planted around, that the spot might look like the rest of the mountain.

DEFEAT WITH HONOR

from the Commentary on the Spring and Autumn Annals

This battle against the Ch'u armies was fought in the year 638 B.C. by descendants of the Shang kings, who continued to rule in the state of Sung.

An army of Ch'u invaded Sung. . . . The Duke of Sung was going to fight, but his Minister of War remonstrated strongly with him, saying, "Heaven has long abandoned the House of Shang. Your Grace may wish to raise it again, but such an attempt would be unpardonable." The Duke, however, would not listen to him, and in the eleventh month . . . he fought with the army of Ch'u by the Hung River. The men of Sung were all drawn up in battle array before the forces of Ch'u had finished crossing the river, and the Minister of War said to the Duke: "They are many and we are few. Pray let us attack them before they have all crossed over." The Duke replied: "It may not be done." . . . Only after the enemy was fully prepared was the attack begun.

The army of Sung suffered a disastrous defeat. The Duke himself was injured in the thigh. . . . The people of the state all blamed the Duke, but he said: "The superior man does not inflict a second wound, or take the gray-haired prisoner. When the ancients had their armies in the field they would not attack an enemy when he was in a defile. Though I am but the unworthy remnant of a fallen dynasty, I would not sound my drums to attack an unprepared enemy."

197

Chronicles

THE AGONY OF EXILE

from a letter to Tzŭ-ch'ing by
Li Ling (*second-first centuries* B.C.)

*Li Ling, a Han general, was defeated by the Huns;
he surrendered instead of committing suicide. Disgraced, he lived out his life among the barbarians.*

Ever since the hour of my surrender until now,
destitute of all resource, I have sat alone with
the bitterness of my grief. All day long I see
none but barbarians around me. Skins and felt
protect me from wind and rain. With mutton
and whey I satisfy my hunger and slake my
thirst. Companions with whom to while time
away, I have none. The whole country is stiff
with black ice. I hear naught but the moaning
of the bitter autumn blast, beneath which all
vegetation has disappeared. I cannot sleep at
night. I turn and listen to the distant sound of
Tartar pipes, to the whinnying of Tartar steeds.
In the morning I sit up and listen still, while
tears course down my cheeks. O Tzŭ-ch'ing,
of what stuff am I, that I should do aught but
grieve? The day of thy departure left me dis-
consolate indeed. I thought of my aged
mother butchered upon the threshold of the
grave. I thought of my innocent wife and
child condemned to the same cruel fate. De-
serving as I might have been of Imperial censure, I am now an object of pity to all. Thy
return was to honor and renown, while I remained behind with infamy and disgrace. Such
is the divergence of man's destiny.

Born within the domain of refinement and
justice, I passed into an environment of vulgar
ignorance. I left behind me obligations to sovereign and family for life amid barbarian
hordes; and now barbarian children will carry
on the line of my forefathers. And yet my
merit was great, my guilt of small account. I
had no fair hearing; and when I pause to think
of these things, I ask to what end I have lived?
With a thrust I could have cleared myself of all
blame: my severed throat would have borne
witness to my resolution; and between me and
my country all would have been over for aye.
But to kill myself would have been of no
avail: I should only have added to my shame.
I therefore steeled myself to obloquy and to
life. There were not wanting those who mis-
took my attitude for compliance, and urged
me to a nobler course; ignorant that the joys
of a foreign land are sources only of a keener
grief.

THE HISTORIAN'S TRUTH

from the Diaries of Action and Repose

The Diaries, *begun during the Han dynasty, were
notes on the emperor's activities. They remained
free of imperial censorship until the Sung dynasty;
then their objectivity and historical value waned.*

The year 642, Summer, fourth month. The
Emperor T'ai-tsung spoke to the Imperial
Censor Ch'u Sui-liang, saying: "Since you, Sir,
are in charge of the Diaries of Action and Repose, may I see what you have written?" Sui-
liang replied: "The historiographers record
the words and deeds of the ruler of men,
noting down all that is good and bad, in
hopes that the ruler will not dare to do evil.
But it is unheard of that the ruler himself
should see what is written." The emperor said:
"If I do something that is not good, do you
then also record it?" Sui-liang replied: "My
office is to wield the brush. How could I dare
not record it?" The Gentleman of the Yellow
Gate, Liu Chi, added: "Even if Sui-liang failed
to record it, everyone else in the empire
would"; to which the emperor replied: "True."

ON A BONE OF BUDDHA

by Han Yü (A.D. 768–824)

This chauvinistic protest to the emperor against displaying a supposed bone of Buddha in the imperial palace nearly cost the life of its author, a Confucian apologist, who was, instead, sent into exile.

The Buddha was born a barbarian; he was unacquainted with the language of the Middle Kingdom, and his dress was of a different cut. His tongue did not speak nor was his body clothed in the manner prescribed by the kings of old; he knew nothing of the duty of minister to prince or the relationship of son to father. Were he still alive today, were he to come to court at the bidding of his country, your majesty would give him no greater reception than an interview in the Strangers' Hall, a ceremonial banquet, and the gift of a suit of clothes, after which you would have him sent under guard to the frontier to prevent him from misleading your people. There is then all the less reason now that he has been dead so long for allowing this decayed and rotten bone, this filthy and disgusting relic to enter the Forbidden Palace.

THE FAMINE

by Ma Mao-ts'ai (*c.*1629)

Throughout its history China has been plagued by famine. The famine described here, in an eyewitness account, took place at the end of the Ming dynasty.

Yenan, the prefecture from which your humble servant comes, has not had any rain for more than a year. Trees and grass are all dried up. During the eighth and ninth months of last year people went to the mountains to collect raspberries which were called grain but actually were no better than chaff. They tasted bitter and could only postpone death for the time being. By the tenth month all the raspberries were gone, and people peeled off tree bark as food. Among tree bark the best was that of the elm. This was so precious that in order to conserve it, people mixed it with the bark of other trees to feed themselves. Somehow they were able to prolong their lives. Towards the end of the year the supply of tree bark was exhausted. . . . there was a dumping ground to the west of Anse, to which two or three infants were abandoned by their parents each morning. Some of these infants cried aloud; others merely whimpered because they had lost all strength to cry. Some yelled for their parents; others, being so hungry as they were, ate their own excrements.

What seemed strange at the beginning was the sudden disappearance of children or single persons once they wandered outside of the city gates. Later it was discovered that some people in the suburb had been eating human flesh and using human bones as fuel for cooking. By then people knew that those who had disappeared were actually killed and eaten. Meanwhile the cannibals themselves became sick as a result of eating other people. Their eyes and faces became red and swollen in a few days; their body temperature kept on rising until they died.

Wherever a person went, he saw dead bodies. Their odor was so odious that it was simply unbearable. Outside of the city wall people dug several pits, and the pits were so large that each of them could contain several hundred dead bodies. When your humble servant passed through the city, three of these pits had been filled up. Two or three miles further away from the city the number of dead bodies that was not buried was even more numerous. If the number of people who perished in a small city like Anse is so large, just imagine the number of those who died in a large city! One only needs to visit one place to know the situation in all other places.

CLEVELAND MUSEUM OF ART,
JOHN L. SEVERANCE FUND

A famine victim   199

Chronicles

COEXISTENCE

by Wang Fu-chih (1619–1692)

Wang, a philosopher born during the Ming dynasty, describes the nomadic Manchu tribesmen who roamed the vast lands that lay northeast of China.

The strength of the barbarians lies in the paucity of their laws and institutions. As long as their shelter, food, and clothing remain crude and barbaric, as long as they continue to foster a violent and savage temper in their people and do not alter their customs, they may enjoy great advantage. And at the same time, because of this China may escape harm. . . . While the barbarians are content to roam about in pursuit of water and pasture, practicing archery and hunting, preserving no distinctions between ruler and subject, possessing only rudimentary marriage and governmental systems . . . China can never . . . rule them. And as long as the barbarians do not realize that cities can be fortified and maintained, that markets bring profit, that fields can be cultivated and taxes exacted, as long as they do not know the glory of elaborate marriage and official systems, then they will continue to look upon China as a . . . bed of thorns.

FOR A MODERN CHINA

by Hsüeh Fu-ch'êng (1838–1894)

Change became inevitable as the wall of isolation between China and the West crumbled. In the nineteenth century, modernists spoke out for reforms.

Western nations rely on intelligence and energy to compete with one another. To come abreast of them, China should plan to promote commerce and open mines; unless we change, the Westerners will be rich and we poor. We should excel in technology and the manufacture of machinery; unless we change, they will be skillful and we clumsy. Steam-ships, trains, and the telegraph should be adopted; unless we change, the Westerners will be quick and we slow. The advantages and disadvantages of treaties, the competence and incompetence of envoys, and the improvement of military organization and strategy should be discussed. Unless we change, the Westerners will co-operate with each other and we shall stand isolated; they will be strong and we shall be weak.

THE BOXERS' WARNING

Anonymous (1900)

The reaction to reform and to cultural incursions by the West culminated in the Boxer Rebellion, during which the following notice was circulated.

Attention: all people in markets and villages of all provinces in China—now, owing to the fact that Catholics and Protestants have vilified our gods and sages, have deceived our emperors and ministers above, and oppressed the Chinese people below, both our gods and our people are angry at them, yet we have to keep silent. This forces us to practice the I-ho magic boxing so as to protect our country, expel the foreign bandits and kill Christian converts, in order to save our people from miserable suffering. After this notice is issued to instruct you villagers, no matter which village you are living in, if there are Christian converts, you ought to get rid of them quickly. The churches which belong to them should be unreservedly burned down. Everyone who intends to spare someone, or to disobey our order by concealing Christian converts, will be punished according to the regulation when we come to his place, and he will be burned to death to prevent his impeding our program. We especially do not want to punish anyone by death without warning him first. We cannot bear to see you suffer innocently. Don't disobey this special notice!

Revolutionaries

REVOLUTIONARY FERVOR

from the Peking Review, May 10, 1968

This story, taken from a Communist periodical, describes how the inspiration of Mao Tse-tung helped defeat a counterrevolutionary attempt at sabotage.

Comrade Liu Hsueh-pao, his heart filled with happiness, saw off the forestry workers who were to join the county's celebration meeting. Into his mind, however, came Chairman Mao's teachings that . . . "just because we have won victory, we must never relax our vigilance against the frenzied plots for revenge by the imperialists and their running dogs." Remaining keenly on the alert, Liu Hsueh-pao patrolled the compound of the station's main building.

As evening fell, the moon rose. A stealthy shadow stole out of the front gate. Liu Hsueh-pao recognized the figure as that of a counter-revolutionary working at the forestry station. . . .

After going out the gate, the counter-revolutionary went along the highway towards the upper reaches of the Tatung River. In that direction lay a vast expanse of forests planted by the workers and a bridge only recently built . . . far-ahead was the new bridge; beyond that, the forest. Lui Hsueh-pao thought of two possibilities: either the man was out to destroy the bridge, or he meant to set fire to the woods. . . .

Alone, Liu Hsueh-pao went ahead. Soon the bridge appeared before him, flanked by steep mountain slopes. Suddenly the counter-revolutionary reappeared. . . . Liu Hsueh-pao rushed forward and tried to grab the counter-revolutionary, but this Kuo-mintang-trained special agent seized him by the legs, and . . . knocked him to the ground.

At this moment Chairman Mao's inspiring words "This army has an indomitable spirit and is determined to vanquish all enemies and never to yield" gave Liu Hsueh-pao immense strength. With a great effort, he managed to get on top of the counter-revolutionary, and, thrusting his right knee into the man's chest, crushed four of his ribs.

Raising his head . . . Liu Hsueh-pao suddenly saw blue sparks spluttering from one of the bridge's arches some eighty meters away. In a flash he realized that the counter-revolutionary must have planted some explosives there, and the fuse was already lit!

His mind blazing with hatred for the enemy, Liu Hsueh-pao. . . . picked up a piece of rock and bashed in the skull of this sinister enemy. . . .

Chairman Mao's teaching rang in his mind: "Be resolute, fear no sacrifice and surmount every difficulty to win victory." . . . His blood coursed through his veins. He decided: "As long as I live, the bridge lives. I will give my life to keep it safe!"

He rushed up to the arch, quickly grabbed the packet of explosives, and dashed away with it under his left arm.

As he ran, he tried to pull out the burning fuse, but failed. He tried to smother it with his fingers, failing again. He had only one thought: to get as far away as possible from the bridge. As he ran, he kept shouting: "Long live Chairman Mao!" "A long, long life to Chairman Mao!" . . . Just when the explosive was about to ignite, Liu Hsueh-pao threw it away with a great effort. . . . The night air of the valley resounded with the explosion and a red glow lit up the earth. . . .

The force of the explosion threw Liu Hsueh-pao to the ground. . . . When he came to, he was surrounded by comrades who had come to his aid. "Don't bother about me . . ." he whispered. "See if the enemy put explosives elsewhere on the bridge. . . ." When he was told that the bridge was intact, he smiled in satisfaction.

THE RULE OF VIRTUE

*According to the tradition begun by Confucian thinkers, good government de-
pended on the employment of virtuous officials rather than on laws or institutions.
The ultimate responsibility for the people's moral conduct belonged, in theory,
to the emperor, whose duty it was to see that economic and social conditions made
it possible for men of all stations to live in harmony, without resorting to crime.*

THE TIGER

from the Book of Rites

When Confucius was crossing the T'ai
mountain, he overheard a woman weeping
and wailing beside a grave. He thereupon sent
one of his disciples to ask what was the matter; and the latter addressed the woman, saying, "Some great sorrow must have come
upon you that you give way to grief like this?"
"Indeed it is so," replied she. "My father-in-
law was killed here by a tiger; after that, my
husband; and now my son has perished by the
same death." "But why, then," inquired Confucius, "do you not go away?" "The government is not harsh," answered the woman.
"There!" cried the Master, turning to his
disciples: "remember that. Bad government is
worse than a tiger."

HEAVEN'S CHOICE

by Pan Piao (A.D. 3–54)

. . . in order for a man to enjoy the blessing of
rulership, he must possess not only the virtue
of shining sageliness and apparent excellence,
but he must be heir to a patrimony of abun-
dant merit and favor long accumulated. Only
then can he, by his pure sincerity, communi-
cate with the divine intelligence and extend
his grace to all living men. Then will he receive good fortune from the spirits and gods,
and all people will come to his rule. There has
never been a case of a man who, the successive
generations having passed without showing
signs of his destiny or recording the merit and
virtue of his family, has been able to rise to
this position of eminence. The mass of people
see that Kao-tsu [first ruler of the Han dy-
nasty] arose from among the common men
and they do not comprehend the reasons for
his rise. They believe that, happening upon a
time of violence and disorder, he was able to

wield his sword, as the wandering political
theorists compare the conquest of the empire
to a deer chase in which success goes to the
luckiest and swiftest. They do not understand
that this sacred vessel, the rule of the empire,
is transmitted according to destiny and cannot
be won either by craft or force. Alas, this is
why there are so many rebellious ministers and
evil sons in the world today. To be so mistaken, one would not only have to be blind to
the way of Heaven, but totally unobservant of
human affairs as well!

PRINCIPLES OF KINGSHIP

by Wu Ching (*died* A.D. 742)

One day in [A.D. 627] . . . T'ai-tsung remarked
to his ministers in attendance as follows: "The
first principle in kingship is to preserve the
people. A king who exploits the people for his
personal gains is like a man who cuts his own
thighs to feed himself. He quenches his hunger for the time being but will die eventually.
To secure peace in the world, the king must
rectify and cultivate himself as an ethical
being. As there is no such thing as a crooked
shadow following a straight object, it is incon-
ceivable that the people can be disloyal when
their rulers are virtuous. What harms the body
is not the objects outside of oneself, however
tempting they are; rather, it is the unlimited
desire for them that brings us disasters. People
love good food and like to be amused with
music and sex. The stronger the desire for
them is, the more harmful the result will be.
For a king such a desire will not only interfere
with his duty of running the government but
also cause disturbances among his subjects.
One irrational remark from the king will make
thousands lose confidence in him. Complaints
will arise; so will revolts. Every time I think
of this, I dare not indulge in idleness."

TOO MUCH GOVERNMENT

attributed to Lao Tzŭ (*born* 604 B.C. ?)

As restrictions and prohibitions are multiplied
. . . the people grow poorer and poorer. When
the people are subjected to overmuch government, the land is thrown into confusion.

FEUDALISM

by Chang Tsai (1020–1066)

To achieve good government in the empire
. . . . the land of the empire should be laid out
in squares and apportioned, with each man receiving one square. This is the basis of the
people's subsistence. In recent times no provision has been made for the people's means of
subsistence, but only for the commandeering
of their labor. Contrary to expectation, the
exalted position of the Son of Heaven has
been used for the monopolizing of everything
productive of profit. With the government
thinking only of the government, and the
people thinking only of themselves, they have
not taken each other into consideration. . . .

The reason a feudal system must be established is that the administration of the empire
must be simplified through delegation of
power before things can be well managed. If
administration is not simplified, then it is impossible to govern well.

THE GREAT SOCIETY

from the Book of Rites

When the Great Way permeates the world, the
world belongs to all of its members. The government is in the hands of the virtuous and the
able, and the people maintain friendly and
faithful relationships among themselves. A
man loves not only his own parents and children but others' as well. The aged are cared
for, the able-bodied have work, and the young

are properly raised. Widows, widowers, or-
phans, the incurably ill, and the crippled—all
of them are adequately supported. All men
have wives, and all women have husbands.
Viewing goods as if they were worthless, people do not hoard them for profit. Viewing
their own ability as if it did not belong to
them, they use it to the benefit of others. Plot-
ting and scheming do not arise, and there are
no such things as thievery and robbery. The
front door need not be closed, day or night.
This is the Great Society.

FLEXIBILITY

by Wang Fu-chih (1619–1692)

The principal function of government is to
make use of worthy men and promote moral
instruction, and in dealing with the people to
bestow on them the greatest humanity and
love. . . . The ancient institutions were designed to govern the ancient world, and cannot be applied to the present day. Therefore
the wise man does not try to set up detailed
systems. One uses what is right for today to
govern the world of today, but this does not
mean that it will be right for a later day. . . .

Times change, conditions are different.
How then can a government go along with
these changes and keep its people from growing idle? There are crises of the moment to be
met in each age, but the expedients used to
meet them are not necessarily worthy of con-
stituting a whole theory of government. . . .
Every age has its different points of laxity and
strictness; every affair has its contingent circumstances. It is better therefore to have no
inflexible rules, lest one use the letter of the
law to do violence to its spirit. Everyone
makes mistakes at times, so that one should
not try to force the world to follow his own
arbitrary views.

THE RULE OF LAW

The scholarly ideal of a state ruled by virtue was unrealistic to Chinese pragmatists. Laws are necessary, they argued, if society is to endure. Criminal codes were therefore instituted as a means of ordering society—despite protests of some officials. The laws were based on such traditional virtues as moderation and filial piety. They were strictly enforced, however, and the penalties were severe.

THE HIGHEST LOYALTY

by Emperor Hsüan Ti (*reigned* 73–48 B.C.)

The affection between father and son and between husband and wife is natural with man. It is not altogether unexpected that after one of the parties has committed a crime, the other tries to conceal it at the risk of his own life. It merely shows how deep this affection is. How can a law be considered wise when it operates in opposition to this natural affection?

Let it be known that from now on a son does not commit a crime if he attempts to conceal the crime of either of his parents; a wife does not commit a crime if she attempts to conceal the crime of her husband; and a grandson does not commit a crime if he attempts to conceal the crime of any of his grandparents. On the other hand, parents are not allowed to conceal the crime committed by their children; a husband is not allowed to conceal a crime committed by his wife; and grandparents are not allowed to conceal a crime committed by their grandchildren. The penalty is death in each case, and the proceedings should be reported to the Governor of Punishments.

CLASSIFYING HOUSEHOLDS

by Liu Hsü (A.D. 897–946)

All households in the nation are to be divided into nine categories in accordance with the amount of properties they possess. Under the supervision of its magistrate, the grading of households in each district should be done once every three years. Such grading should be then examined, checked, and made official by the provincial authorities.

One hundred households form a hamlet, and five hamlets form a township. A neighborhood consists of four households, and a *pao* is composed of five households. Those who live in cities are organized into wards, and those in the countryside are grouped into villages. All people in each of the organizational units—village, ward, neighborhood, or hamlet—are urged to emulate one another in good behavior.

The four classes of people—scholars, farmers, artisans, and merchants—earn their livelihood by engaging in their respective professions; they should not compete with people socially below them for the purpose of making profits. Artisans, merchants, and people of miscellaneous occupation are not allowed to associate themselves with scholars.

After a person is born, he or she is classified as an infant. When he reaches the age of four, he is called a child. A child becomes a junior adult when he is sixteen. He attains full adulthood when he reaches the age of twenty-one. Beginning in his sixtieth year, he is classified as a senior citizen.

SLAVERY

by Ma Tuan-lin (*thirteenth century* A.D.)

In accordance with the suggestion made by responsible officials, the limitation of slave ownership should be as follows: For kings and dukes the maximum number of male and female slaves each of them is allowed to own is 200; for counts and imperial princesses, 100; and for counts who reside in the capital and its environs and for all officials and commoners, 30. Slaves over the age of sixty or below that of ten are not included in this limitation.

AGAINST A PENAL CODE

from the Commentary on the Spring and Autumn Annals

The former kings reached their decisions in criminal cases after careful deliberation on the particular circumstances of the case in hand;

they did not set up general laws because they feared that this might give rise to a contentious spirit among the people. But as crimes could not be prevented, they set before them the barrier of righteousness, sought to bring them to rectitude, caused them to act in conformity with right, maintained them with good faith, and cherished them with benevolence. They also instituted places of salary and position to encourage them to conform, and strictly laid down punishments to awe them from excesses. Fearing that these were insufficient, they taught them loyalty, urged them by their conduct, instructed them in what was most important, employed them in a spirit of harmony, came before them in a spirit of seriousness, met exigencies with vigor, and gave their decisions with firmness. And in addition to this they sought to have sage and wise persons in the highest positions, intelligent discriminating persons in all offices, leaders of loyalty and sincerity, and teachers of gentle kindness. In this way the people were successfully dealt with, and disasters and disorders did not arise.

But when the people know what the exact laws are, then they do not stand in awe of their superiors. And they come to have a contentious spirit, and make their appeal to verbal technicalities, hoping thus to be successful in their argument. They can no longer be managed.

A MORAL CODE

by Sung Lien (1310–1381)

If a family deliberately creates rumors that throw doubts on a maiden's character and thus creates a situation in which she will not receive a proposal for marriage from any family except the one which has created these rumors but is fully aware of her innocence, the head of this family will receive fifty-seven blows by a wooden stick, and the girl in question, if she

has already been married into this family, is free to leave.

An official who flirts with a man's wife and thus causes the man to desert his wife will receive sixty-seven blows by a wooden stick. He will be dismissed from his present post and will be demoted by two ranks when and if he is reinstated. . . .

A man is held responsible if his son has illicit sexual relations with a woman. The responsibility remains the same even if he has taken the initiative to report these relations to the government. He is not held responsible, however, if he has warned his son against, and has done his best to prevent, such relations before they take place.

WEDDINGS AND FUNERALS

by Wang Shou-jen (1472–1528)

Men and women should be married when they reach the marriageable age. Wedding is often delayed when the family of the prospective bride complains of the insufficient amount of betrothal money that has been paid, or when the family of the prospective groom regards the amount of dowry as inadequate. In each case . . . the parties concerned [should be informed] that the amount of betrothal money or dowry should vary with the ability to pay and that weddings should not be delayed on financial grounds.

After the death of one's parents, funeral services should be conducted in such a way as to demonstrate adequately the sense of loss which he feels. The amount of expenses should not exceed his ability to pay. What good does it do to the deceased that their survivors risk financial bankruptcy in order to perform the most elaborate Buddhist rituals or to give the most ostentatious banquets? . . .

Artisans at work

205

SCHOOLS OF THOUGHT

The Chinese philosophers have always been concerned more with the practical application of wisdom to problems of human relations than with great metaphysical questions of immortality and the existence of a deity. Not only scholars have felt the influence of philosophy; the doctrines of the sages—particularly Confucianism—have shaped the very character and culture of the Chinese people.

CONFUCIUS

from the Analects

The thoughts and deeds of K'ung Fu-tzǔ (whose name is Latinized as Confucius) were compiled in the Analects *by the Master's disciples after his death.*

The Master said, At fifteen I set my heart upon learning. At thirty, I had planted my feet firm upon the ground. At forty, I no longer suffered from perplexities. At fifty, I knew what were the biddings of Heaven. At sixty, I heard them with docile ear. At seventy, I could follow the dictates of my own heart; for what I desired no longer overstepped the boundaries of right.

The Master said [to a disciple] . . . shall I teach you what knowledge is? When you know a thing, to recognize that you know it, and when you do not know a thing, to recognize that you do not know it. That is knowledge.

The Master said, In serving his father and mother a man may gently remonstrate with them. But if he sees that he has failed to change their opinion, he should resume an attitude of deference and not thwart them; may feel discouraged, but not resentful.

The Master said, Only one who bursts with eagerness do I instruct; only one who bubbles with excitement, do I enlighten. . . .

The Master said, I have never yet seen anyone whose desire to build up his moral power was as strong as sexual desire.

The Master said, Do I regard myself as a possessor of wisdom? Far from it. But if even a simple peasant comes in all sincerity and asks me a question, I am ready to thrash the matter out, with all its pros and cons, to the very end.

Master K'ung said, Highest are those who are born wise. Next are those who become wise by learning. After them come those who have to toil painfully in order to acquire learning. Finally, to the lowest class of the common people belong those who toil painfully without ever managing to learn.

Tzu-kung asked saying, Is there any single saying that one can act upon all day and every day? The Master said, Perhaps the saying about consideration: "Never do to others what you would not like them to do to you."

Tzu-chang asked Master K'ung about Goodness. Master K'ung said, He who could put the Five into practice everywhere under Heaven would be Good. Tzu-chang begged to hear what these were. The Master said, Courtesy, breadth, good faith, diligence and clemency. "He who is courteous is not scorned, he who is broad wins the multitude, he who is of good faith is trusted by the people, he who is diligent succeeds in all he undertakes, he who is clement can get service from the people."

The Master said, It is only the very wisest and the very stupidest who cannot change.

THE WAY

attributed to Lao Tzǔ (*born* 604 B.C. ?)

The followers of Taoism taught that man could find immortality by discovering, through mystical intuition, the essence of all nature—the Tao, or Way.

The Tao which can be expressed in words is not the eternal Tao; the name which can be uttered is not its eternal name. Without a name, it is the Beginning of Heaven and

Earth; with a name, it is the Mother of all things. Only one who is ever free from desire can apprehend its spiritual essence; he who is ever a slave to desire can see no more than its outer fringe. . . .

Tao eludes the sense of sight, and is therefore called colorless. It eludes the sense of hearing, and is therefore called soundless. It eludes the sense of touch, and is therefore called incorporeal. . . . We may call it the form of the formless, the image of the imageless, the fleeting and the indeterminable.

It is the Way of Heaven to take from those who have too much, and give to those who have too little. But the way of man is not so. He takes away from those who have too little, to add to his own superabundance. What man is there that can take of his own superabundance and give it to mankind? Only he who possesses Tao.

Keep behind, and you shall be put in front; keep out, and you shall be kept in.

Goodness strives not, and therefore it is not rebuked.

He that humbles himself shall be preserved entire. He that bends shall be made straight. He that is empty shall be filled. He that is worn out shall be renewed. He who has little shall succeed. He who has much shall go astray.

When the superior scholar hears of Tao, he diligently practices it. When the average scholar hears of Tao, he sometimes retains it, sometimes loses it. When the inferior scholar hears of Tao, he loudly laughs at it. Were it not thus ridiculed, it would not be worthy of the name Tao.

If Tao prevails on earth, horses will be used for purposes of agriculture. If Tao does not prevail, war-horses will be bred on the common.

The Great Way is very smooth, but the people love the by-paths.

MAN'S GOODNESS

attributed to Mencius (372–289 B.C.)

Mencius (Mêng Tzŭ), who made popular the doctrines of Confucius, preached a return to the virtues practiced in the time of the mythical Sage kings.

The trees on the Bull Mountain were once beautiful. But being too near the capital of a great state, they were hewn down. . . . Even so, nourished by the rain and dew and with the force of growth operating day and night, the stumps sent forth fresh sprouts. But soon cattle and sheep came to browse on them, and in the end the mountain became bare again. Seeing it thus, people now imagine that it was never wooded. But is this the nature of the mountain?

So it is with human nature. How can it be said that man is devoid of human-heartedness and righteousness? He has only lost his good feelings in the same way that the trees have been felled. Assailed day after day, can the heart retain its goodness? Even so, nourished by the calm air of dawn and with the force of life operating day and night, man develops in his heart desires and aversions that are proper to humanity. But soon these good feelings are fettered and destroyed by the inroads of the day's activity. Thus, fettered again and again, they wither until the nourishing influence of night is no longer able to keep them alive. So in the end man reverts to a state not much different from that of birds and beasts, and seeing him thus, people imagine that man never had good feelings. But is such the nature of man?

Schools of Thought

THE SMALL MAN

from an appendix of the Book of Changes

The I Ching, *or* Book of Changes, *dating perhaps from Shang or Chou times, contained moral instruction, but was used mostly to foretell the future.*

The Master said:—"The small man is not ashamed of what is not benevolent, nor does he fear to do what is not righteous. Without the prospect of gain he does not stimulate himself to what is good, nor does he correct himself without being moved. Self-correction, however, in what is small will make him careful in what would be of greater consequence; —and this is the happiness of the small man. . . .

"If acts of goodness be not accumulated, they are not sufficient to give its finish to one's name; if acts of evil be not accumulated, they are not sufficient to destroy one's life. The small man thinks that small acts of goodness are of no benefit, and does not do them; and that small deeds of evil do not harm, and does not abstain from them. Hence his wickedness becomes great till it cannot be covered, and his guilt becomes great till it cannot be pardoned. . . ."

A GOLDEN RULE

by Mo Tzŭ (*c*.470–*c*.391 B.C.)

Mohism, one of the hundred schools of philosophy that flourished around the time of Confucius, taught a doctrine of universal love and utilitarianism.

Mo Tzu said: It is the business of the benevolent man to try to promote what is beneficial to the world and to eliminate what is harmful. Now at the present time, what brings the greatest harm to the world? Great states attacking small ones, great families overthrowing small ones, the strong oppressing the weak, the many harrying the few, the cunning deceiving the stupid, the eminent lording it over the humble—these are harmful to the world. . . . If men were to regard the cities of others as they regard their own, then who would raise up his city to attack the city of another? It would be like attacking his own. If men were to regard the families of others as they regard their own, then who would raise up his family to overthrow that of another? It would be like overthrowing his own. Now when states and cities do not attack and make war on each other and families and individuals do not overthrow or injure one another, is this a harm or a benefit to the world? Surely it is a benefit.

When we inquire into the cause of such benefits, what do we find has produced them? Do they come about from hating others and trying to injure them? Surely not! They come from loving others and trying to benefit them.

SEIZE THE DAY

by Yang Chu (*c*.440–*c*.360 B.C.)

Completely opposed to Mo Tzŭ's altruism is Yang Chu's hedonism, which sprang from a fatalistic interpretation of man's position in the universe.

There is not one hour free from some anxiety. What then is the purpose of life? What then is the happiness of life? It is in rich food and fine clothing and in music and beauty.

Some die at the age of ten; some, at one hundred. The wise and benevolent die as well as the cruel and imbecile. Therefore, let us hasten to enjoy life and pay no attention to death.

The teachings of Buddhism, summarized here by the historian Wei Shou, are said to have reached China from India in the first century A.D. Distinctively

Confucius receiving a visitor

Chinese interpretations of Buddhism are based on the Lotus of the Wonderful Law, *which preaches salvation for all. Chinese Buddhism reached its most profound expression in the Ch'an, or Zen, school, of which the earliest proponent is Lu Hui-nêng.*

TOWARD ENLIGHTENMENT

by Wei Shou (A.D. 506–572)

The essential teaching of Buddhism can be summarized in one statement: i.e., the sufferings inherent in the endless cycle of births and rebirths are caused by man's attachment to this world. There are three worlds altogether, the past, the present, and the future. The important thing is to understand that despite his transmission from one world to another a person's spiritual self cannot be obliterated. Those who do good things will be rewarded; those who do bad things will be punished. A great deed is the gradual accumulation of many small deeds: a coarse, rustic nature can be refined through constant effort. Whatever forms life may take, the ultimate goal of all lives is the attainment of enlightenment, an enlightenment which can be achieved only through hard, diligent work. By then there will be no more births and rebirths, and the Way of Buddha will be finally attained.

THE LOTUS

attributed to the Buddha (*c.*563–*c.*483 B.C.)

Any among the living beings,
Who have come into contact with former
                                   Buddhas,
Have learned the Law and practiced charity,
Or have undergone discipline and endured
                       forbearance and humiliation,
Or have made serious efforts at concentration
                           and understanding, etc.,

And cultivated various kinds of blessing and
                                    wisdom—
All of these people,
Have reached the level of Buddhahood. . . .

Those people who, for the sake of the Buddha,
Installed images,
Or have had them carved,
Have reached the level of Buddhahood. . . .

Those who with a happy frame of mind
Have sung the glory of the Buddha,
Even with a very small sound, ...

Or have worshiped,
Or have merely folded their hands, ...

Or have uttered one "Namo" [Praise be . . .],
All have reached the level of Buddhahood.

PURIFICATION

by Lu Hui-nêng (A.D. 637–712)

Purification of mind comes first through freedom from taint of jealousy, anger, avarice, or hatred. . . . this will bring one to the state of an imperturbable mind. . . . Being free from impediments, one then becomes full of wisdom . . . , which enables one to be respectful toward superiors . . . and sympathetic with the poor. . . . After that, one feels a sense of *liberation.* . . .

Make it a rule to be straightforward on all occasions. . . . Don't let your mind be crooked and practice straightforwardness with your lips only. . . . When . . . our outward appearance and our inner feelings harmonize with each other, it is a case of the equilibrium of tranquillity and wisdom. . . . Those under delusion . . . don't realize that straightforwardness is the holy place, the Pure Land.

209

CEREMONY

Through observance of ritual, man's desires might be held within bounds, and society kept from dissolving into chaos. In Confucian tradition the ancient rites were the means by which an attempt could be made to re-create the peace, wisdom, and virtue that obtained in early China. It was believed that the neglect and corruption of those rites by later rulers caused spiritual and social disorder.

RITES AND MUSIC

from the Book of Rites

Man is born in stillness, for stillness is his nature given by Heaven. In response to external things he becomes active, activity being the expression of the desires of his nature. . . . If these likes and dislikes are not controlled within him and his understanding is beguiled by the external world, then he cannot return to his true self. . . . Then his heart will turn to revolt and deception, and his actions will become dissolute and rebellious. . . . Therefore the former kings set up rites and music that men might be controlled by them. . . . Music comes from within, rites from without. Music coming from within is characterized by stillness, while rites which are from without are characterized by order. Great music must be easy, great rites simple. Music induces an end to anger, rites an end to strife. . . . Music is the harmony of Heaven and earth, rites are their order. Through harmony all things are transformed; through order all are distinguished. Music arises from Heaven; rites are patterned after earth. . . . Therefore the sage creates music in response to Heaven, and sets up rites to match earth. When music and rites are fully realized, Heaven and earth function in perfect order.

THE PURPOSE OF RITUAL

from the Book of Rites

One day Yu-tzǔ and Tzǔ-yu saw a child weeping for the loss of its parents. Thereupon the former observed, "I never could understand why mourners should necessarily jump about to show their grief, and would long ago have got rid of the custom. Now here you have an honest expression of feeling, and that is all there should ever be."

"My friend," replied Tzǔ-yu, "the mourn-ing ceremonial, with all its material accompaniments, is at once a check upon undue emotion and a guarantee against any lack of proper respect. Simply to give vent to the feelings is the way of barbarians. That is not our way.

"Consider. A man who is pleased will show it in his face. He will sing. He will get excited. He will dance. So, too, a man who is vexed will look sad. He will sigh. He will beat his breast. He will jump about. The due regulation of these emotions is the function of a set ceremonial.

"Further. A man dies and becomes an object of loathing. A dead body is shunned. Therefore, a shroud is prepared, and other paraphernalia of burial, in order that the survivors may cease to loathe. At death there is a sacrifice of wine and meat; when the funeral cortège is about to start, there is another; and after burial there is yet another. Yet no one ever saw the spirit of the departed come to taste of the food.

"These have been our customs from remote antiquity. They have not been discarded, because, in consequence, men no more shun the dead. What you may censure in those who perform the ceremonial is no blemish in the ceremonial itself."

THE RIVER GOD'S WEDDING

by Ch'u Shao-sun (*first century* B.C.)

Hsi-men Pao was appointed as magistrate of Yeh [in Honan province]. . . . After arriving at his post, he asked the local elders from what they suffered most. "The marriage of the River God," they replied; "it is the main reason for our being so poor." . . .

Each year before the wedding took place, said the elders, the town chief and the town treasurer imposed heavy taxation upon the people. Of the several million standard coins they collected they spent two or three thou-

A musical performance

sand on the wedding and divided the rest among the sorceresses and themselves. Shortly before the wedding took place, the sorceresses went from house to house and, seeing an attractive maiden, would designate her as the prospective bride. The girl would then be washed clean from head to toe, and new silk clothes would be made for her wedding dress. To wait for the scheduled wedding, she went through a period of fasting and penance in her own house. Meanwhile a structure on a raft, called penance hall, was built on the bank of the river and richly decorated with yellow and golden silk. . . . On the day of her wedding to the River God, the raft structure was placed on the river with her in it. It floated downstream for many miles before it submerged into the water. . . . People said that if the River God did not receive his bride, he would cause flood and would bring death to all people in this area.

Upon hearing this story, Hsi-men Pao told the elders that at the next wedding of the River God he would like the local officials and the sorceresses to inform him in advance so that he could attend the wedding himself. The elders said that they would be happy to comply with his demand.

On the day of the wedding Hsi-men Pao arrived at the river bank. There were about three thousand people watching the procedure, including the town chief, wealthy and influential citizens of the community, and the elders. Besides, there was the chief sorceress, aged seventy or over, accompanied by ten of her disciples who, dressed in unlined garments made of silk, stood behind her. Hsi-men Pao told the officials in charge that he would like to see the bride himself to make sure that she was attractive enough to be the River God's wife. After the girl was brought before him, he announced to the local officials and the sorceresses that this girl was too plain for the role

which she was supposed to play and that he was wondering whether the chief sorceress would be kind enough to inform the River God to wait for a few days until a more attractive girl could be found as his bride. He then ordered the soldiers to throw the chief sorceress into the river.

A moment later Hsi-men Pao said that he could not understand why the chief sorceress had not returned and that a disciple of hers should be sent to hurry her. A young sorceress was then thrown into the river. Neither did she return; so another young sorceress was thrown into the river to hurry the first one. . . .

"You cannot trust women," Hsi-men commented. "They cannot deliver even a simple message. May I bother the town chief for this important mission?" The town chief was then thrown into the river.

The magistrate stood attentively, facing the river and bowing his head in respect. The elders and the officials were as frightened as they were surprised. For a long time the magistrate waited for the messengers' return, but in vain. "What should we do since none of them has returned?" he asked. He suggested that the town treasurer and a member of the local gentry should be sent to the river to fetch them. Upon hearing this both of them prostrated themselves and knocked their heads so hard against the ground that blood gushed out, entailing the change of color on the ground. "Maybe we should wait for a while and see whether our messengers will return by themselves," said the magistrate.

A moment later, Hsi-men Pao spoke again. "Arise, dear treasurer. Since the River God has obviously decided to retain our messengers as his permanent guests, there is no sense for you to go there now. In fact, I think that all of you should proceed home at this moment." From then on, nobody in Yeh ever dared to speak of the marriage of the River God.

THE SOCIAL CODE

An important element of the ritual promoted by the Confucians was the observance of manners. Showing reverence for one's superiors and respect for all others preserved the order of society and fostered an awareness of one's own position. In theory the rules of courtesy and dress were the outward expression of harmonious relationships. Modern revolutionaries, however, saw such formalities as tools of oppression and overthrew the rules along with the rulers.

A GENTLEMAN'S ATTIRE

from the Analects

A gentleman does not wear facings of purple or mauve, nor in undress does he use pink or roan. In hot weather he wears an unlined gown of fine thread loosely woven, but puts on an outside garment before going out-of-doors. With a black robe he wears black lambskin; with a robe of undyed silk, fawn. With a yellow robe, fox fur. On his undress robe the fur cuffs are long; but the right is shorter than the left. His bedclothes must be half as long again as a man's height. The thicker kinds of fox and badger are for home wear. Except when in mourning, he wears all his girdle-ornaments. Apart from his Court apron, all his skirts are wider at the bottom than at the waist. Lambskin dyed black and a hat of dark-dyed silk must not be worn when making visits of condolence. At the Announcement of the New Moon he must go to Court in full Court dress.

THE GENTLE VIRTUES

by Yen Tseng (*first century* B.C.)

A gentleman regards tasteful food as destructive to his stomach and wealth as an invitation to danger. He has no use for jealousy, envy, slandering, or flattery. He believes that cruelty will boomerang against its practitioner, and betrayal will eventually entrap the betrayer. To him sexual indulgence is the road to a family's destruction, and a habitual drinker will surely wind up in the gutter.

A gentleman, on the other hand, will embrace the virtues of loyalty and filial piety as a means to acquire personal wealth, and rely on temperance and thrift as the most reliable source of financial adequacy. He criticizes himself three times everyday and instructs his descendants to do likewise until eternity to come.

AN EXCEPTION TO THE RULE

attributed to Mencius (372–289 B.C.)

A philosopher asked Mencius, saying, "That men and women, in giving and receiving, shall not touch hands,—is such the rule of propriety?" "It is," replied Mencius. "But supposing," said the philosopher, "that a sister-in-law was drowning, should a man not give her a hand and pull her out?" "A man," answered Mencius, "who could see his sister-in-law drown and not give her his hand, would be a wolfish brute. That men and women, in giving and receiving, do not touch hands, is a rule of propriety; but when a sister-in-law is drowning, to give her a hand and pull her out comes under the head of exceptions to the rule."

RESPONSIBILITIES

from a letter by Tsêng Kuo-fan (1811–1872)

Since Uncle Ch'eng has moved to the new residence, you are now the lord of our old homestead, the Golden House. My grandfather, the honorable Hsing-kang, attached great importance to the successful management of the household. First, he insisted that every member of our family should get up early in the morning. Second, the house should be washed and swept regularly to keep it clean. Third, the offering of sacrifices to the deceased ancestors should be performed in the most sincere manner. Fourth, all of our neighbors, relatives, and clan members should be well treated. Whenever they came to our house, they were always received with great respect. We gave them financial help if they were in need. We offered them our good offices if they were involved in lawsuits; congratulated them on wedding and other festival occasions; provided comfort when they were sick; and sent them condolences after the death of any of their family members.

Besides the four items described above, the honorable Hsing-kang paid constant attention to the study of books and the raising of vegetables. Recently when I wrote letters home, I often reminded you of the importance of "books, vegetables, fish, and hogs." I want you to know that whenever I did this, I merely followed the tradition established by my grandfather.

THE CULTIVATED MAN

by Lü K'un (1536–1618)

A gentleman does not have any of the ten attributes commonly shared by others. These ten attributes are those of a soldier, a woman, a juvenile, a vulgar man, a prodigal son, a country bumpkin, a defendant in front of a judge, a female slave, an informer, and finally, a merchant.

He should hide a large portion of whatever goodness he might have and thus cultivate his "ethical profoundness." Likewise he should conceal to a great extent the shortcomings of others and thus enlarge his "magnanimity." Patience is essential to planning, and a peaceful mind is a prerequisite to the management of affairs. Modesty is the most important item in the preservation of one's life, and tolerance and forgiveness should be the basic attitude towards others. To cultivate his mind, a gentleman should not be unduly concerned with such things as affluence or poverty, life or death, constancy or change.

OVERTHROWING OLD WAYS

by Mao Tse-tung (1893–   )

The old rule that forbids women and poor people to attend banquets in the ancestral temple has also been broken. On one occasion the women of Paikwo, Hengshan, marched into their ancestral temple, sat down on the seats and ate and drank, while the grand patri-

A dinner party

archs could only look on. At another place the poor peasants, not admitted to the banquets in the temples, swarmed in and ate and drank their fill, while the frightened local bullies, bad gentry, and gentlemen in long gowns all took to their heels. . . . Forbidding superstition and smashing idols has become quite the vogue in Liling. In its northern districts the peasants forbade the festival processions in honor of the god of pestilence. There were many idols in the Taoist temple on Fupo hill, Lukow, but they were all piled up in a corner to make room for the district headquarters of the Kuomintang, and no peasant raised any objection. When a death occurs in a family, such practices as sacrifice to the gods, performance of Taoist or Buddhist rites, and offering of sacred lamps are becoming rare. . . . In the Lungfeng Nunnery in the North Third district, the peasants and school teachers chopped up the wooden idols to cook meat. More than thirty idols in the Tungfu Temple in the South district were burnt by the students together with the peasants; only two small idols, generally known as "His Excellency Pao," were rescued by an old peasant who said, "Don't commit a sin!" In places where the power of the peasants is predominant, only the older peasants and the women still believe in gods, while the young and middle-aged peasants no longer do so. Since it is the young and middle-aged peasants who are in control of the peasant association, the movement to overthrow theocratic authority and eradicate superstition is going on everywhere.

PLEASURES AND PASTIMES

The peasant who spent his life bent in toil on the land seldom had time or energy for learning, literature, and the arts—though scholars, artists, and statesmen did rise from the peasantry. Generally, high culture was the pursuit of the wealthy and the leisured. But every class had its diversions. Some could afford more than a glance from the women of pleasure; prostitution was legal in China until the Communist takeover. For others there were wine and song, lavish meals, boat rides, the theatre, and the storytellers in the teahouses.

A VISIT TO DRUNK-LAND

by Wang Chi (*sixth-seventh centuries* A.D.)

This country is many thousand miles from the Middle Kingdom. It is a vast, boundless plain, without mountains or undulations of any kind. The climate is equable, there being neither night, nor day, nor cold, nor heat. The manners and customs are everywhere the same.

There are no villages nor congregations of persons. The inhabitants are ethereal in disposition, and know neither love, hate, joy, nor anger. They inhale the breeze and sip the dew, eating none of the five cereals. Calm in repose, slow of gait, they mingle with birds, beasts, fishes, and scaly creatures, ignorant of boats, chariots, weapons, or implements in general.

The Yellow Emperor went on a visit to the capital of Drunk-Land, and when he came back, he was quite out of conceit with the empire, the government of which seemed to him but paltry trifling with knotted cords. . . .

Alas, I could not bear that the pure and peaceful domain of Drunk-Land should come to be regarded as a preserve of the ancients. So I went there myself.

A SEA OF LOTUS FLOWERS

by Chang Tai (1597–*c.*1684)

The people in Hangchow. . . . go to the lake in large numbers, ostensibly for the purpose of watching the moon. They generously tip the gate keepers, and then go straight to the shore of the lake where the sedan-chair bearers, holding the torches high, help them into the boat. Once in the boat, they order the boatmen to row to Tuanch'iao as fast as possible so that they will not be late for the elaborate Buddhist rituals. Thus before ten o'clock there is nothing to hear except noise and nothing to see except crowds. All boats, large and small, rush towards the shore at the same time: all one can see is poles clashing against poles, boats bumping into boats, shoulders rubbing against shoulders, and faces meeting faces.

It does not take long before all of these excitements are over. The soldiers cry aloud to pave the way for the officials to return home, soon after the banquets have come to a close. The sedan-chair bearers rush the boatmen to row faster, lest the city gates will be closed before they reach there. Along the roads are lamps and torches that shine like stars; they move in groups that follow one another. Meanwhile those who have spent the evening on the shore are also rushing towards the city gates before they are closed. The crowd becomes thinner and thinner until it eventually disappears.

It is only then that we anchor our boats against the shore of Tuanch'iao. We sit on the stone steps that have begun to feel cool, and we call upon our guests to drink as much as they can. At this time the moon looks like a mirror only recently cleaned; the mountains are more beautiful than ever; and the lake seems to have once again washed her own face. Those who love soft music and leisurely drinking have finally emerged; so do those who until then have hidden themselves under the shadows of the trees. To them we send our invitation; and if they are too modest to accept, we drag them by their hands. Here come the friendly poets and the cultured prostitutes with whom we share our wine and music. The merriment continues until moonlight becomes feeble and the day is about to dawn. Our guests bid us good-bye; and we, finally, return to our own boat. The boat wanders its way among a sea of lotus flowers, while we sleep soundly in it. The air is full of fragrance: can there be a better environment to induce a beautiful dream?

RIVER HOUSES

by Chang Tai (1597–*c*.1684)

The river houses along the Ch'inhuai River can serve any or all of the following purposes: temporary housing, social gathering, and sexual indulgence. Though the rent is high, rarely has been a room vacant. . . .

Outside each river house is an exposed terrace protected by red railings and enclosed with open silk. To assure privacy, bamboo curtains and silk screens are used to separate one section of the terrace from the other. In summer months the girls sit leisurely on the terrace after their bath; and when a breeze gently lifts up the edge of their skirts, one smells a scent of jasmine, heavenly enchanting. They wear light silk and keep themselves cool with round fans. The hair on the temples is loose, and the curls, casually tied together, are leaning towards one side. They are soft, charming, and irresistible.

COOKING

by Yüan Mei (1715–1797)

Cookery is like matrimony. Two things served together should match. Clear should go with clear, thick with thick, hard with hard, and soft with soft. I have known people mix grated lobster with birds'-nests, and mint with chicken or pork!

The cooks of today think nothing of mixing in one soup the meat of chicken, duck, pig, and goose. But these chickens, ducks, pigs, and geese have doubtless souls. And these souls will most certainly file plaints in the next world on the way they have been treated in this. A good cook will use plenty of different dishes. Each article of food will be made to exhibit its own characteristics, while each made dish will be characterized by one dominant flavor. Then the palate of the gour-

mand will respond without fail, and the flowers of the soul blossom forth. . . .

Don't cut bamboo-shoots with an oniony knife. . . . A good cook frequently wipes his knife, frequently changes his cloth, frequently scrapes his board, and frequently washes his hands. If smoke or ashes from his pipe, perspiration drops from his head, insects from the wall, or smuts from the saucepan get mixed up with the food, though he were a very chef among chefs, yet would men hold their noses and decline.

WIT AND HUMOR

by Han Fei (*died* 233 B.C.)

While working in the fields, a farmer saw a rabbit running against a tree. The rabbit was instantly killed.

He took the rabbit home, cooked it, and found it delicious.

In the second day, he gave up his farming and sat under the same tree, hoping that the same thing would happen again. It never did.

from the Documents of the Warring States

A mussel had opened its shell and was sunning itself on the beach when a snipe pecked at its flesh. It quickly closed its shell, and caught and tightly held the snipe's beak. The mussel could not go back to the river; nor could the snipe walk away.

"If it does not rain for two days, soon the mussel will be dead," thought the snipe. "If I keep his beak between my shells for two days, soon there will be a dead snipe," thought the mussel.

While the mussel and the snipe were angry at each other and neither one wished to make any concessions, a fisherman walked by and caught both of them.

Preparing fish

THE IMPERIAL COURT

The ideal ruler of China was virtuous; the ideal official was taken into the government for his shining character and scholarly achievements. However, as these excerpts show, China had its share of tyrants. When the ruler was corrupt, his court was probably decadent as well. An influential patron could nullify the results of official examinations, and intrigues and bribery were commonplace.

THE GENERAL TS'AO TS'AO
by Ch'ên Shou (A.D. 233–297)

As a person, [the General] Ts'ao Ts'ao [died A.D. 220] was frivolous and undignified. He loved music and was often surrounded by entertainers and prostitutes from morning to night. He wore clothes made of light silk and attached to his belt a small bag which contained his handkerchief and other personal effects. Sometimes he put on a conical cap when receiving visitors. During a conversation he was outspoken and joked a great deal; often did he laugh so loudly that he buried his head among the dishes on the table, soiling his headwear. How frivolous he really was!

However, he was strict and harsh in the enforcement of his laws. If he suspected a general to be superior to him in military strategy, he would find some legal excuse to put him to death. He would not hesitate to kill his long-time followers or friends if he found that they had complaints against him. Once he decided to kill a man, no weeping or pleading could make him change his mind. . . .

Once marching his soldiers in a wheat field, he gave the order that under no circumstances would they be allowed to damage the crop and that those who did would be immediately put to death. Observing his order, all of his cavalrymen alighted from their mounts and gently pushed the plants aside so as to thread their way through. Ts'ao Ts'ao's own mount, however, suddenly jumped into the field and caused considerable damage to the crop. Ts'ao ordered the law enforcer to carry out the punishment that was to be inflicted upon himself.

"According to the *Spring and Autumn Annals*," said the law enforcer, "penalty should not be imposed upon the most superior."

"If I am not punished for violating my own law, how can I expect obedience from my subordinates?" said Ts'ao Ts'ao. "However, since I am the commander-in-chief, I cannot very well commit suicide at this moment. Let me punish myself." He unsheathed his sword, cut off his long hair, and threw it to the ground.

NUMBER ONE POET
by Hsüeh Yung-jo (*ninth century* A.D.)

Chang Chiu-kao [younger brother of the prime minister] was regarded as the most promising young talent in the literary circle; in fact, some of Princess T'aip'ing's friends, invoking her name, had already passed his poems on to the examiners in the capital, so that he would be rated "number one" when the examination took place. Wang Wei was about to take the same examination, and when he heard about this arrangement, he reported it to Prince Ch'i [the princess' brother] and pleaded for help.

"The Princess is a very powerful person, and we cannot openly defy her wishes," said Prince Ch'i. "However, I have a plan. . . ." Wang followed Prince Ch'i to the Princess' residence.

"Knowing that Your Ladyship is at home, I have taken the liberty of bringing you food and music," Prince Ch'i went in and reported. Then he gave the order that a banquet be set up immediately. The musicians, meanwhile, came in one after another in an orderly fashion. In the front row among the musicians stood Wang Wei who was young, handsome, and elegant. The Princess took a look at him and then asked Prince Ch'i who the young man was.

"He is an expert musician," the Prince replied.

The Prince then ordered Wang to play the new song which the latter had recently composed. The song was so sad that all people

The emperor's sedan chair

present were visibly moved. . . . The Princess was immensely impressed.

"This young man not only knows music," said Prince Ch'i; "he has no peers in the field of poetry."

The Princess was even more surprised. "Have you brought some of your poems with you?" she asked.

Wang Wei took out the poems which he had prepared and presented them to the Princess. Reading them, the Princess was astonished beyond belief. "These are the poems that I have studied and recited regularly," said she. "I always thought that they were the works of the ancient great. Are they your work?" . . .

"Will not the nation be proud to have this young man as the 'number one' in this year's metropolitan examination?" said Prince Ch'i.

"Why do you not ask him to participate in the examination?" asked the Princess.

"He said that he will not take the examination under any circumstances unless he has Your Ladyship's blessings," Prince Ch'i replied. "But it is reported that Your Ladyship has already recommended Chang Chiu-kao as the 'number one.'"

"I personally had nothing to do with that recommendation," said the Princess. "I did it at other people's request." Then turning to Wang Wei, she added: "Go ahead and take the examination. I shall do my part to help." . . .

Later, the Princess summoned the examiners to her residence and ordered her servants to transmit to them her wishes. Wang Wei was then designated as "number one" and passed the metropolitan examination in his first attempt.

BOOT LICKING

by Tsung Ch'ên (*sixteenth century*)

How indeed does an official find favor in the present day with his chief? Morning and evening he must whip up his horse and go dance attendance at the great man's door. If the porter refuses to admit him, then honeyed words, a coaxing air, and money drawn from the sleeve, may prevail. The porter takes in his card; but the great man does not come out. So he waits in the stable among grooms. . . . At nightfall, the porter who has pocketed the money comes forth and says his master is tired and begs to be excused, and will he call again next day. So he is forced to come once more as requested. He sits all night in his clothes. At cockcrow he jumps up, performs his toilette, and gallops off and knocks at the entrance gate. . . . And the porter, another fee to the good, gets up and lets him in; and then he waits again in the stable as before, until perhaps the great man comes out and summons him to an audience.

Now, with many an obeisance, he cringes timidly towards the foot of the dais steps; and when the great man says "Come!" he prostrates himself twice and remains long without rising. At length he goes up to offer his present, which the great man refuses. He entreats acceptance; but in vain. He implores, with many instances; whereupon the great man bids a servant take it. Then two more prostrations, long drawn out; after which he arises, and with five or six salutations he takes his leave.

On going forth, he bows to the porter, saying, "It's all right with your master. Next time I come you need make no delay." The porter returns the bow, well pleased with his share in the business. Meanwhile, our friend springs on his horse, and when he meets an acquaintance flourishes his whip and cries out, "I have just been with His Excellency. He treated me very kindly, very kindly indeed." And then he goes into detail, upon which his friends begin to be more respectful to him as a protégé of His Excellency.

THE FAMILY TRADITION

Confucius is quoted by a disciple as saying that "filial piety is the basis of virtue and the source of all instruction." Such has been the Chinese tradition ever since. A man learned his responsibilities to society by serving and revering his parents. Woman's role was doubly demanding, for she had not only to please her husband (even to the point of finding him a concubine) but her parents-in-law too. If widowed, her activities were drastically restricted by society.

FATHERLY ADVICE

by Chu Hsi (1130–1200)

When mounting the wall of a city, do not point with the finger; when on the top, do not call out.

When at a friend's house, do not persist in asking for anything you may wish to have. When going upstairs, utter a loud "Ahem!" If you see two pairs of shoes outside and hear voices, you may go in; but if you hear nothing, remain outside. Do not trample on the shoes of other guests, nor step on the mat spread for food; but pick up your skirts and pass quickly to your allotted place. Do not be in a hurry to arrive, nor in haste to get away.

Do not bother the gods with too many prayers. Do not make allowances for your own shortcomings. Do not seek to know what has not yet come to pass.

THE DUTIFUL SON

by Hou Fang-yü (1618–1654)

Many years ago there was in Ch'uanchou a dutiful son named T'ang Yen who cut a piece of flesh from his right arm to feed his father. . . . Commenting on this incident, the historian Yao Lai maintained that to mutilate one's body, for whatever purpose, is incompatible with the concept of righteous conduct and should not be regarded as a good example to follow. Since then people have considered this statement the final word on this subject. . . . [However] what situation [could] be more compelling than the suffering of unbearable pain by one's parents as a result of injury or illness? If a person decides to mutilate his own body so that his parents can live, I cannot see any reason why he should not be allowed to do so. Furthermore, a man who mutilates himself will be on the verge of death; unless he is

absolutely sincere, he would not have taken such a step in the first place. It is wrong to compare him with those hypocrites who take drastic actions for the sole purpose of earning an undeserved reputation. His example will inspire others to show the same boundless love for their parents.

FILIAL PIETY

from the Book of Documents

The king says, "Fêng, such chief criminals are greatly abhorred, and how much more detestable are the unfilial and unbrotherly—the son who does not reverently discharge his duty to his father, but greatly wounds his father's heart; the father who can no longer love his son, but hates him; and the younger brother who does not think of the manifest will of Heaven, and refuses to respect his elder brother, so that the elder brother . . . is very unbrotherly to his junior. . . . You must deal speedily with such offenders. . . ."

BROTHERS

by Yen Chih-t'ui (A.D. 531–595)

Brothers come from the same origin and are consequently of the same spirit, even though they are separate in form. While they are little, they tag along with the same parents, eat at the same table, and wear each other's clothes. They study the same subjects when they are in school, and travel in the same areas when they are old enough to be out of their home. Even if one of them acts improperly, the others will love him just the same. The situation begins to change, however, when they reach adulthood and are married. Each of them has his own wife and children, and the brotherly love, however great it has been, will suffer some degree of deterioration.

Domestic tasks

EULOGY TO WANG

by T'ang Shun-chih (1507–1560)

In the first three years after her marriage, Wang had two miscarriages. From then on she was greatly concerned with the fact that my brother might not have an heir. One day, returning home from a trip that he had made with me to Yihsing, my brother saw a strange girl in his room. Surprised, he asked his wife who the girl was; he was told that this was the concubine that she had bought for him. Protesting that he, barely over twenty, was too young to have a concubine, he sent the girl home without being intimate with her. Five or six years later when there was still no male child, she again bought a concubine for her husband. She personally dressed up the girl, being fearful that the latter might not be attractive enough for her husband. The arrival of the concubine did not in any way affect the relationship between Wang and her husband which remained affectionate. In fact, she encouraged her husband to stay with his concubine for as many evenings as he wished. . . .

It seems that with her ability and virtue she should have enjoyed a long life and been rewarded with many sons. Yet she died young without a child and, more ironically, died of childbirth. These are the things we mortals simply cannot understand. After two miscarriages early in her married life, she did not expect any more pregnancy; instead, she was praying for the pregnancy of the concubine after the latter had been brought in to our household. When later Wang did become pregnant, people said that possibly Heaven had decided to reward her for her lack of jealousy. Yet she died because of this pregnancy. Why? Why?

WIDOWHOOD

by Chou Chi (*Ch'ing dynasty*)

A concubine is not legally tied with the man with whom she lives because their union does not come about through proper rituals. Yet she is legally entitled to her son born of this union. On the other hand, a widow who chooses to remarry is forced to cut off all ties with her children. The law places her in an inferior position, lower than that of a concubine. Not wishing to leave her children, a widow has no choice except to comply with what the society approves or demands, namely, continuous widowhood. . . . Knowing the difficulty of maintaining widowhood, many women choose to commit suicide after the death of their husbands, leaving behind not only their parents and parents-in-law to whom they owe gratitude but also their children who need their love and care.

I believe that a widow who chooses to remarry should be treated in the same manner as a concubine. She is to cut off all ties with her former husband's family according to the custom, but she should be allowed to maintain relationship with her children. This new rule, if adopted, will be beneficial to all concerned for two reasons. First, her parents and parents-in-law cannot force her to continue her widowhood by denying her the access to her children; and, second, her continuous widowhood, if she chooses that status, will be voluntary and therefore genuine.

THE INQUISITIVE MIND

Inventions, such as gunpowder, the compass, and printing, appeared in China long before knowledge of them reached Europe. But astronomy, chemistry, medicine, and the other sciences were tied too closely to occultism and superstition to earn the respect of the scholars who could have contributed to their development.

THE UNIVERSE

by Chang Hêng (A.D. 78–139)

Heaven is like an egg, and the earth is like the yolk of the egg. Alone it dwells inside. Heaven is great and earth is small. Inside and outside of heaven there is water. Heaven wraps around the earth as the shell encloses the yolk. Heaven and earth each are borne up and stand upon their vital force, floating upon the water.

from the Treatise on Astronomy

Heaven is like an umbrella, earth like an overturned dish. Both heaven and earth are high in the middle and slope down at the edges. The point beneath the north pole is the center of both heaven and earth. This is the highest point of earth, and from here it slopes down on all sides like water flowing downward. The sun, moon, and stars alternately shine and are hidden and this makes the day and night. The highest point in the center of heaven, where the sun is at the winter solstice, is 60,000 li from the horizontal line representing the level of the edges of heaven. The height of the earth at its highest point beneath the north pole is also 60,000 li. The highest point of the earth is separated from the horizontal line representing the level of the edges of heaven by 20,000 li. Since the highest point of heaven and earth correspond, the sun is constantly at a distance of 80,000 li from the earth.

by Wang Ch'ung (A.D. *c.* 27–97)

Heaven is flat just as the earth is flat, and the rising and setting of the sun is due to the fact that it revolves along with heaven. . . . To the gaze of men it appears that heaven and earth unite at a distance of no more than ten li. This is only the effect of distance, however, for they do not actually come together. In the same way when we seem to see the sun set, it does not actually set. The illusion of setting is the effect of distance. . . .

TOWARD IMMORTALITY

by Ko Hung (A.D. 253–*c.*333)

Pao-p'u Tzu said: I have investigated and read books on the nourishment of human nature and collected formulas for everlasting existence. Those I have perused number thousands of volumes. They all consider reconverted cinnabar [after it has been turned into mercury] and gold fluid to be the most important. Thus these two things represent the acme of the way to immortality. . . . If these two medicines are eaten, they will strengthen our bodies, and therefore enable us not to grow old nor to die. This is of course seeking assistance from external substances to strengthen ourselves. It is like feeding fat to the lamp so it will not die out. If we smear copperas on our feet, they will not deteriorate even if they remain in water. This is to borrow the strength of the copper to protect our flesh. Gold fluid and reconverted cinnabar, however, upon entering our body, permeate our whole system. . . .

INVENTING MOVABLE TYPE

by Shên Kua (1030–1093)

During the Ch'ing-li period (1041–1048) a commoner named Pi Sheng first invented the movable type. Each type was made of moistened clay upon which was carved one Chinese character. The portion that formed the character was as thin as the edge of a small coin. The type was then hardened by fire and thus made permanent.

To proceed with the process of printing, a printer smeared an iron plate with a mixture of turpentine, resin, wax, and burned paper ash. Pieces of movable type were then placed on the plate closely together and were arranged in such a way as to reflect the text of a book to be printed. They were confined within the plate by an iron fence fastened tightly to the plate.

The iron plate was then placed on a gentle fire in order to melt the mixture previously described. A wooden board with smooth surface was pressed upon the type so that the heads of all pieces would appear on the same level. The plate was then ready for printing. . . .

The fact that moistened clay, instead of wood, was used as the material to make movable type was because wood was subject to change and tended to distort the Chinese character carved on it.

DR. CHANG

by Ts'ao Hsüeh-ch'in (*c.* 1719–1763)

"Having felt the pulse of your honorable wife," said the doctor [Dr. Chang to Chia Yung], "I would like to venture the following opinions. Her left pulse is heavy and slow, and the beat of her left joint is feeble and concealed. Her right pulse is weak and thin, and the beat of her right joint is spiritless and empty. The heaviness and slowness of her left pulse result from the weakening of her heart which in turn generate the element of 'fire,' and the feeble and concealed beat of her left joint comes as a result of the lack of sufficient blood in her liver. The weak and thin beat of her right pulse can be attributed to the feebleness of her lungs, and the lack of spirit in her right joint results from the fact that the liver, which represents the element of 'wood,' has completely dominated the spleen which represents the element of 'earth.'

"The generation of 'fire' that results from a weakening of the heart affects a woman's menstruation which, consequently, becomes irregular. It also causes sleeplessness at night.

The lack of sufficient blood in her liver results in swelling and pain below the ribs, lateness in menstruation, and burning sensation inside the heart. The feebleness of her lungs causes periodical dizziness as if she were sitting in a boat, and also perspiration during the early hours of the morning. When the liver has completely controlled and dominated the spleen, a person does not feel like to drink or eat; she is tired easily; and her four limbs, being limp, have no strength. . . . From what I can observe by feeling the pulse, your mistress is a very ambitious and highly intelligent person. If a person is too intelligent, she is bound to have more than her fair share of unhappiness. An intelligent person worries often; and worries affect the spleen adversely and make the liver unusually strong and dominant. The net result is the irregularity of her menstruation. The irregularity takes the form of lateness rather than early arrival. . . . If she had taken tranquilizing drugs, her illness would not have deteriorated to such an extent. As far as I can see, this is a clear case of 'strong fire' and 'weak water.' The purpose of my prescription is to re-establish the balance." The doctor wrote down the prescription. . . . [It contained such elements as fungus, cooked earth, peony roots, roasted rice, *japonica*, clam powder, wine, seven lotus-seeds minus kernels, and two large plums.]

Looking over the prescription, Chia Yung said: "This looks very good to me. Please tell me: Is my wife's life really in danger?"

"An intelligent man like you should know that when a person is as sick as your honorable wife is, nobody can forecast the outcome," Dr. Chang replied. "Let her take this prescription first, and we shall see what fate has in store for us. If I were you, I would not expect too much improvement before this winter. We shall place our hope sometime in the spring." [A short time later the patient died.]

THE GOOD EARTH

Always heavily dependent on agriculture, the Chinese early devised schemes for regulating the use of land and for guarding against famine. A minister of a Chou dynasty duke here questions the efficacy of one way of dealing with drought. Another method, the grain storage program, is mentioned in the essay on the value of agriculture by Ch'ao Ts'o. As the anecdote of the snake catcher of Yungchow illustrates, there was even a solution to the problem of taxation.

THE VALUE OF AGRICULTURE

by Ch'ao Ts'o (*died* 155 B.C.)

Crime begins in poverty; poverty in insufficiency of food; insufficiency of food in neglect of agriculture. Without agriculture, man has no tie to bind him to the soil. Without such tie he readily leaves his birthplace and his home. He is like unto the birds of the air or the beasts of the field. . . .

As man is constituted, he must eat twice daily, or hunger; he must wear clothes, or be cold. And if the stomach cannot get food and the body clothes, the love of the fondest mother cannot keep her children at her side. How then should a sovereign keep his subjects gathered around him?

The wise ruler knows this. Therefore he concentrates the energies of his people upon agriculture. He levies light taxes. He extends the system of grain storage, to provide for his subjects at times when their resources fail.

PRODUCTION INCENTIVES

by Ch'ao Ts'o (*died* 155 B.C.)

To promote agricultural production is our most urgent task today. To do so, we shall place a high priority on the value of grain. Grain, in fact, should be used as a means of reward and punishment. Let the order be issued that those who contribute grain to the treasury be granted official titles, or given clemency should they be found to have committed crimes. By using this device we achieve three purposes simultaneously: the rich will acquire the coveted titles, the poor will become financially better off, and the government will have grain at its disposal. Taking the surplus from the rich to meet governmental expenses, we do not need to tax heavily the poor; the surplus will go wherever it is needed. Once such an order is issued, it will benefit all people concerned.

BURNING A WIZARD

from the Commentary on the Spring and Autumn Annals

Thereupon the duke wished to burn a wizard; but his chief minister said to him, "That will avail nothing against the drought. Rather mend the city walls; diminish consumption; be economical; and devote every energy to gathering in the harvest. This is the proper course to take: what can a wizard do for you? If God now desires his death, he might as well have never been born. And if he can cause a drought, to burn him would only make it worse."

The duke followed this advice; and in the ensuing season, although there was distress, it was not very bad.

POPULATION PROBLEM

by Hung Liang-chi (1746–1809)

There has never been a people which did not delight in peaceful rule, nor a people who did not wish peaceful rule to endure for a long time. Peaceful rule having lasted now for more than one hundred years, it may be considered of long duration. But if we consider the population, we can see that it has increased five times over what it was thirty years ago, ten times over what it was sixty years ago, and at least twenty times over what it was one hundred and some tens of years ago. . . . Who can be surprised at the frequency with which people die from exposure and starvation, exhaustion and despair?

"Does Heaven and earth have no way to take care of this?" one may ask. Flood, drought, and pestilence—that is nature's way of regulating things. But the number of those who suffer misfortune from flood, drought, and pestilence is only a few. "Does the ruler and his government have no way to deal with it?" To have all land utilized and the people exert themselves to the utmost; to move people into newly opened fields in the border land; to reduce taxes, where they have increased in weight and number, so as to bring them into line with former levels; to prohibit extravagance and stop the monopolizing of land; to open the government granaries in times of flood, drought, and pestilence and give the people food—these are about all that the ruler and his government can do to regulate and ameliorate things.

THE SNAKE CATCHER

by Liu Tsung-yüan (A.D. 773–819)

The wilderness outside Yungchow produces strange snakes whose black bodies are spangled with white dots and stripes. They are so poisonous that whatever trees, shrubs, or grass they touch will soon wither and die. . . .

Because of the medicinal qualities these snakes possess, the imperial physicans recommended that the government collect them, and the government followed the recommendation by imposing Yungchow an annual quota of two snakes as part of the tax load. . . . Those who handed their catches to the government would be exempt from taxation. Responding to the government's call, a large number of the Yungchow people were anxious to catch these snakes. However, only the Chiang family has survived this undertaking. . . .

I had the opportunity of meeting with Mr. Chiang, and I asked him how he liked his job of catching snakes. "My grandfather died of it; so did my father," he replied. "I have been in it for twelve years since the death of my father, and I myself almost died on several occasions. . . . If I did not have my present duty, my life would be much worse. My family has lived in this area for three generations, totaling

A snake seller

HONOLULU ACADEMY OF ARTS

sixty years. During these years the people became poorer and poorer, and all my neighbors had a difficult time to maintain a tolerable livelihood. They could not meet their tax payments, even though they had contributed all that their land produced and everything that their houses contained. . . .

"Whenever the tax collector came to our township, he caused so much disturbance and fear that even chickens and dogs could not enjoy their tranquillity. I woke up from my sleep and, seeing my snake in the jar, I went back to my bed with peace of mind. I fed my snake dutifully, and when the time arrived, I delivered it to the government as my taxes.

"Thus only twice a year I risk my life when I attempt to catch the snakes. For the rest of the year I enjoy what the land produces, and I have a pleasant time. Who among my neighbors has the sense of peace and serenity that I have? Should I die while catching snakes, I shall still have lived longer than most of my neighbors who have died a long time ago. How can I complain that the snakes are poisonous?"

FOREIGN DEVILS

The imperious tone taken by China in dealings with the West contributed to the strained relations that finally erupted into the Opium War. Before the war broke out in 1839, a Chinese commissioner sent this letter to Queen Victoria.

A DIPLOMATIC NOTE

by Lin Tsê-hsü (1785–1850)

A communication: magnificently our great Emperor soothes and pacifies China and the foreign countries, regarding all with the same kindness. If there is profit, then he shares it with the peoples of the world; if there is harm, then he removes it on behalf of the world. This is because he takes the mind of heaven and earth as his mind.

The kings of your honorable country by a tradition handed down from generation to generation have always been noted for their politeness and submissiveness. We have read your successive tributary memorials saying, "In general our countrymen who go to trade in China have always received His Majesty the Emperor's gracious treatment and equal justice," and so on. Privately we are delighted with the way in which the honorable rulers of your country deeply understand the grand principles and are grateful for the Celestial grace. For this reason the Celestial Court in soothing those from afar has redoubled its polite and kind treatment. The profit from trade has been enjoyed by them continuously for two hundred years. This is the source from which your country has become known for its wealth.

But after a long period of commercial intercourse, there appear among the crowd of barbarians both good persons and bad, unevenly. Consequently there are those who smuggle opium to seduce the Chinese people and so cause the spread of the poison to all provinces. Such persons who only care to profit themselves, and disregard their harm to others, are not tolerated by the laws of heaven and are unanimously hated by human beings. His Majesty the Emperor, upon hearing of this, is in a towering rage. . . . Only in several places of India under your control such as Bengal, Madras, Bombay, Patna, Benares, and Malwa has opium been planted from hill to hill, and ponds have been opened for its manufacture. For months and years work is continued in order to accumulate the poison. The obnoxious odor ascends, irritating heaven and frightening the spirits. Indeed you, O King, can eradicate the opium plant in these places, hoe over the fields entirely, and sow in its stead the five grains [i.e., millet, barley, wheat, etc.]. Anyone who dares again attempt to plant and manufacture opium should be severely punished. . . . Now consider this: if the barbarians do not bring opium, then how can the Chinese people resell it, and how can they smoke it? The fact is that the wicked barbarians beguile the Chinese people into a death trap. How then can we grant life only to these barbarians? He who takes the life of even one person still has to atone for it with his own life; yet is the harm done by opium limited to the taking of one life only? Therefore in the new regulations, in regard to those barbarians who bring opium to China, the penalty is fixed at decapitation or strangulation. This is what is called getting rid of a harmful thing on behalf of mankind . . . The barbarian merchants of your country, if they wish to do business for a prolonged period, are required to obey our statutes respectfully and to cut off permanently the source of opium. They must by no means try to test the effectiveness of the law with their lives. May you, O King, check your wicked and sift your vicious people before they come to China, in order to guarantee the peace of your nation, to show further the sincerity of your politeness and submissiveness, and to let the two countries enjoy together the blessings of peace. How fortunate, how fortunate indeed! After receiving this dispatch will you immediately give us a prompt reply regarding the details and circumstances of your cutting off the opium traffic. Be sure not to put this off.

In a Manchu dynasty painting, two foreign dignitaries (right) and a group of musicians are clothed in European fashion, but the artist has given them long fingernails and Oriental features.

9 Travelers and Traders

This T'ang dynasty pottery figure shows a bearded trader carrying a wineskin. His features and his headgear suggest that he comes from the Near East.

There is very little evidence that the Chinese had any contact with distant foreign peoples or knew of their existence before the second century B.C. The foreigners they did know were their traditional foes, the nomadic peoples of the Mongolian steppe. Lack of records makes it difficult to assess what knowledge the Chinese of the early classical period had of the peoples of what is now south China, and the lands beyond. It has been conjectured that in the reign of the first emperor of Ch'in (221–210 B.C.) the seacoast people already knew of Japan and other islands, such as the Ryukyu group, at no great distance from the coast of Shantung. The conjecture is based on the fact that the emperor sent an expedition to discover the Isles of the Immortals in the Eastern Sea. But it was not until the empire had recovered from the devastating wars that preceded its foundation that real and continuing contact was made with western Asia, India, and the south. This occurred during the reign of the Emperor Wu (140–87 B.C.).

The original reason for making contact with the lands of the west was military, to seek the alliance of a tribe called the Yüeh-chih; these were enemies of the Hsiung-nu Tatars, with whom the emperor was at war. Having been defeated by the Hsiung-nu, the Yüeh-chih had retired to the west. In 128 B.C. the Emperor Wu decided to send an envoy to find them and persuade them to come east again and co-operate with the Han armies against the Hsiung-nu. The man chosen as envoy was Chang Ch'ien, an intrepid traveler and loyal official, whose account of his voyage and of the lands he discovered has been preserved in the Han history.

Chang Ch'ien set out toward the west with one hundred followers. He was quickly captured by the Hsiung-nu and held captive for a year. Then he escaped and continued his journey. He crossed the deserts of Sinkiang and reached the I-li valley, where he hoped to find the Yüeh-chih. But they had been driven from that country by another tribe, and so Chang Ch'ien continued on westward until he reached the kingdom that the Chinese called Ta Yüan, situated in what is now Soviet Central Asia. The Yüeh-chih were not there either, so Chang Ch'ien continued onward until he found them in lands to which they had recently migrated, between the rivers Oxus and Syr Darya. This country, north of present-day Afghanistan, was known as Ta Hsia. After many adventures, including another captivity by the Hsiung-nu, Chang Ch'ien returned to China and reported that the Yüeh-chih had no intention of returning to the east. But the countries he had discovered were thenceforth to play a very important role in Chinese culture.

Ta Yüan, known to the West as Fergana, is the same as Sogdiana, one of the easternmost provinces of Alexander the Great's empire. (See map on page 228.) Ta Hsia is Bactria, and like Sogdiana, had been Greek or Macedonian territory until the Yüeh-chih conquered it. Both lands are in the Soviet Union today, located in the territories of the Uzbek, Kirgiz, and Tadzhik republics. The Yüeh-chih have been identified as the Asii, or Asiani, of Greek writers. They were a mixed people and included a subtribe, called Tocharians by the Greeks. There is evidence that the Tocharians spoke a language of Indo-European origin, having affinities with Celtic. The Yüeh-chih conquest of Ta Hsia, or Bactria, was recent when Chang Ch'ien reached the country, and a great many of the conquered inhabitants still spoke Greek.

Chang Ch'ien realized that the people he encountered were highly civilized. "The people of Ta Yüan are sedentary and cultivate the soil," he wrote. "They have superb horses which sweat blood when they perspire. There are cities, mansions and houses as in China . . . Ta Hsia is southwest of Ta Yüan and has similar customs. When your servant was in Ta Hsia he saw big bamboos and cloth of Shu [Ssǔch'uan province, China]. When he asked how they obtained these things they told him that their merchants brought them from Shen Tu [that is, India] which is a country several hundreds of li southeast of Ta Hsia and is a sedentary nation like Ta Hsia. Both Ta Hsia and Ta Yüan are tributary to An Hsi [Parthia]."

Chang Ch'ien had reached the fringes of the Hellenistic world, and he identified the great lands of India and Persia, although he did not visit them. His belief that he saw products of Ssǔch'uan in Ta Hsia is probably mistaken; more likely these things came from some part of India. Acting on Chang Ch'ien's information, Emperor Wu tried to send expeditions and envoys to India through southwest China and Assam, but the dangers of the route prevented them from getting through. As a consequence of their efforts, the Chinese found out a great deal about what is now southwest China and profited from this knowledge to invade and conquer an independent southern kingdom then centered on Canton.

In later years Emperor Wu sent envoys to Ta Yüan to obtain some of the famous horses, which he needed in order to breed better stock for his cavalry. The Ta Yüan people refused to sell, so the emperor organized a military expedition to conquer their distant country. It failed, but a subsequent and very costly expedition was successful, and Ta Yüan was brought under Chinese suzerainty. This was the beginning of that contact with western Asia that has been called the Silk Road. China exported silk, whose production was then a Chinese secret and monopoly, and in return obtained horses and other trade goods. It was along the Silk Road that the grape vine was brought to China. Half a century after the time of Chang Ch'ien, the Chinese were induced to interfere in the political affairs of the last Greek kingdoms in India. The prince they supported, Hermaeus, king of Parapanisadae, the last Greek king to reign in India, held his court at Cophen in the Kabul valley of modern Afghanistan. Ultimately he was driven out by a nomadic invasion, at a time when China was too preoccupied with internal troubles to help him.

In the Later Han period, in A.D. 73, the Chinese once more took an active interest in Central Asia. A famous administrator, Pan Ch'ao, was sent to restore Chinese authority, which had been allowed to lapse; for thirty years he carried on this mission with great success. All the petty states of Sinkiang became Chinese tributaries. Pan Ch'ao ended his career by advancing with an army of seventy thousand men, many of them local levies, to the shores of the Caspian Sea. He then sent out envoys to learn about the countries farther west. The Han history has incorporated their reports, but it has always been rather difficult to identify the places that the envoys visited. Persia was certainly one. There is no

doubt that the Chinese also reached the eastern provinces of the Roman empire, but it is not known whether this was done by way of Mesopotamia or, as now seems more probable, by sailing along the coast of the Black Sea.

Direct contact with Rome was obstructed by the Persians, who gave misleading information and actually restrained Chinese emissaries to the West. They did not want the silk trade with Rome to bypass their empire, which as a middleman derived great profit from it. Chinese descriptions of the Roman empire are accurate in part; in part they are a confusion of information obtained at widely separated periods. They mention institutions of republican Rome at the same time as those of imperial date. There are some vague references to the western provinces of the Roman empire and to the "land where the sun sets," which was said to be a two-hundred-day journey west of the Black Sea.

In A.D. 166, near the end of the Later Han period, there is a record of an embassy sent to China by An Tun, king of Ta Ch'in. An Tun is the Emperor Marcus Aurelius Antoninus, and Ta Ch'in is the old Chinese name for the

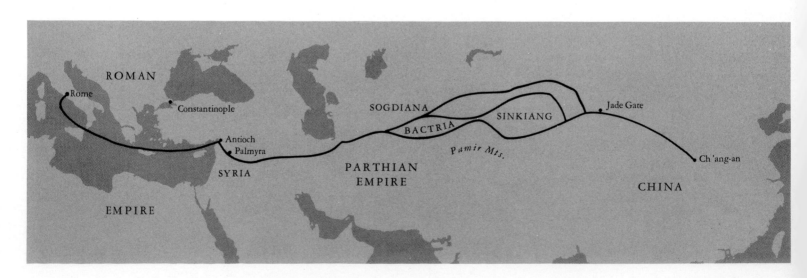

Roman empire. The Chinese doubted whether the envoys were really official, for the presents that they brought were evidently of southeast Asian origin. They suspected that the envoys were really merchants. Whatever they were, their arrival is the first definite proof that the sea route from the West to China was already in operation, going around Arabia and across the Indian Ocean, where sailing was aided by the monsoon. Another embassy arrived shortly after the fall of the Han dynasty; this one was official, for the name of the envoy was recorded, but its Chinese form had never been identified with a Latin or Greek name. The Chinese sent their own envoy back with him, but he died early in the voyage. The discovery in Thailand of Roman products, lamps and other objects, also confirms that the sea trade route was open and that it touched all the major ports along the south coast of Asia.

One of the most important consequences of the opening of these new routes was that along them Buddhism came to China. Both the land and the sea routes were used by the Buddhist missionaries from India and by the Chinese pilgrims who soon went to India to visit the holy places and learn Sanskrit in order to translate the Buddhist scriptures. Some of these pilgrims have left accounts of their travels; the most notable was Fa Hsien, who in A.D. 399 traveled across Central Asia to India. He found Buddhism flourishing in Central Asia and in what is now Afghanistan, but decaying in India. After several years he returned to China by the sea route, shunning the dreadful crossing of the Hindu Kush mountains. He sailed from Bengal to Ceylon, and thence to Java, which was not yet a Buddhist country. Ultimately he took ship for China. His destination was Canton, but he landed on the Shantung coast, after the captain had lost his reckoning and the travelers had passed seventy

days at sea without sighting land. It is clear that the sea route was no pleasure cruise. Later, pilgrims found that Sumatra, which had become a Buddhist center, was a good place to make a long stay and learn Sanskrit, which the numerous Brahmans at the king's court were very willing to teach. These pilgrims were probably the earliest Chinese to settle, even temporarily, in any part of southeast Asia.

There is no doubt that in the period from the first century B.C. to the early seventh century A.D. Chinese knowledge of the outer world increased enormously. In Han times, some knowledge of Japan was acquired; Han documents contain the earliest records we possess of Japanese history. By the early seventh century, the end of the period of division in China, Japan was emerging as a centralized state. Soon it was eagerly copying and learning the arts of advanced civilization from its great T'ang neighbor. The cities of Nara and Heian-kyo (Kyoto) were modeled on T'ang dynasty Ch'ang-an, and even today Kyoto retains some of the street names copied from Ch'ang-an. Around the same time Buddhism came to Japan, brought by both Chinese and Korean monks. It was also in this period that early contacts developed with the lands south of China. Almost all that is known of the early history of southeast Asia has been preserved in the dynastic histories of China from the time of the Later Han and its immediate successors.

All this knowledge was reported to the court by diplomatic envoys and Buddhist pilgrims, and then preserved in the archives. With few exceptions the reporters are anonymous. It was not a custom among the Chinese to record the sending of an embassy to some foreign country. Foreign embassies are recorded only in so far as they enhance the prestige of the emperor, for, according to theory,

Travelers crossing a desert are seen in a painting dating from the Mongol period. The men, probably merchants, have unloaded their two-humped, Bactrian camels. One of their number (foreground) tends to the cooking.

A Mongol groom, dressed in a red gown and high-crowned hat, leads a dappled horse in this Yüan dynasty painting. The Chinese imported horses by the thousands from neighboring lands.

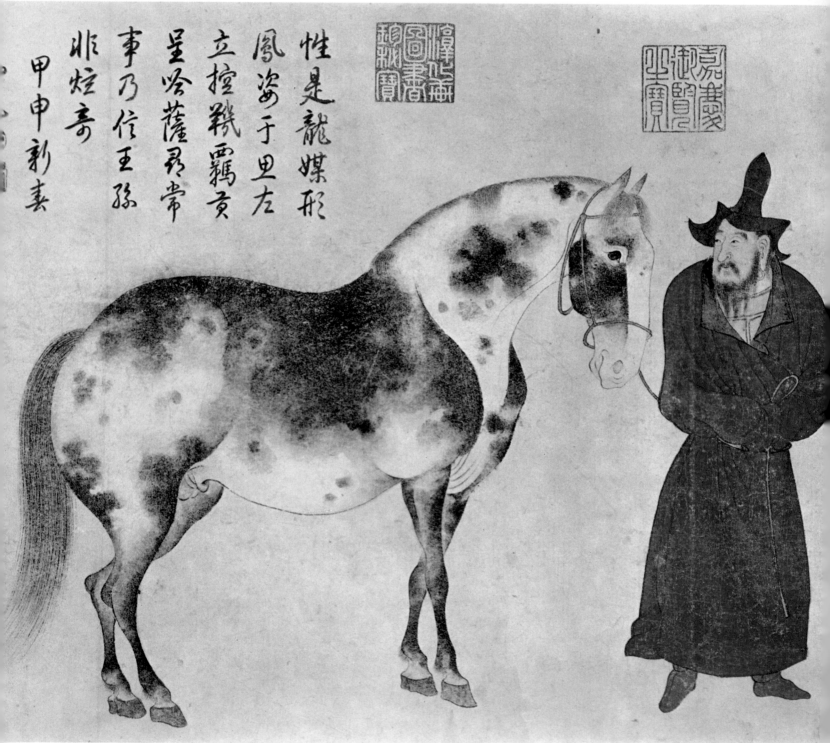

性是龍媒形
鳳姿于里左
立控鞚鞴貢
呈答薩羅常
事乃信王孫
非炫奇
甲申新春

it was always assumed that relations with foreigners were relations between suzerain and tributary, even if such was not always the case. If the emperor sent an envoy to seek foreign aid, no mention is made of it, although the information about other countries that appears in the dynastic history suggests that this was done.

We know that the T'ang court (A.D. 618–906) had a wide diplomatic contact with western Asia and with Byzantium. Embassies from these distant lands, and the names of their rulers, are recorded. Reciprocal Chinese embassies were certainly sent, because the Chinese histories of the T'ang dynasty give fascinating details of Constantinople that were certainly not gained at second hand and that often provide information unavailable from Western sources. Strange objects were imported from far-off lands. These exerted their influences on Chinese art; there are T'ang bowls decorated in a debased Hellenistic style, and at the tomb of the seventh-century Emperor Kao Tsung, there is a very accurate sculpture of an ostrich, which was brought from Arabia or Africa. Black slaves were also imported from Asia.

The ninth-century Arab chronicler Abu Zaid records that his countryman Ibn Wahab of Basra told him of an interview that he had had with the T'ang Emperor I Tsung in A.D. 872. The emperor knew all about Islam and had a picture of Mohammed, which he showed to Ibn Wahab. He had heard of Noah and the Flood, but said the story was a legend, as the flood did not reach China. The emperor had pictures of Moses and of Jesus with the apostles. He knew their histories also. It would seem that the ninth-century T'ang educated elite knew more about the Western world than did their successors at the Manchu court in the early nineteenth century.

Contacts at the time were, in fact, widespread. Nestorian Christians, exiles from the Byzantine empire, spread their teaching throughout Asia and established themselves in China, with imperial permission, early in the T'ang dynasty. They built their church in Ch'ang-an, the capital; when it fell into disrepair late in the eighth century, they rebuilt it, commemorating the event on a stone tablet, which is still preserved and still legible. On the tablet they explicitly claimed that their religion derived from the Roman empire.

There was a large community of Persian refugees in Ch'ang-an, who had escaped during the Arab conquest of the Sassanian empire. They included the last king, Yezdegerd, his son and heir, Firouz, and his grandson, who became a general of the T'ang imperial guard. They were allowed to erect a Zoroastrian temple, but their community does not seem to have survived the troubles at the end of the T'ang period. That they were esteemed, and moved in literate circles, can be shown from the fact that the famous contemporary poet Li Po is known to have spoken Persian, although there is no evidence that he read the language.

Ch'ang-an was then probably the largest city in the world, and except for Constantinople, the most advanced in all arts and culture. It is not surprising that the two great powers of East and West, too distant to quarrel, should have enjoyed cultural contacts. It has been suggested that the Byzantine motive for maintaining contact was to find in China an ally that would threaten the Arab caliphate from the rear, and thus take away heavy pressure from the Eastern Roman empire. China did clash with the Arabs in Central Asia, and came off worse, but the incident was far away on a distant frontier and had no lasting importance to the court.

In the T'ang period the Chinese were in the habit of burying in their tombs clay figures

of those who were to attend the spirit of the deceased in the world to come. The striking fact about these T'ang grave figures is that a very high proportion of foreign types is shown among them. The portraits are lifelike, and the clothing of the figures is colorfully painted. The grave figures represent a variety of races, from all parts of Asia and from Europe and Africa. Central Asians, with their prominent Armenoid features, were usually shown as grooms and camel men; Indians as dancers and singers; Africans as domestic slaves; Syrians or Greeks as jugglers and entertainers. What is conspicuous is that all are obviously employees; no social equals from foreign lands are represented. This may be because such friends would have no place in the afterlife, and it seems to suggest that Chinese contacts with foreigners were essentially based on the employer-servant relationship. Sometimes this relationship took the form of that between teacher and pupil, as can be seen from accounts of visits to T'ang China by Japanese Buddhist pilgrims, who flocked there for instruction and to visit the shrines. This is in piquant contrast to the relationsip between overseas Chinese and Westerners in the nineteenth century.

The Chinese probably borrowed certain customs made familiar to them by these foreign residents. Grave figures show a whole team of girls playing polo—a game later forgotten in China and certainly one that later ages would not have thought suitable for girls. (A group of such figures appears on pages 110–111.)

It is unfortunate that evidence of Chinese travel and contact with foreigners can so often only be deduced from the introduction of a new fashion or custom rather than from direct literary description. The Northern Sung period (A.D. 960–1126) and the succeeding age (1127–1279), during which China was divided, with the foreign Chin dynasty in the north and the Sung still in the south, seem to have been times when Chinese trade with other parts of the world increased while travel abroad diminished. The decline of Buddhism in India, and the Moslem invasions that converted Central Asia and India's Buddhist northwest to Islam, ended the era of Chinese pilgrimage to the holy land of Buddhism. The greatly expanded overseas trade with western Asia was conducted by Arab merchants and seamen rather than by Chinese. It is from this age that we have the most comprehensive account of west Asia and Europe that was produced by the scholarship of old China, the book called *All the Foreigners*, by Chao Ju-kua. The title could also be translated *All the Barbarians*, but that would be misleading, unless "barbarian" is read in the old classical sense, meaning a people who speak an incomprehensible, alien tongue.

Chao was a distant relative of the imperial family and high official, who held the post of Inspector of Foreign Trade in Fukien province early in the twelfth century. There is no evidence that he traveled; but he was greatly interested in gathering information about the countries from which foreign merchants came. The south coast was now a thriving region, fully incorporated into the Chinese empire and nation. Arab merchants traded at ports such as Canton, Ch'uan-chou in Fukien, and Kanp'u, the port of the Southern Sung capital Hangchou. It is clear that Chao Ju-kua collected his information from these merchants, for the information is most complete for countries that were within the orbit of Arab trade or authority. Thus Persia and Iraq, Egypt and the east coast of Africa, are fully described, with notes on such details as the unsolved mystery of the source of the Nile. African animals unknown in China, such as the giraffe, are also mentioned. Chao's informant also told him about Madagascar, and described it as the center of the trade in Negro slaves.

The Mediterranean countries were well known to the Arabs who visited China. Sicily, which had been part of the Byzantine empire, is described as being inhabited by people whose "clothing, customs, and language are the same as those of Lu Mei" (that is, "Rum," which was the Arabic name for the Byzantine, or Roman, empire). Whether Chao's informant

was correct in saying that the Sicilians of the twelfth century still spoke Greek, or whether he meant Italian, the language of another part of "Rum," is not clear. Mount Etna is described, but here Chao Ju-kua either did not understand what he was told or his informant was ignorant of the real character of volcanic eruptions, for Chao states that once "every five years fire and stones break out and flow down as far as the sea, and then go back again. The trees and woods through which the fire passes are not burned, but the stones in its path are turned to ashes." There are no active volcanoes in China by which this misunderstanding could have been corrected.

Chao also mentions Spain and Morocco, but not in terms that suggest that he had talked with anyone who had been to those lands. He was told that to the north of Spain "if one travels by land for two hundred days, the days are only six hours long." If we exclude possible references in the Han account of the Roman empire, this is the first mention of northwest Europe in Chinese literature. It clearly indicates that Chao's information originated from a traveler who had wintered in some city of northern Europe. Another Chinese account, of a little later date, reports that in that region there is no night. This account must be based on the report of a seaman who had sailed to Scandinavia or the Baltic in summer, the only season safe for such a journey.

The arrival of a caravan in a small Chinese village is depicted in a set of Han dynasty funerary figures. The merchants proceed past the "ghost screen" (left), erected by residents as a defense against evil spirits, and enter the village, where a group of dancers (right) performs in the street.

233

One of the oldest surviving pieces of silk, dating from around A.D. 50, is this embroidered fragment found in the Syrian trading city of Palmyra.

Chinese exports were carried to the east as well as the west: the dish above, which is decorated with a lotus pattern, was discovered in the Philippines.

234

In the year A.D. 1080 the Chinese court received an embassy from the "king of Fu Lin, Mieh Li Yi Ling Kai Sa," the Byzantine Emperor Milissenus Nicephorus Caesar. The long name of the ambassador is also cited, but cannot easily be equated with any known Greek of that period. Whoever he was, his mission probably was to enlist the aid of China against the Turks, who were then pressing hard on the Eastern Roman empire. The Sung were not in a position to undertake any such war, and two other embassies from Constantinople, between 1081 and 1091, were equally fruitless. It is almost certain that Chinese embassies went in turn to Constantinople; Chao Ju-kua, who was in a position to have spoken to the officials sent on such missions, describes the court of Constantinople and the ritual at an imperial audience in detail that could only be learned from one who had been present at such an audience. This is an experience that no Arab merchant was likely to have had. Chao's observations on the Byzantine empire in general, and on Constantinople in particular, are accurate and precise.

It is known that many Arabs stayed in China for long periods. They had large colonies in the southern ports, which are mentioned, along with communities of Jews, by Arab writers. In some respects, especially in their apparent monopoly of long-distance overseas trade, the Arabs in the T'ang and Sung periods seem to have played in China the economic role that Europeans were later to assume. But the political consequences of that role were quite different. There is no evidence that the Arabs ever tried to gain special privileges or seize control of Chinese ports and cities. It was not only the lack of local bases that kept them from trying to do so; the Moslem rulers of such places as Malacca in Malaya could have provided the necessary bases, not too distant from south China. It must have been the strength of China rather than the relative weakness of the Moslem states of southeast Asia that deterred any thought of invasion or conquest.

There is no question that overseas trade with nearby Japan and Korea, and with the distant lands of western Asia, India, and

southeast Asia, played a much greater part in the Chinese economy in the Sung period than at any other time until the late seventeenth century, when trade with Europe began to flourish. Silk and porcelain were beginning to be produced in bulk in factories—although production was still wholly by hand. Sung celadon, made largely for export, has been found as far afield as Zanzibar. Some modern historians have conjectured that China was ripe for a great industrial revolution by the end of the Sung period and had fully reached the stage of mercantile economy. But no further development occurred.

The age of Mongol rule in China, beginning in 1280, is one of the periods of Chinese history best known to the West. Everyone has heard of Kublai Khan; the name of Marco Polo is a household word. The Venetian traveler, who accompanied his father and uncle on a voyage to China and then stayed there for seventeen years, was the earliest European to give a first-hand record of a visit to China. He is only the best known of many travelers who came to China during the rule of

the Mongol emperors. Their travels were made possible by the unity of the continental-sized empire that Genghis Khan, the founder of Mongol power, had built up by ruthless conquest. Under Genghis' successors, who completed his work, not only all China but Korea, Central Asia, India, Persia, much of Asia Minor, and most of Russia came under Mongol sway. It became possible to travel, under the law of the great Khan, from points near the eastern coast of the Mediterranean all the way across Asia to the coast of China. Never before, and never since, has this vast area been under the control of a single government. Papal envoys, hoping to convert the pagan Mongol world ruler to Christianity and so deal a fatal blow to the rival religion of Islam, also traveled to the Khan's court at Peking and wrote accounts of their journeys. Arabs came too, and men from every country of western Asia and eastern Europe. The Mongols employed many of them to administer their huge dominions; Marco Polo was by no means the only foreigner in Mongol service. As never before, China was open to

Tribute paid by foreigners to the T'ang emperors often took exotic forms, as this detail from a seventh-century handscroll illustrates. Envoys from southeast Asia are shown bearing elephant tusks, peacock feathers, caged birds, an ibex and a spotted mountain goat, and several oddly shaped pieces of petrified driftwood, which was used in landscaping Chinese gardens.

235

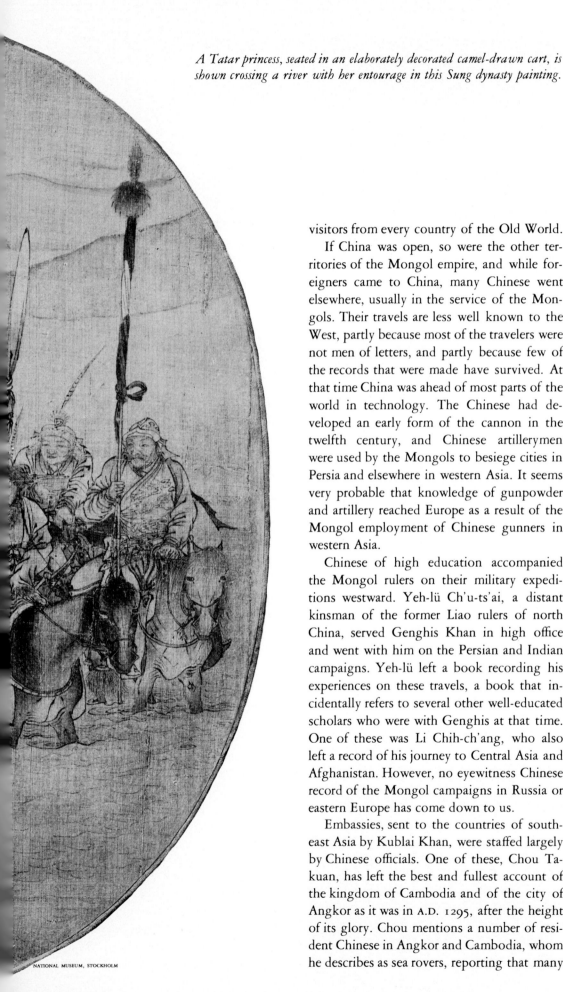

A Tatar princess, seated in an elaborately decorated camel-drawn cart, is shown crossing a river with her entourage in this Sung dynasty painting.

visitors from every country of the Old World.

If China was open, so were the other territories of the Mongol empire, and while foreigners came to China, many Chinese went elsewhere, usually in the service of the Mongols. Their travels are less well known to the West, partly because most of the travelers were not men of letters, and partly because few of the records that were made have survived. At that time China was ahead of most parts of the world in technology. The Chinese had developed an early form of the cannon in the twelfth century, and Chinese artillerymen were used by the Mongols to besiege cities in Persia and elsewhere in western Asia. It seems very probable that knowledge of gunpowder and artillery reached Europe as a result of the Mongol employment of Chinese gunners in western Asia.

Chinese of high education accompanied the Mongol rulers on their military expeditions westward. Yeh-lü Ch'u-ts'ai, a distant kinsman of the former Liao rulers of north China, served Genghis Khan in high office and went with him on the Persian and Indian campaigns. Yeh-lü left a book recording his experiences on these travels, a book that incidentally refers to several other well-educated scholars who were with Genghis at that time. One of these was Li Chih-ch'ang, who also left a record of his journey to Central Asia and Afghanistan. However, no eyewitness Chinese record of the Mongol campaigns in Russia or eastern Europe has come down to us.

Embassies, sent to the countries of southeast Asia by Kublai Khan, were staffed largely by Chinese officials. One of these, Chou Ta-kuan, has left the best and fullest account of the kingdom of Cambodia and of the city of Angkor as it was in A.D. 1295, after the height of its glory. Chou mentions a number of resident Chinese in Angkor and Cambodia, whom he describes as sea rovers, reporting that many

237

A fourteenth-century French work, The Book of Marvels, *provides among its wonders an illustrated account of Marco Polo's adventures in Cathay. Two illuminations from the book are shown here: at right, gold is being delivered to Kublai Khan's countinghouse in Hangchou; at far right, the Great Khan's soldiers are depicted conquering a walled city in Japan.*

of them took Cambodian wives and settled abroad permanently. This is one of the earliest and best-authenticated indications of Chinese settlement in southeast Asia. The fact that the immigrants had been sea rovers strongly suggests that they, like their successors, were from the southeast provinces of Fukien and Kuangtung.

The Mongol world-empire dissolved after the death of Kublai. The trade and unrestricted travel of the early Mongol period decreased. Central and western Asia were now in the hands of rival khans, who were often at war with each other. No universal ruler kept the roads safe and clear as Genghis Khan had. From this time onward the land route to the West declined in importance, replaced by the sea route, which had already become conspicuous long before the Portuguese found their way to the Indian Ocean. Even in Marco Polo's lifetime the sea route was an acceptable alternative. Marco came to China overland,

but he returned to Venice by sea, along the coasts of India and Persia, discharging his last duty to Kublai by escorting a Tatar princess to the court of the khan who ruled Persia.

The decline of the land route across Asia, and the rise of the sea route through the Indian Ocean to the Red Sea, were strikingly illustrated by the policy of the Ming dynasty (A.D. 1368–1644), which drove the alien Mongols from the throne. Unlike all the preceding powerful dynasties, the Ming did not occupy Sinkiang except for Hami, the oasis nearest China. On the other hand, early in the fifteenth century, when the empire was at peace, they engaged in a series of large overseas expeditions, unique in Chinese history and peculiar in their motivation and organization. These were enterprises conducted by the court, not by the civil service or other regular government organs. They were commanded by a court eunuch, an unlikely choice for an admiral, but one that proved most successful.

The expeditions were large, but not primarily military in purpose. They traded, but that was not their major objective. They explored lands thitherto unknown to the Chinese, partly out of curiosity and partly to satisfy the taste for rarities that the ladies of the court indulged. Perhaps the real motive was to "show the flag," to display to the small kingdoms of southeast Asia the power and glory of the new Ming dynasty and establish its prestige in lands that the Mongols had once threatened or invaded. But this motive hardly called for the fleets to cross the Indian Ocean to Africa, visit the Red Sea and the Persian Gulf, or penetrate into the southern islands of Indonesia, where no Mongol had ever been seen.

Chêng Ho, the admiral, was probably a man of rare genius and great enterprise. He had a free hand when he left China, and he conducted his fleet wherever he chose to go. He detached small squadrons or single ships to explore obscure islands and ports. It seems certain that he was inspired by that love of discovery and exploration that was to move so many Europeans in the following centuries to voyage to the ends of the earth. There were seven great expeditions altogether between 1405 and 1433. They carried a force of seventy thousand men, in specially constructed great ships, much larger than those subsequently built in China. The earliest voyages, more political in aim than the later ones, established Chinese suzerainty in the kingdoms of Malaya, Java, Sumatra, and in Ceylon. Kings who refused to acknowledge the Ming emperor were dethroned, and more subservient rulers installed. But such action was rarely called for. Recognition of the distant Ming emperor did no harm, and the lavish gifts distributed to compliant kings by the Chinese admiral smoothed the path. In Malacca, then the chief port of Malaya, the Chinese had very good relations with the sultan; the city became the principal overseas Chinese base. Before the rise of Singapore centuries later, Malacca was the strategic center in control of the narrow Strait of Malacca, which provides access to the Indian Ocean. The sultan and his successors made several visits to Peking to pay homage in person.

Subsequent voyages extended to Burma, the coasts of India, Ceylon, and the Philippines. In the Philippines, which did not have organized kingdoms or a literate culture, the Chinese for a time seem to have contemplated outright annexation. The southern islands of Indonesia were explored, it would seem, less by men of the main fleet than by venturesome

The first giraffe ever seen in China is pictured along with a turbaned attendant; it was sent to Emperor Yung Lo in 1414 as tribute from a foreign king.

sailors from individual ships. Timor, which lies closest to Australia, was certainly visited. This can be proved by recorded evidence and by a linguistic oddity. The Chinese call Timor "Ti Wen"; the second sound is written with a character that is pronounced "wen" in every dialect of China except that of Fu-chou, in which it is sounded as "mo." Now Chêng Ho raised his fleet and manned it at Fu-chou; the men of that city have not been very prominent in overseas settlement in subsequent centuries, but to them Timor remains "Ti Mo," as they named it early in the fifteenth century.

Later voyages sailed up the west coast of India into the Persian Gulf, and around the south coast of Arabia and Aden and into the Red Sea. The pearls of the Persian Gulf were probably the main attraction. As a result of the knowledge gained from earlier voyages, the last expedition sailed down the coast of east Africa, perhaps as far as Zanzibar. From that region the Chinese brought back, all the way to Peking, a live giraffe, which was presented to the Emperor Yung Lo and which lived for several years on the palace grounds. Yung Lo had its portrait painted, and the picture (shown at left) still survives. Flatterers told the emperor that the giraffe was a Chi Lin, a mythical animal said to appear only when a sage ruled the empire. Yung Lo was not deceived; an old and hard-bitten soldier who had played a large part in the wars that founded the dynasty, he replied, "I am no sage and that beast is no Chi Lin."

The great seaborne expeditions were financed by the court, out of revenues that were beyond the control of the state treasury. The Mongols had reserved a huge tract of land north of the Huai River in southern Shantung and northern Anhui provinces as a hunting park. It was an empty, desolate region. The original inhabitants had either fled or perished in the destructive Mongol invasion, and no one had been allowed to settle the land thereafter. This great and fertile area became imperial property under the Ming dynasty. Yung Lo decided he had no use for it and sold it off to new settlers, thus obtaining a large income independent of the government's ordinary revenues. These funds were used to sustain the naval expeditions. The Ming sea expeditions were abnormal in many ways; no doubt this explains why they were discontinued after Yung Lo's death and never resumed. The admiral Chêng Ho was also dead, but he was not forgotten. Today he is revered among the overseas Chinese as the semidivine hero of their ancestors and the founder of their communities.

The civil service had always opposed these expeditions, which had been sent out by the court and commanded by a eunuch. The civil service always disliked the power of the eunuchs and sought to diminish it. So when the emperor and Chêng Ho were dead and another expedition was proposed by the court, the civil service used its well-known ability to obstruct. The sailing papers were "lost"; every device was employed to delay and frustrate the expedition, until the young emperor who had succeeded to the throne wearied of the effort required for the project and gave up. Thus China abandoned a naval supremacy in the southern seas, which, had it been maintained and consolidated, could have excluded the Portuguese from the region and changed the course of history. Two of Chêng Ho's captains have left partially preserved accounts of their voyages and discoveries, and the dynastic history includes a rather short record of the expeditions; but until modern times the expeditions were largely forgotten in China.

In later centuries Ming rulers took little interest in the foreign lands that Chêng Ho had visited and explored. The rise of Japanese piracy and the subsequent intrusion into east-

ern waters of the Portuguese and the Dutch, who often attacked Chinese ships, discouraged travel and weakened Chinese contact with the lands overseas. A spirit of self-sufficiency, of stay-at-home complacency, began to dominate China, in sharp contrast to the inquiring attitude of the T'ang and Sung periods. When newcomers arrived from the West in the sixteenth century, the response of China to them was conservative and aloof. No effort was made to enter into contact with the home countries of the visitors, and their attempts to establish diplomatic relations with the court were repulsed. The last seaborne expedition of Chêng Ho sailed in 1433, sixty-five years before Vasco da Gama rounded the Cape of Good Hope. In 1514, less than a century after the Chinese had dominated the southern seas, a Portuguese traveler arrived at Canton; with its arrival began the long era of Western contact and intrusion into China that has ended only in our own time.

Western intrusion was so slight at first that the Chinese can be forgiven for paying very little attention to its implications. They were accustomed to the harmless Moslem traders from Malaya and Indonesia. They did not appreciate the fact that the home bases of the Portuguese, and of the Dutch and English who followed them, were very far away. That these foreigners were able to reach China at all pointed to a superior sailing technique and a resolute search for wealth and conquest. In the third century A.D. a seaborne embassy from Rome had been welcomed, and the Chinese considered sending an ambassador back with it; there was no reason why China in the sixteenth century would refuse to follow this precedent. Portuguese navigators could have been brought to court, treated well (even if as tribute bearers), and courteously entertained; they would have been glad to carry a Chinese envoy back to Lisbon, thereby enhancing their prestige among their own countrymen.

Such was not the policy of the later Ming, and still less was it the policy of their successors, the Manchus. Their reaction was to limit trade to one port, Canton, and hamper all other intercourse. Diplomatic relations were refused, and even embassies were unwelcome. Early missionaries did manage to take back to Rome one or two converts, but these were men without official standing, of no social prestige, and, for the most part, rather fearful of ever returning to China. The opportunity of discovering at first hand the real nature of the European nations and of their civilization was thrown away. The consequences of this ignorance were to be disastrous for China.

The Manchus went further than the Ming in obstructing both foreign traders and Chinese who wanted travel abroad. Resistance to the Manchu conquest of 1644–1659 had been strongest and most prolonged in the south. The Manchu dynasty felt that all southerners were disloyal, and that those who went abroad were refugees from political justice or rebels seeking foreign help. They therefore prohibited all travel and emigration. Those who left clandestinely were liable to the death penalty if they returned. Many Chinese did migrate to Java and to Malaya, but they were malcontents or the very poor, and most never attempted to return. Until Western pressures forced the Manchu government to raise this prohibition, very few Chinese could travel, and even fewer could do so in safety. Those who went abroad received no protection from their government and were treated as criminals.

In the nineteenth century, when China was growing weak and was already almost powerless at sea, the European nations that had established colonial dominions in Indonesia, Malaya, and Indochina wanted cheap laborers who would be more willing to work than the natives were. They found the Chinese very suitable, and by political pressure forced the Manchus to permit emigration. Great numbers of Chinese from the southern provinces profited by this relaxation to go to the Nanyang, or the southern sea countries, as they were collectively known. The vast majority were poor laborers or small merchants, who could not travel to distant countries for pleasure or instruction. They came to earn a living, to escape from an overcrowded countryside, or to evade political persecution. Many years were to pass before the prosperous sons and grandsons of these poor immigrants could afford to send their children to England, Holland, or other Western countries for higher education. These were the first Chinese to live in the West; they did not come directly from China, and many of them never went there in their lives.

It was not until the second half of the nineteenth century that China established its first diplomatic missions in Europe and the United States, and that the first Chinese students, men destined for official careers, were permitted to study abroad. As their numbers grew, their influence was to become immense; they were wholly inimical to the Manchu regime and later to the whole system of government and society. Most of them were of the scholar class, but whatever their social origin, they became revolutionaries abroad. The impact of the West on China has often been seen as resulting from the influence of Western traders and missionaries, backed by gunboats. But the ideas and policies of the returned students—those who had "drunk foreign ink"—proved to be a much more profound and enduring influence. They did not always bring back to China what their Western teachers would have liked them to learn; but they did bring back explosive new thoughts, which have remolded China through the fires of a long revolution.

10　The Later Empire

(1260 *to* 1912)

The Manchu Emperor K'ang Hsi ascended China's throne in 1662. During his long reign Outer Mongolia and Tibet were brought under Chinese rule.

The Mongol dynasty, which is known in China as the Yüan, is officially listed as coming to the throne in A.D. 1260, although it was not until 1279 that the rival Southern Sung dynasty was finally suppressed. In terms of effective authority over the greater part of China, the duration of the Yüan dynasty was brief. An old man of eighty would have seen the triumph of the Ming in 1368 and still remembered, as a young boy, the last years of the reign of Kublai Khan, who conquered south China for the Mongols. Two long lifetimes would have covered the whole period of Mongol rule. This helps to explain why Mongol rule made in the end so slight an impression on Chinese civilization, despite the fact that it involved the first conquest of all China by an alien people. After the fall of the Mongols in 1368, the Ming were able to restore the basic system of government and education because Chinese traditions had not faded out. The innovations made under Mongol rule never took deep root.

For a time it appeared as if the conquest would destroy Chinese culture and even the nation itself. The campaigns of Genghis Khan in 1205, 1209, and 1215, and those of his immediate successors, were ruthless in the extreme. Cities were annihilated, and tens of thousands of homeless refugees fled to the mountains, where they starved or survived as vast hordes of wandering mendicants. Great areas of land went out of cultivation. Much of this land was turned into hunting parks by the Mongol khans. At first they saw no value in the alien practice of agriculture, and even considered massacring the entire Chinese peasantry and turning the countryside back to grass. However, the Mongols were soon to find that in peacetime such ruthless methods were unsatisfactory. Wandering refugees could neither cultivate the soil to support themselves nor pay taxes to support the state.

Money may not have been very important in the economy of the Mongolian steppe, but for the administration of a vast, settled empire—even a devastated one—it was essential. It became necessary to impose some degree of order, to refrain from massacre, and to get the peasants back to the farms and let them earn enough to pay taxes.

Moreover, there were still other wars to wage and finance. Genghis was not only the conqueror of north China but also the invader of Central Asia. His immediate successors invaded Asia Minor, Persia, Russia, and even Hungary. Huge hordes (the word *horde* is Mongol for "army") swept across Asia; they had to be provisioned, armed, and kept under central command. All this cost great sums, which China could provide, for it was by far the richest country under Mongol rule.

Under the first Mongol rulers, including Kublai Khan himself, the Chinese governmental system was suppressed and the civil service examinations were discontinued. The civil service was recruited from a host of miscellaneous foreign adventurers, of whom Marco Polo is best known to the West; most were Arab, Persian, or Central Asian Moslems. Some of these men were able; many were corrupt. Few spoke or read Chinese, and hardly any of them made the effort to learn the language. In seventeen years of service under Kublai, Marco Polo certainly learned little Chinese. All these men did learn Mongolian, which was the official language of the empire, although it had only recently acquired a written form. Many Yüan dynasty edicts and inscriptions are written in a barbarous style that combines semicolloquial Chinese with transliterated Mongolian words and neologisms. Some edicts have survived, inscribed on huge stone monuments. From them one can imagine what might have happened to the Chinese language and culture had Mongol rule endured for many centuries; the old tongue would have been distorted into a new language, and the use of Chinese as a living medium of thought would have survived only among a few scholars. Such Yüan dynasty inscriptions are parallel to the "dog Latin" of the early Middle Ages in Europe.

In the later years of the dynasty, after Kublai's death, the Chinese civil service examinations were revived, although it would seem that they were used only for the appointment of a relatively small percentage of government officials. The reason for their revival must have lain in the difficulty the Mongol emperors had in recruiting officials from western Asia after that region no longer paid allegiance to Peking. The Mongol khans who ruled western Asia had turned Moslem to keep in touch with the vast majority of their subjects. Kublai and his successors in China remained Buddhist, adopting the Tibetan Lamaist form of Buddhism, which had been little known in China before the Mongol period.

By rejecting the Confucian system of government and education for many years and adopting a form of Buddhism quite foreign to China, the Yüan dynasty rulers ensured that they would remain aliens in the eyes of their Chinese subjects. This may have been a conscious choice; the Mongols were relatively few, and the Chinese, even after their population had been greatly reduced during the Mongol conquest, were still numerous. The Mongol rulers may not have been well versed in Chinese history, but they cannot have failed to note that earlier northern invaders —the Wei of the fifth and sixth centuries and the later Liao and Chin—had become assimilated to Chinese culture and had lost their native languages and customs. To the end the Mongols consciously resisted being swallowed up by their Chinese subjects. One of the ministers of the last Mongol emperor,

A contemporary portrait shows the Mongol conqueror Kublai Khan, who reunited northern and southern China.

fearing revolt with the evident rise of Chinese unrest, actually proposed the massacre of all Chinese bearing the commonest surnames—Chang, Wang, Liu, Li, Chao. This would have destroyed more than two thirds of the population.

In the reign of Kublai no such fears disturbed the Mongols. Kublai, who thanks to the work of Marco Polo is perhaps the best known to the West of all emperors of China, secured internal tranquillity for the Chinese empire and restored a measure of prosperity. It is evident from Marco's observations that these happier conditions were most conspicuous in the south, the former domain of the Southern Sung. The south had largely escaped the full fury of the original Mongol invasions. Quinsay (which is Hang-chou, the site of the former Sung capital) was described by Marco Polo as a more magnificent city than he could ever have conceived of—far larger, more populous, and richer than any in Europe, a center of refined art and skilled handicraft, of learning and administration, of trade and manufacture. Quinsay may then have been only a pale reflection of the city as it had been under the Sung dynasty, but it captivated the imagination of Marco, "Il Milione," the man who always spoke of "millions" in his tales of China.

Kublai expanded the confines of the Chinese empire by incorporating the present southwestern province of Yünnan, which had up to that time been an independent kingdom. He sought also to reduce Burma and Vietnam, but their unhealthy climate and jungle-covered terrain defeated his efforts. It was easy to defeat the armies of their kings in battle; but the pacification of the people who had taken refuge in the jungles was a task that the Mongol cavalry was not well fitted to undertake. Kublai withdrew his armies, content to exact tribute from these unrewarding lands and to

exert nominal suzerainty over them.

The Great Khan also launched two expeditions against Japan, each of which landed in the southwestern island of Kyushu. Fleets for the invasion were provided by his Korean tributaries and by the south China ports and provinces. It may be suspected that neither the Koreans nor the south Chinese undertook these duties with much enthusiasm; both had only recently suffered Mongol conquest. Through incompetence or indifference, the fleets were badly handled. Caught by summer typhoons, they were scattered with great loss of life. The Mongol troops that landed were defeated by the resolute defense of the Japanese feudal chivalry. Both expeditions were dismal failures for the Mongol emperor; and the "Divine Wind," the typhoon that scattered and destroyed the fleet of the invaders, has remained in Japan a symbol of the protection that the gods extended to their favored land.

The Mongols were essentially a land people; they had no understanding of what sea warfare and overseas expeditions involved. In spite of the failure of his invasions of Japan, Kublai also invaded Java, an easier prey because it was less united than Japan. Nevertheless, the expedition had only a limited and transitory success. The Mongol armies dethroned some kings and installed more subservient monarchs in their place. The tropical climate took a heavy toll of the Mongol soldiery, and it was found best to claim suzerainty, exact tribute, and depart—leaving the country to its own rulers.

After the conquest of China had been completed with the incorporation of Yünnan, there were further attempts to extend Mongol rule in eastern Asia, but they were all unsuccessful. The Mongols had reached the limit of their range. After the death of Kublai no further conquests were attempted, and before

many years had passed, his weak and short-lived successors were more concerned to defend what they held than to acquire new dominions. In the thirty-nine years between the death of Kublai and the accession of the last Mongol emperor in 1333, six short reigns, the longest only thirteen years, enfeebled the dynasty. The last Mongol ruler, Tohan Timur, reigned for thirty-five years over a disintegrating empire and ended his life as a fugitive. Mongol rule either had to rise or fall. No stability seemed possible without the stimulus of aggressive war; once that ceased, the loss of vitality and purpose became all too apparent, and decline was swift.

The contributions of the Mongol period to the Chinese civilization are not easily defined; the most obvious benefit was the reopening of communications between China and Europe, which stimulated exploration and discovery. But this exerted more influence on the European peoples than it did on the Chinese and was an unintentional side effect of Mongol rule. Chinese literary effort was diverted from the study of the classics to the fields of drama and fiction; this may have been a consequence of the abandonment of the examination system. Under the Mongols the style of government was more autocratic than had traditionally been the case in China and less under the influence of prestigious officials. Foreign officials, with no support in the country or interest in it either, could exercise very little restraint over the whims of the autocrat. Per-

By 1204 Genghis Khan, grandfather of Kublai, had united the Mongols under his rule. In the next twenty years his troops invaded Korea, Turkistan, and Persia, among other countries. A Persian miniature, above, portrays the white-bearded warrior seated in a garden beneath an umbrella.

247

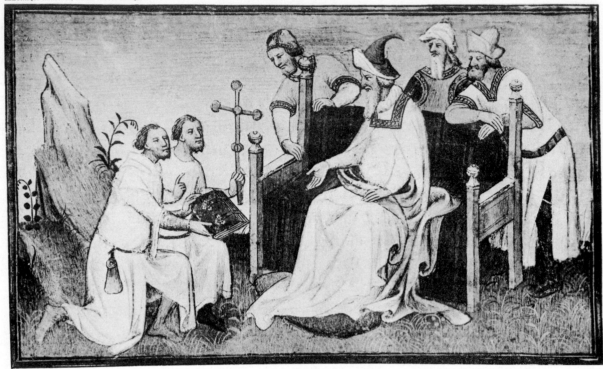

The thirteenth-century Venetian merchants Nicolo and Maffeo Polo were the first Europeans to travel in China. Their audience with Kublai Khan (seated) is the subject of this fourteenth-century French miniature, one of a series of views depicting events described in the diary of Nicolo Polo's son, Marco.

haps the major contribution of the Mongol rule was, then, an undesirable one: the growth in the absolute authority of the monarch and the weakening of those traditional checks that had been developed in the earlier empire to restrain and guide the power of the throne.

The revolt of the Chinese against Mongol rule, which culminated in 1368 with the establishment of the Ming dynasty, was not a straightforward uprising that gradually achieved victory. It began as an incoherent series of rebellions in different parts of the empire. Many of these rebellions were suppressed by the Mongol government; others coalesced to form larger movements. The rebels were not in alliance with each other, but fiercely competitive. In one sense the multiple uprisings were a national revolt against alien rule, but they were not co-ordinated in the manner of modern nationalist movements. Rather, they involved open, uninhibited strife among leaders, each of whom hoped to acquire the power to form a new dynasty. Since all the rebels were Chinese, the revolts assumed the nature of a national uprising.

The Mongol regime had become corrupt and incompetent; it had lost the Mandate of Heaven, which, according to many scholars,

it may never have enjoyed to begin with. The educated class expected the successful pretender to the throne to turn to them to restore Chinese methods of government; along with this restoration, their own influence would be restored. They were not to be disappointed. However, even the most firm believer among them in the Mandate of Heaven theory may have been somewhat surprised at the choice that Heaven made for deputy on earth.

Chu Yüan-chang, who is known by his posthumous dynastic title of Hung Wu, was a man of the most obscure origin, with no advantages other than his natural ability, which was certainly very great. His parents were poor peasants. Driven from their small farm by famine, they had sold the boy to a Buddhist monastery to save both his life and their own. After some years as a novice monk, Chu Yüan-chang ran away and became a bandit. In the confusion of the age, with revolts breaking out on all sides, it was a logical step for him to join one such revolt along with his band of outlaws. A doughty fighter, and as he was to prove, a military leader of great ability, he rose in the ranks of rebellion and emerged as one of the main contenders for the leadership of the national uprising. During this time his ac-

Two Mongol attempts to conquer Japan met with disaster. A detail from a thirteenth-century Japanese scroll depicts a rare event—a Mongol retreat.

tivity was directed as much, or more, against rivals in the southeastern provinces as it was against the Mongol government.

Chu was a man of the lower Yangtze region, the richest in China. As part of the old Southern Sung empire it had escaped the worst ravages of the Mongol conquest. This region was also among the most populous in China, and Chu recognized that its control would be the key to victory. Once he had eliminated his Chinese rivals there, he could deal at his leisure with distant pretenders and with the Mongols in the north; their fate was inevitable. By the year 1366 he had achieved the destruction of his Chinese rivals and taken their forces under his command. With the capture of Nanking in 1356, he acquired a city that had in former times been the capital of the southern dynasties. Here he proclaimed his new dynasty, choosing as title "Ming," which means "brilliant." In earlier times new dynasties had been named after the area over which the founder had maintained some military authority or feudal power. Han was originally the name of a kingdom, and T'ang that of a hereditary dukedom; Sung was the classical name of the part of Honan from which the founder of the Sung dynasty came. But Chu Yüan-chang was a peasant with no real claim to territorial titles. So he called his new regime by a name of good omen, thereby perhaps emphasizing its univeral claim. Nearly three hundred years later the Manchus were to follow this example; they called their dynasty Ch'ing, meaning "pure," instead of naming it after the kingdom they had formed in Manchuria before conquering China.

Chu's innovation may also reflect the changed social conditions of the new age. The great scholar families, which had continued in office generation by generation under the T'ang and Sung, lost their status and their influence under the Mongols. Many of them

had probably been almost wiped out in the conquest. In the Sung period, old names such as Ssŭ-ma, dating back to Han and earlier times, were still prominent in Shensi, the original home of the Ssŭ-ma clan. Famous double surnames of great antiquity, such as Ssŭ-ma and Ssŭ-tu, Shang-kuan and Ou-yang, were borne by many great men of the Sung dynasty. But after the Mongol period no more is heard of these ancient families except for some branches surviving in the far south, in Kuangtung, which in T'ang times had been a place of exile for disgraced officials, and in Sung times the last stronghold of Southern Sung power.

After the establishment of the new dynasty at Nanking, the conquest of the north and the expulsion of the Mongols from China were no longer the immediate concern of the emperor. He left these problems to his great general, Hsü Ta, and to his warlike second son, who later reigned as the Emperor Yung Lo. It is said that in the final advance that drove the unresisting Mongols from Peking, Hsü Ta commanded an army of a quarter of a million men. Even if the figure is exaggerated, it is evident that the new dynasty had huge resources at its disposal. It was, nevertheless, some years more before the Mongol armies in the mountainous southwestern provinces were overcome.

Yünnan was the last stronghold of the Mongols, who long remained there, cut off from their compatriots north of the Great Wall. When Yünnan was pacified, the emperor settled a large part of his now-superfluous army in the remote province. This gave Yünnan a predominantly Chinese character in spite of the many non-Chinese peoples that inhabited it. It was perhaps the last major example of an ancient practice—settling a victorious army on lands it conquered in order to disband it in safety and avoid the risk of dis-

The Forbidden City, Peking's imperial palace, was built by the Ming Emperor Yung Lo. A processional way leads over a canal and through a gatehouse (at rear) to the Hall of Supreme Harmony, the audience room.

Hung Wu, the commoner who became the first Ming emperor, was one of China's most able and autocratic rulers.

charging upon the home provinces a great host of ex-soldiers who were landless and unable to earn a peaceful livelihood.

The Emperor Hung Wu was probably almost illiterate all of his life. Yet he had the good sense to realize that it was essential for the stability of his new empire to enlist the support of the scholar gentry and to take steps toward restoring the T'ang and Sung system of government. The examinations, the civil service, and the educational system were all revived on the old models. The emperor won the support of the scholars, but he did not always treat them with respect, as had his T'ang and Sung predecessors. His rule was unchallenged absolutism, exercised with little restraint. An authoritarian, accustomed all his life to enforcing military discipline upon a rebel army, he brooked no opposition; he was wont to have ministers of high position flogged in his presence if they offended him. Fallen or disgraced ministers were not sent off to the country as district magistrates, but were likely to suffer decapitation. Such procedures would have been unthinkable in T'ang and Sung times.

The unbending character of the emperor, precedents set by the Mongols, and changed social conditions, all encouraged the growth of absolutism. The new ministers were fine scholars, but they lacked the social background of their Sung models, and the newly restored civil service did not have the cohesive power and solidarity that the civil service had shown in the past. "Rule like the T'ang and Sung" was the emperor's motto, inscribed on his tomb in Nanking, but the emperor did not really achieve this ideal; Ming rule was harsher than that of the T'ang and Sung.

After a long reign as sole master of the Chinese world, Chu Yüan-chang died in 1398. He had restored the empire and consolidated the dynasty's authority; no doubt he felt that he

had achieved the Mandate of Heaven and achieved it in a way unparalleled by his predecessors. He had done it alone. No family privilege, no hereditary power, no education, no wealth, and no high office had been his, yet he had built up an empire not only larger than that of the greatest native dynasties of the past but one far more populous and strongly united under a powerful centralized government. These may not be the goals of modern statesmanship, but they certainly corresponded to what was meant by obtaining the Mandate of Heaven.

There are advantages and disadvantages to longevity in an absolute monarch: long life may give stability to the realm, but it may also result in weakness if the throne passes to a child. Such was the misfortune of the Ming. The crown prince died before his father did, leaving a boy of fifteen as heir to the empire. This young prince had an uncle, the formidable prince of Yen, an old and experienced soldier, the conqueror of the Mongols and the viceroy of the north, and resident of the city now called Peking. The prince of Yen had pursued the Mongols across the Gobi desert into what is now Siberia, leading a Chinese army farther north than any had ever traveled before (or since). He was not disposed to accept a boy as his master. Before the old emperor had been a year in his tomb, the prince of Yen had found a pretext for revolt and was marching southward.

The government of the boy-emperor was weak and distracted. His soldiers were unwilling to oppose the heroic prince of Yen; many feared for their careers if they defied the likely winner. The young emperor's defense collapsed; Nanking was taken by storm and the palace set on fire. In the confusion the young emperor disappeared; his body could not be identified among the slain. The prince of Yen took the throne. He removed the capital to his

The imperial palace at Peking was largely reconstructed during Ming times. This elaborately ornamented Ming dynasty lion stands guard at a temple entrance outside the Forbidden City.

The flood control and irrigation programs initiated by the Manchu dynasty Emperor K'ang Hsi benefited China's peasantry as much as the emperor's patronage benefited China's scholars. The painting above, which depicts a royal progress made in 1689, shows a group of K'ang Hsi's subjects kneeling respectfully as the emperor passes.

own northern headquarters, which he named Peking (*Pei-ching*, the "Northern Capital"), leaving Nanking (the "Southern Capital") as a secondary center.

The new emperor, Yung Lo, as he is known to history, was not really certain that his nephew had died at Nanking. He searched for any evidence of his fate, but could never obtain convincing proof of either his death or his survival. Very many years later, when Yung Lo was long dead and his great-grandson was on the throne, an aged Buddhist monk came to Peking and revealed to one of the oldest of the palace eunuchs that he was the long-lost emperor. The old eunuch recognized him. The embarrassing situation was resolved by permitting the aged ex-emperor to live out the last months of his long life in a monastery in the Western Hills near Peking. Officially, he had died long before at Nanking.

Yung Lo was not troubled by other competitors and reigned in Peking until 1424 with great magnificence. It was during his reign

that the maritime expeditions were sent out to the southern oceans and across to Africa. It was he who built the city of Peking as it now stands within the old walls. It is recorded that the emperor gave his contractors ten years to build the palace enclosure, the Forbidden City. They did the job in five, employing a million men. When Yung Lo died, the Ming dynasty, dating from the conquest of the north and the expulsion of the Mongols from Peking, had already survived for fifty-six years. The dynasty was to endure for more than two hundred years after Yung Lo's death.

The Emperor Yung Lo had named Peking the capital in part because it was his own long-established base, and in part because he believed that unless the government was seated close to the Mongol frontier, it would lose control over the conquered Mongol tribes and perhaps overlook the vital task of frontier defense. The emperor believed that the court, by residing at so northern a city as Peking, within forty miles of the Great Wall,

254

would be constantly alert to the growth of dangers from the steppe. On the other hand, the court was exposed to the danger of sudden raids. And, it can be argued, the threat from the north, emphasized by the transfer of the capital, preoccupied the later emperors to the point that they ignored the needs of other parts of China.

The reasons why the present regime has restored Peking as the capital are also geographical and are, therefore, related to those that had induced Yung Lo to establish his court in the city. Peking still commands the communications between Manchuria and the north China plain, and also the passes that lead into China through the mountains from Inner Mongolia. In Ming times the lands beyond the passes were in hostile hands or were frontier districts exposed to enemy attack. In modern times these same regions are great centers of industry and mineral resources, and are among the most industrially developed parts of China. Peking commands the communi-

cations between the regions of heavy industry and the predominantly agricultural provinces south of the Great Wall. A government that controls Manchuria and Inner Mongolia finds Peking a vital center of communications.

For some years, throughout the reign of Yung Lo and his immediate successors, there was no apparent risk in locating the capital at Peking. Mongol power was crushed, and the Mongol tribes were fragmented and, nominally at least, under Chinese suzerainty. The Ming had made southern Manchuria, as far north as modern Mukden, a province and had incorporated it into their empire. The still-weak Manchu tribes had no unity and were under Ming sovereignty. The defeat of the Mongols had set the seal on a long, slow process of change in the balance of power between China and the nomadic peoples of the Mongolian steppe. It was partly a matter of population. The Chinese empire numbered at least one hundred million people. The Mongolian population, limited by the barren

255

This portrait of Emperor Yung Chêng wearing European dress was probably painted by Giuseppe Castiglione, a Jesuit whose artistic ability made him popular with the Chinese court.

nature and the pastoral economy of its country, did not exceed ten millions—the number of inhabitants that live in Mongolia today.

Ever since the end of the T'ang dynasty, danger had begun to threaten from the northeast region, Manchuria. This was a fertile country able to sustain a larger population than Mongolia. Being suitable for agriculture, Manchuria was more easily influenced by the neighboring civilization of China and more amenable to central organization. The Khitan and the Chin Tatars had profited from these circumstances in early Sung times to grow strong enough to menace China. Indeed, Mongol power was founded on Genghis Khan's conquest of the Chin and of Manchuria. Under Ming suzerainty, the Manchu tribes learned to govern themselves in the Chinese manner and to form a coherent and stable monarchy. Like the Khitans centuries earlier, they developed a formidable military power hostile to the Chinese.

The Ming suffered from the chance misfortune of a rapid succession of short reigns. Yung Lo's heir died within ten months of his succession; his son, Yung Lo's grandson, reigned only ten years. And so, a few years after the death of the formidable Yung Lo, the throne was occupied by his great-grandson, a boy of eight, the Emperor Cheng T'ung. The child's mother ruled the empire as regent, and the result was the rise to influence of palace eunuchs once again. In 1443 Cheng T'ung came of age and took over the government. He had been born and bred in the palace, and from his earliest childhood he had received the deference and indulgence that eunuch servitors showed to the titular sovereign. He put his entire trust in these flattering attendants and in particular singled out one, Wang Chên, for the highest mark of favor.

In 1449, when the young emperor had been in charge of the government for seven years,

Wang Chên persuaded him to leave Peking on an expedition to punish a rebel Mongol chief who was raiding the frontier. This was not a serious matter; any competent general could quite easily have dealt with it. Wang Chên's real purpose was to get the emperor to visit his native place, the district of Huai Lai, just beyond the Wall. The prestige of an imperial visit would establish his family's influence in the region. The emperor not only agreed, but with reckless folly made Wang Chên, a man with no military experience, commander in chief of the army.

The veteran generals felt insulted; they gave the new commander in chief little help, and he made fatal errors. Having bungled the campaign, he found it necessary to withdraw; but he insisted on postponing his retreat in order to bring the emperor to his native place. This resulted in a situation whereby the army was caught by the Mongols, easily surrounded, and deprived of food and water. The Mongols scored a complete victory, slaying Wang Chên and many of the best officers in the Chinese army, and capturing the emperor himself.

It was a chance disaster, not a catastrophe. Reinforcements arrived to safeguard the capital, and the emperor's younger brother was enthroned in his stead. The Mongol Khan found his prisoner an embarrassment and a politically useless hostage. Cheng T'ung had an engaging personality, and he easily won friends and supporters. When his brother, who reigned as Ching T'ai for eight years, became sick, the ministers at court obtained Cheng T'ung's release and restored him to the throne, even before his brother was dead. He reigned another seven years under a new reign title, T'ien Shun, "conforming to (the will of) Heaven," which may, or may not, have been an appropriate description of his career.

The period from the late fifteenth century to the first half of the sixteenth century was a time of peace and prosperity, marked by great artistic achievements. The reign titles of the emperors whose lives covered these years—Ch'eng Hua, Hung Chih, Cheng Te, and Chia Ching—are very well known, not because these emperors were great administrators or warriors, but because these titles are inscribed on the Ming porcelain produced at the imperial factories during their reigns. This was also the age in which a new literary form, the novel, rose to prominence. The dramatic events of the foundation and of the fall of the Ming dynasty are separated by more than two hundred fifty years. This was a long era in which imperial authority was, for the most part, respected and effective, in which great cultural development continued, and in which the prosperity and population of the empire increased. The Ming period was not, as it is often represented, a time of cultural stagnation, the beginning of the decline of the Chinese civilization, although in the later Ming period China did begin to be outstripped by Europe in technological development. The European Renaissance is contemporary with the middle Ming period; the dawn of the scientific age in the mid-seventeenth century is contemporary with the last years of the dynasty. But the charge can be laid that although the Ming undoubtedly restored, embellished, and developed the Chinese cultural tradition, they did not change it. Neither greed nor fear stimulated the ruling class to question the age-old assumptions and authority of their classical education.

The long reign of Wan Li (1573–1620) was the last long period of stability the Ming dynasty knew. For more than a century the corruption of the government had increased steadily. Eunuch influence reappeared in the early sixteenth century and was never again eliminated. The eunuchs took bribes, sold offices, and blackmailed officeholders into paying large sums to avoid dismissal. One chief eunuch early in the sixteenth century accumulated a fortune of 251,583,600 ounces of silver as well as vast quantities of precious gems, gold, and property before he was dismissed for corruption. The empire must have been rich indeed to sustain peculation on this scale.

All this misgovernment and waste was contemporaneous with high artistic achievement, especially in the making of porcelain. When the tomb of the Emperor Wan Li was opened some ten years ago, it was found to contain an immense treasure, not only in silver and gold ingots, but in every type of porcelain produced in Wan Li's reign, which was famous for the quality of its porcelain. There were also rare and delicate works of jewelry and gold. All this treasure is now displayed in the museum at Peking. It must be assumed that the still-unopened tombs of Wan Li's predecessors contain treasures of art and bullion even more extensive and impressive. The Ming government not only allowed eunuchs to extort immense amounts of money, but buried vast revenues in the tomb of each monarch.

The price paid for these extravagances was increasing weakness and growing disorder in the provinces. Around the year 1592 a costly and largely unsuccessful war in Korea with Japan drained the resources of the empire. The Japanese finally withdrew from an enterprise whose scope and magnitude they had badly misjudged. China was left as suzerain of Korea, but control of Korea was an empty honor. China had wasted great resources, and the war had enabled the Manchu tribes, who were potentially much more dangerous than the Japanese, to grow strong and prepare for revolt. Nonetheless, it is doubtful whether the Manchus alone would have been strong enough to conquer China. Their numbers were very small compared to the vast population of the empire, and the Ming professional

Chinese fascination with Western culture is evident in another portrait attributed to Castiglione; it depicts Ch'ien Lung's armor-clad favorite, known as the "Fragrant Concubine."

257

army was well led and equipped. But the outbreak of rebellion within the empire, and the utter mismanagement of its suppression, opened the road to the Manchus.

As a result of eunuch corruption and of the incompetence of the monarchs who succeeded Wan Li—men who were ignorant of what was going on, largely because the eunuchs concealed the truth—the rebellion was permitted to gain a head start. The leader of the rebellion in northwest China was Li Tzǔ-ch'êng. In 1640 he moved east and conquered the great province of Honan, lying athwart the communications route between Peking and the Yangtze valley. Attempts to counter him were badly directed. In 1644 Li suddenly moved north and swept down on Peking from the Shansi mountains. The defense of the capital had been committed to eunuchs; this was a gross folly. The eunuchs fled, and the last Ming emperor, abandoned and alone, hanged himself from a tree on the Mei Shan, or Coal Hill, within the palace grounds. Li Tzǔ-ch'êng entered the city and proclaimed himself "emperor" of the new dynasty of Shun.

The army of the frontier was stationed at Shan-hai Kuan, a gate of the Great Wall at the point where the Wall reaches the seacoast.

The army was commanded by an able general, Wu San-kuei. Had Wu accepted the new dynasty, it would have been secure, and the Manchus could have done little to destroy it. But because of a quarrel over one of his concubines, whom Li Tzǔ-ch'êng had found in Peking and had taken into his own harem, Wu San-kuei was alienated. Perhaps he also thought himself a more fitting successor to the Ming emperor. He broke off negotiations with the rebel leader and, instead, concluded an agreement with the Manchus. According to this agreement, Wu was entrusted with the task of driving out the rebels and crushing

them; he accepted the Manchu boy-king as emperor and permitted the Manchu armies to enter China unopposed. Li Tzǔ-ch'êng was defeated and driven west; there he was relentlessly pursued and finally destroyed. The Manchus, uncontested, occupied north China and set up their rule in Peking.

No other dynasty had come to power in this unusual way, and the consequences of the Manchus' peaceful occupation of the north, and the long hard struggle they encountered in conquering the south, marked their dynasty until its end in 1912. While Manchu armies eliminated Ming pretenders from the

During Emperor Ch'ien Lung's sixty-year-long reign, expeditionary forces were sent to quell disturbances in Yünnan, subdue Vietnamese and Burmese rebels, and conquer Nepal and the island of Taiwan. Shown above is a war fleet sent out by Ch'ien Lung.

259

Court eunuchs, princes, and numerous other attendants trail behind Emperor Ch'ien Lung's closed palanquin (center right) in this detail from an eighteenth-century French engraving. As the royal procession passes in total silence through Peking's streets, Ch'ien Lung's mother, the empress dowager, kneels on the ground beside her sedan chair (top right). The jerrybuilt booths seen at rear were erected to hide the squalor of Peking's streets.

Yangtze region, Wu San-kuei and two other Chinese collaborators were left in charge of the conquest and pacification of the southeastern and southwestern provinces. The rule of the Manchu emperor in south China was nominal; administration remained in the hands of the three Chinese princes of the south. For the first eighteen years of Manchu rule it seemed possible that the regime would not endure. When the young Manchu Emperor Shun Chih came of age, he proved to be a retiring, contemplative man, with no taste or ability for government. There is a strong tradition that he finally fled, disguised as a monk, to a temple in the Western Hills, where he ended his life as a hermit. He died in 1662 and was succeeded by his son, a boy of sixteen, who reigned for sixty-one years as the great Emperor K'ang Hsi.

K'ang Hsi assumed authority from the first; there was no regency. In a few years the young monarch suppressed the southeastern Chinese princes. Finally came the inevitable

clash with his greatest potential rival, Wu San-kuei, who was established in the far southwest, in Yünnan province, from which he had driven the last Ming pretender into exile in Burma. Although Wu San-kuei was now an old man, he was still formidable. His campaign was in progress and far from failing when he suddenly died. His death saved the Manchu dynasty. The sons of Wu San-kuei were incompetent, and they quarreled among themselves. K'ang Hsi was soon able to eliminate them and seize all of mainland China. He was still defied for some years by one Ming general and his son, who had established their own regime on the island of Taiwan. This general, Chêng Ch'êng-kung, known as Koxinga (the Portuguese interpretation of his imperial name, Kuo-hsing-yeh), ruled the island till his death and was succeeded by his son. When the turn came for Chêng Ch'êng-kung's grandsons to succeed, their quarrels opened the door to Manchu conquest of Taiwan. The similarity to the contemporary his tory of mainland China and Taiwan has not escaped the notice of modern Chinese.

In terms of political reality, the Manchu, or Ch'ing, dynasty's rule in China was established and consolidated by K'ang Hsi in a long reign that extended over the first two decades of the eighteenth century. The emperor's character and achievements made a deep impression on the Jesuit missionaries, who were the first Europeans to reside in Peking. They were full of praise for the firm government of the new dynasty, the discipline of its Manchu armies, and the vast extent of its territories. After his pacification of China, K'ang Hsi went on to bring Inner Mongolia under Chinese suzerainty and to restore Chinese rule in Sinkiang (the rule had lapsed since the end of the T'ang dynasty). The Chinese empire was expanded to dimensions never before attained (if one excludes the heterogeneous domain of the Mongol rulers). Later Tibet was brought under Chinese control, and the reduction of Outer Mongolia was completed, eliminating finally the nomad threat that had hung over the northern borders of China since the dawn of history. Korea, Annam, Burma, Thailand, and Nepal were made to acknowledge the suzerainty of the Ch'ing emperor.

Under the Manchus, Chinese imperialism was more extensive, sustained, and successful than it had been under any other dynasty since the Han. Manchu military dominance lasted for a full century and a half, until the death of the Emperor Ch'ien Lung in 1799. Ch'ien Lung had reigned for sixty years; he had abdicated in order to avoid reigning longer than his august grandfather. It was during the last years of Ch'ien Lung's reign that Nepal was conquered by an expedition that crossed the Himalayas, a feat that was unprecedented, very costly, and certainly not worth the effort.

Within the Manchu empire, which was held under firm control, the government was conducted on the lines of the Ming regime; indeed, the Manchu dynasty hardly changed any Ming institutions. The civil service continued to provide the ruling elite, although Manchus were admitted and a certain proportion of places was reserved for them. The Manchu people were not permitted to engage in commerce or farming; they could serve only in the army and the civil service, receiving a regular "tribute allowance" of free grain. They were enlisted in a military organization called the Eight Banners; and Manchu garrisons were established in separate walled enclosures within the great cities of China. Intermarriage with Chinese was forbidden.

With these measures the Manchus imposed a military-feudal system, entirely under the control of the emperor, upon the old Ming civil service. There was some friction, but the system worked well enough for several generations. It worked, that is to say, so long as the Manchu Bannermen remained active soldiers, on frequent campaigns in the Mongolian steppe or other border regions. Such service kept them alert and virile. But with the all-too-successful reign of Ch'ien Lung, this active service came to an end for lack of enemies to conquer, and the Bannermen were left to lounge in their garrison cities, living off tribute rice and forbidden to work. They were, for the most part, unequipped with the scholarship necessary to enter the civil service, despite the fact that entrance standards were less strict for them than for the Chinese. Inevitably they became useless drones.

It was the fate of the Manchu dynasty to be successful only in the early period; later rulers were unable to sustain the high level of ability set by the three successive early rulers, K'ang Hsi, Yung Chêng, and Ch'ien Lung, whose reigns cover the second half of the seventeenth century and the entire span of the eighteenth.

During this long period, except toward the very end of Ch'ien Lung's reign, China was internally at peace. There were no serious rebellions. The external danger to the northern provinces had been ended by the Manchu conquests. The Great Wall was allowed to fall into disrepair. The population greatly increased, probably doubling or trebling during this period; but the area of agricultural land did not expand commensurately. The Manchu conquests were made in steppe countries, which were useless to Chinese farmers. Manchuria, which could have been settled by the growing Chinese population, was the homeland of the dynasty, and Chinese were forbidden to settle there, lest the native stock be swamped by immigration (as it was to be in the nineteenth century). But all this—and its attendant prosperity—was marred by overriding failures: there was no governmental reform and there were no changes in the economy.

The Manchu emperors were very conscious of their "barbarian" origin. While they were in one way proud of their race and of its achievements, they knew that they counted for nothing in the eyes of their Chinese subjects unless they proved themselves to be good Chinese classical scholars, faithful disciples of Confucian philosophy, careful imitators of Chinese systems of government, and conservative guardians of the old traditions of Chinese culture. They had to write philosophic essays modeled on those of the Sung scholars, paint like the Ming artists, write poetry in the T'ang manner, govern in accordance with the precepts of the remote past, or, at least, they had to pay lip-service to these ideals. The Manchu emperors set about these tasks with devotion and success. K'ang Hsi was a good scholar; Yung Chêng, a clever and skillful ruler; Ch'ien Lung, among many other accomplishments, an excellent poet and a discriminating student of history. They worked hard and annotated and read an enormous number of memorials and state papers that survive to attest to their energy. But they distrusted every form of innovation, fearing that any change would be attributed to their "barbarian" tastes.

The Ch'ing emperors were dazzled by the splendor of their own achievements and inheritance. So long as they were accepted by the Chinese educated class, the views and ideas of barbarians were of no significance. As they patronized conservative opinions and disregarded all suggestions for change, they received very few foreign ideas. Their government was probably more absolutist than that of the Ming, far removed from the tempered autocracy of T'ang and Sung. The great ability of K'ang Hsi, Yung Chêng, and Ch'ien Lung exalted the monarch far above his advisers, but no successor was able to sustain this position or emulate these rulers. A government designed by and for emperors of very unusual ability was quite unsuitable for more ordinary mortals, who blundered on, sticking to precedents set by the great early rulers and blind to the fact that their policies were outdated and had thus become dangerous.

The death of Ch'ien Lung at the very end of the eighteenth century was a landmark in Chinese history. Up to that time, in spite of increasing corruption that was concealed from the aging emperor, the old system stood apparently intact—magnificent and all-powerful. But foreign observers, such as the shrewd British ambassador Lord Macartney, could see and record the presence of elements that were undermining the whole fabric of state. Lord Macartney compared the empire to a great ship, which once well found and seaworthy, had grown too old, with its timbers rotting, so that it could never withstand a storm and could not be rebuilt on the same keel. He proved to be a far-sighted prophet.

Life in the City

In the fourth century B.C. the Chinese philosopher Mencius proposed that all China's farmland be divided into immutable eight-family units. His scheme, which was adopted by later generations, called for the sectioning off of arable acreage into squares of nine equal units. Eight of these units were tilled by peasant families; the ninth was worked collectively by the eight families to provide the government with taxes. Generally, the families grew too large to support themselves on their allotted acreage, and the younger members were forced to leave the land and move to the cities. As a result, China's already crowded urban centers overflowed their perimeters. By the seventh century A.D. the T'ang capital of Ch'ang-an, for example, boasted a population of nearly two million inhabitants, and its walls enclosed an area of thirty square miles.

By the time of the Mongol dynasty, China's cities were transformed into "lively, mercantile, pleasure-seeking" metropolises. An increasingly active class of entrepreneurs ran factories, shops, and pushcart businesses. Prosperity attracted to the towns peddlers and charlatans, professional storytellers and singing girls. Open-air bazaars sold caged crickets, fishing tackle, beauty products, such as eyebrow black, and, according to Marco Polo, "every kind of vegetables and fruits."

The congestion and commercial bustle of such a city is the subject of the scroll entitled *Life along the River on the Eve of the Ch'ing Ming Festival*, sections of which appear on the following pages. The scroll, a twelfth-century masterpiece by Chang Tse-tuan, depicts the life along a river or canal in Pien-ching (modern K'ai-feng), the capital of the Northern Sung empire. The following pages reveal the scroll in the Occidental fashion, from left to right. Readers who wish to examine the scroll in the proper Oriental manner should turn first to page 279 and then follow the pages backward in order to inspect the painting from right to left.

In the painting on the opposite page, by the Southern Sung artist Li Sung, a buxom woman and her brood examine the varied wares of a knick-knack peddler who carries, according to the artist's description, "five hundred articles." 265

In the crowded streets and open-air shops of the Northern Sung capital, citizens assemble to gossip and transact their business. At left, a scholar, wearing a wide-brimmed hat and attended by three grooms, rides past the residence of a wealthy patent medicine dealer; beside the medicine shop, water-carriers load their buckets at a well. At far right, a crowd listens to a storyteller.

As a caravan of Bactrian camels passes beneath one of Pien-ching's formidable main gates (at right), wealthy inhabitants of the city, in sedan chairs and on horseback, arrive at a cheng-tien, or "wineshop," which is draped with hangings (upper left); there the city's elite socialize on the upper two floors. At right center, beside the gate, peasants chat outside a letter writer's stall.

Tranquillity pervades this stretch of street: sedan bearers rest and talk under the willows at far left, and off-duty soldiers nap outside the doorway of their quarters (top center). The small restaurants and wineshops on either side of the street are all but deserted. A wheelwright labors with his assistant at far right; across the street a bearded fortuneteller entertains a crowd.

Heavy-bottomed houseboats are moored along the banks of the Pien canal, as produce-filled barges are rowed and pulled alongside them. The waterway was the city's main supply route for food and other merchandise. Two seated figures can be seen conversing on the roof of one of the boats at left. At lower right, guests of a canalside inn lounge in a second-story room.

The canal's strong current has turned askew the barge at right center, and dozens of passers-by line the arching Rainbow Bridge to shout encouragement to the bargemen. Small stalls offering dry goods, medicines, and comestibles have been set up along the bridge to tempt pedestrians bound for the spring festival. In the restaurants at lower right, drink is dispensed to travelers.

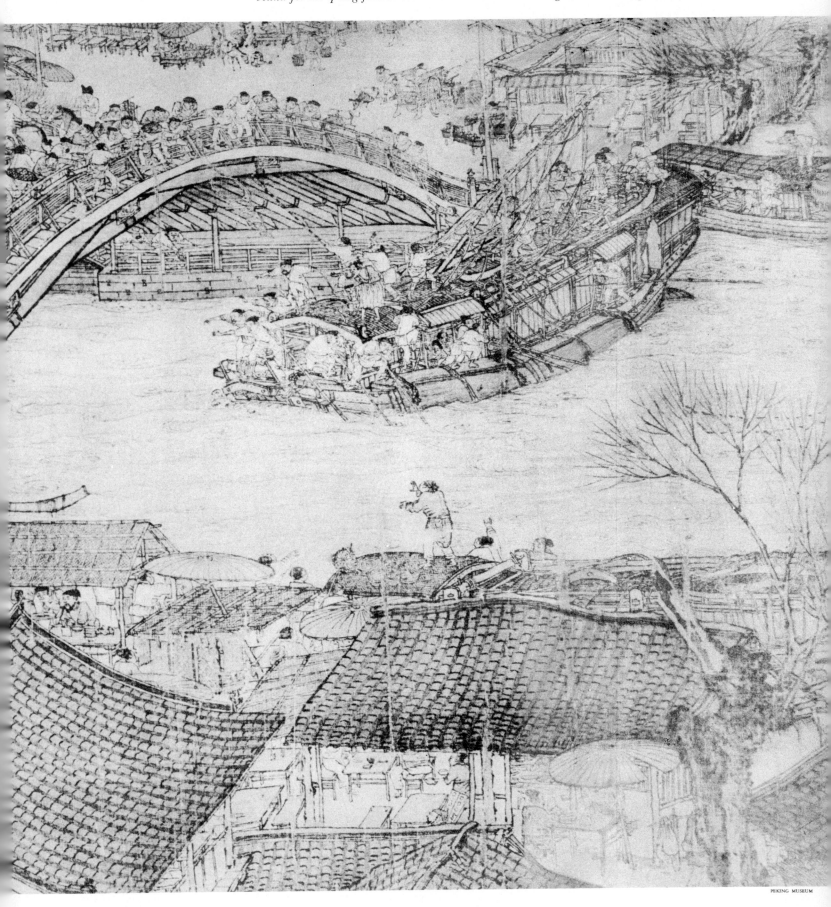

As a group of peasants at lower right makes its way into the countryside, shopkeepers on the outskirts of the Sung capital prepare for the day's customers. The rice paddies at top stand empty, as does the small raised pavilion at upper left. At left center, workers unload sacks of grain from a barge while an overseer (who is sitting in comfort on one of the sacks) gives directions.

11 The Scholar's World

The scholar Fu Shêng (above), who spent the greater part of his life teaching the Confucian classics, hid a precious text attributed to Confucius during the book burning of 213 B.C. Years later, when literature was restored to favor, ninety-year-old Fu Shêng revealed his long-hidden manuscript.

The word *shih*, which came to mean a scholar, a literate member of the upper class, originally meant a warrior of the feudal aristocracy. (The Japanese borrowed the word and long continued to use it to mean "warrior.") The word's later definition is almost contrary to its earlier meaning, for in China a clear distinction came to be drawn between men of the sword and men of the pen. Yet it is not hard to see how the evolution of meaning occurred. The first feudal nobles were scholars as well as soldiers. The philosophers of the Chou period, Confucius, Mencius, Mo Tzŭ, and others, were all members of the aristocratic class. There was no separate role for scholars as such; they were members of the governing, landowning elite, and served as warriors and priests and civil administrators in the developing kingdoms.

The revolution that overthrew the feudal system and instituted the unified imperial state eliminated the old aristocracy as a class. Its place was taken by the literate landowners, who became squires rather than feudal lords of their domains. This new class was the mainstay of the new empire, providing civil and military officials, and teachers and scholars.

The reconstruction of early literature after the Ch'in dynasty burning of the books assured high prestige to those members of the new elite with scholarly tastes. At the same time the adoption of Confucianism as the orthodox philosophy and source of all education tended to make members of the governing class more scholarly.

The fact that men of the ruling class were scholars as well as soldiers goes far to explain why in the disturbed times that prevailed, with the fall of the early empire and the subsequent barbarian invasions, there was no Dark Age. Although the power went to soldiers, these soldiers were not barbarian mercenaries, nor, for the most part, illiterate adventurers. They were members of the landowning literate class, who were now forced to take to arms to defend their property and privileges, which a failing court and disorganized civil service could no longer protect. The result was a narrowing of the bounds of the scholar class, but not a deterioration in its quality.

In the period of division, from the late third century A.D. to the end of the sixth century, the scholar gentry who had no close connections with great families had relatively small chances of careers and success; those who had good connections could and did rise high in the government. The old forms of the civil service persisted, even though the civil service was now controlled by the military aristocrats and their clients. Men of learning were still sought out and employed, works of literature were produced, and poetry, in particular, flourished. It cannot be said that the scholarly members of the ruling class had superior status—this was reserved for men who wielded military authority—but they were respected and revered.

The growth of Buddhism also provided men of speculative or religious temperament a new avenue for the development of the taste for learning. It might be imagined, comparing China to contemporary Europe, that the new interest in Buddhism would gradually draw scholars away from military and civil service and bring about a sharp division between literate priest and illiterate warrior. (Such a division occurred in Europe in the early Middle Ages.) But this did not happen in China. Confucian philosophy and ethics never yielded place to Buddhism; Confucianism became rather hidebound, with few new inspirations and few great teachers, but it remained firmly in control of education and the bureaucracy. The secular-minded scholars maintained a steady opposition to any excessive Buddhist authority, although they themselves often retired to Buddhist monasteries after a life-

time of civil service. Their opposition was manifested by their ouster of the fervently Buddhist Liang dynasty Emperor Wu Ti, after his long reign in the sixth century. Not being a conquering, militant creed, Buddhism did not give the military aristocracy a direct part in religious life.

The role of the scholar in the period of division was less important than it had been under the Han empire, but it was not insignificant. The scholars had lost political power rather than moral authority or intellectual quality. The reunification of the empire under the Sui and then the T'ang dynasties was to confer a new and much more prominent role upon the scholar class—a role that was to be maintained almost continuously until modern times. This development resulted from the fact that the new T'ang dynasty was exposed to the ambitions of the great military aristocratic families that had dominated the central government for more than three centuries. The T'ang imperial family itself came from this class; the T'ang had experienced the ambition and seized the prize, which they were determined to hold. The logic of their situation required the elimination or enfeeblement of the military aristocracy, who were China's officers and civil administrators. Once the empire was united and at peace, soldiers could be sent to guard the frontiers, a politically neutral occupation that removed them from court. But administrators still had to be found and employed, and if these were clients of the great aristocrats, the power of the aristocrats remained dangerous.

The solution—arrived at by the founder of the T'ang dynasty, the Emperor T'ai Tsung, and developed by his heirs—was to create a class of civil servants, to be recruited by public examination from among the literate gentry. The examinations were difficult; and the men of ability who passed them were not usually

A detail of a copy of a tenth-century scroll shows a group of scholars seated in a study, listening to one of their number read from a book. The scholar in the foreground is sitting in an armchair made from gnarled tree roots.

the favored clients of the aristocratic military lords. Thus the power of the aristocracy was broken, and a new world was opened to the scholars.

It became the aim of education to prepare young men to pass the civil service examinations. Passing the examinations was the road to power and wealth. Gradually the number of scholars in the civil service increased. The shift in power from military aristocrats to civil officials was steady. Even when political life appeared to return power to the military, as happened at the end of the T'ang period, the return proved to be ephemeral, being merely the temporary seizure of authority by professional soldiers in an age of confusion. Under the Sung dynasty, when unity and peace were restored, the scholar-official came into his own; indeed, scholar-officials were more powerful than ever before. Centuries later, Europeans were to call members of this class Mandarins (the word, derived from Malay by way of Portuguese, originally meant "counselor"). The essential characteristic of the Mandarin was not family descent, but learning.

The new scholar gentry assumed, or chose to assume, that they had always been in the

seat of authority. In their histories they treated the military aristocrats who had preceded them in power as if they had been officials like themselves, men who had attained authority by passing an examination and not by possessing family connections. They simply did not admit that a social change had occurred. The scholars themselves created the myth of changeless China, possibly as a result of their subconscious need to identify with the most ancient legends of the race, legends that they revered and took as the model for all conduct and government.

Throughout much of Chinese history, no group could rival the scholars in influence. The absence of a powerful priestly class made the Chinese scholar the guardian of conventional morality and ethics as well as an educator and administrator. In most parts of Europe education was controlled by the Church, even after the Reformation; but in Europe the clerics and schoolmasters were not also the magistrates, judges, treasury officials, and civil servants, as they were in China. After the early T'ang period there was, for the most part, no hereditary aristocracy in China (as there was in Europe). The relatives of the emperor did bear titles, but these decreased in prestige by one degree with every generation; after six generations the emperor's relatives were left with only the distinction of bearing the imperial surname and of being remote members of the imperial clan. They did not have authority by virtue of possessing titles. They could sometimes become public servants by passing the examination, but in many cases they were actually debarred from holding certain offices. The merchant was relatively unimportant, too, except in a limited number of large trading cities on the coast or along the Yangtze River. Merchants and artisans were traditionally assigned a lower status than either scholars or peasants. Consequently there was no powerful middle class either. Society was broadly divided into two dominant classes: the scholar gentry, who provided the ruling elite; and the peasants, who provided the food and the revenue. By the end of the T'ang dynasty, society was firmly established on this pattern (from which it never really departed until the Communist revolution of 1948–1949).

Under the Sung, public examinations became necessary for entry into the civil service. A great store of knowledge about literature was the indispensable requisite for candidates; the examinations tended to concentrate more and more on this material. The effect on education was to eliminate all disciplines that did not contribute toward passing the civil service examination. The Chinese people have a great natural aptitude for mathematics and a talent for invention, making them remarkable technicians. But these qualities found no outlet in the educational system that the scholar-bureaucrats imposed on the nation.

Education was made difficult. The writing style employed by pupils had to be classical; the colloquial language could not be used; the ideographs were more complex than was necessary. Simplification would have made liter-

acy too accessible. This situation was self-reinforcing; those who had mastered a difficult education were not disposed to make it easier for others. Government service was the goal of all the scholar gentry, but no government could have employed all members of the class; it was necessary to limit the number of possible candidates for government posts by making the examinations harder.

Education became rarefied under the Sung, and even more so under the Ming, after the alien Mongols had been expelled in the late fourteenth century. Under the Mongols, Chinese learning had for a time been of little account. The founder of the Ming dynasty was almost illiterate, but he realized that his cause could benefit if he gave scholars employment and restored their status. When he triumphed, the old civil service was fully restored, with the examinations and the educational system modeled on the Sung pattern. The Ming government was more autocratic than the Sung had been, however, and it was less influenced by its scholarly ministers. The scholar got back his place, but he did not get back all his old prestige and power. In an empire with a population that exceeded one hundred fifty millions it was difficult to rise to the top. Competition was stronger than it had been, and education more than ever essential; the examinations tended to become narrow and scholastic. Since the court could choose among so many potential officials, it had little need to pay deference to any; they could all be replaced. The invention of printing in T'ang times, and its spread in the Sung period, had made education easier to acquire. As a result of this, the number of literates increased greatly in proportion to the general population, forcing families with a long tradition of officeholding to compete with many rivals.

Studies of the history of Ming and Manchu dynasty officials have shown conclusively that

After the T'ang dynasty, athletic activity was discouraged among Chinese scholars, who were urged to walk with a shuffling gait and with shoulders hunched forward, like the two scholars shown above.
CINCINNATI ART MUSEUM

the majority increasingly tended to come from certain parts of the country—the lower Yangtze region, the area around Canton, and Ssŭch'uan. In these regions a high level of prosperity, based on favorable agricultural factors and such specialized products as tea and silk, made it possible for the gentry to pay for a long and expensive education. Fewer officials came from the old centers of Chinese scholarship and culture—the provinces of Shantung, Honan, Shensi, and Hopei, where Peking is located. These regions were never insignificant, but they were no longer dominant. In Sung times officials from these regions had been more numerous and more conspicuous than the southerners were.

In prosperous regions scholar families were able to establish schools and attract talented teachers to them. These men, who were often retired officials, knew the ways of the civil service; they could teach methods and procedures that were acceptable to their colleagues in office and to examiners. Students in the favored areas enjoyed the advantages of good libraries and of schools that were staffed by able and experienced men. The students came from families who could afford to put their sons through the long period of training. One of the claims often made for the Chinese imperial civil service is that it opened the road to government service to all capable young men regardless of class or region. This was true in theory and may have been near the truth in practice in middle T'ang or in Sung times; but it was ceasing to be true under the Ming dynasty and especially under the Manchu. Novels of Ming and Ch'ing times often have as heroes brilliant scholars who pass the examinations at a very early age and rise to the highest posts while still young. These tales are fictions in more senses than one; they are wish-fulfillment fantasies. The road to office was long and hard, and the best starting point was membership in a wealthy landed family in the lower Yangtze region or in Kuangtung province.

Record of the family origin of men of distinction is found in the dynastic histories from Han times onward; but before Ming times these entries cover at best only the most

As this detail from a copy of a Sung dynasty scroll indicates, the scholar's life had its frivolous moments. Diversions included the playing of musical instruments and of board games.

prominent men of each generation. From later periods the family records of less famous men survive. In T'ang times admission to the capital's imperial training college (or university, as it has sometimes been called) was the best road to office. This institution had one of the finest libraries in the empire. Great libraries were probably not easily found in the provinces, even in the prosperous ones. The population of T'ang dynasty Ch'ang-an, which was so much larger than that of the greatest provincial centers, suggests that residence in Ch'ang-an was a social advantage for prospective officials. In Ming and later times the capital, Peking, was not the pre-eminent center of learning and culture, being outshone by Su-chou and Hang-chou, and by Canton, the great intellectual center of the south. In the nineteenth century the glories of Su-chou were largely transferred to the great new center of Shanghai.

The way of life of scholar families is well known from the records of the last six hundred years. How far the same pattern of life was true of earlier times must be conjectural.

Scholar-gentry families may have been landed gentry, but they lived from the land, not on it. The city was their home, and their country estate provided the income. It is characteristic of China that the countryside, which was dominated by landed gentry, exhibits so few stately houses. China has no castles dating from a warlike past, no great mansions where grandees dwelt on their estates. Even the houses of the landlords who actually did reside in the country were neither luxurious nor large. They were more commodious and better built certainly than the peasants' farmhouses, but otherwise there was not much difference between the two. In modern times such houses were often taken over complete with their furniture and made the office of a commune committee or a collective farm.

For the future scholar-official, education began at a very early age. From the age of four the child was taught to trace large characters on paper, learning the order in which the strokes should be written. When he reached seven years, he was already literate in the sense that he could read and write a number of char-

285

acters (but without having been taught their meaning in any but a very rudimentary sense); and he began to learn the *Thousand Character Classic*, a rhyming Confucian moralistic essay, which has the distinction of comprising one thousand characters, all different, rhymed in four-character lines. The young schoolboy had to memorize this work—without any explanation of its meaning. In this task he was assisted by the teacher. The pupil stood with his back to the master, who held a cane. Any slip was promptly corrected with a whack on the backside. This system was traditionally known as backing.

After the *Thousand Character Classic*, the student proceeded to learn other classical texts: *The Great Learning* and the *Book of Odes*. Methods of instruction were similar; the pupil did not have an explanation of the meaning of these works until he knew them by heart. It was purely an exercise in memorization, very effective for training an almost photographic memory no doubt, but useful for little else. Not until the pupil was word perfect was he permitted to go further. Then the learned commentaries that had accumulated around the Confucian classical texts through the centuries were enlisted to help his progress. As the years passed, a proficient student acquired something close to total recall of the Confucian texts.

The dynastic histories were added to the curriculum. In parts, these texts are difficult, but by the time a comparatively young student reached them, he could read them with ease. Buddhist texts were excluded from the curriculum, and so were the famous novels of the Ming and Ch'ing periods. Woe betide the young student caught reading one of these works!

Youth had few recreations. Almost no sport was allowed. The scholar never ran, jumped, or swam. There was a kind of foot-ball, which involved the skillful use of the foot to keep a ball off the ground, but even the novels condemned this sport as the frivolous amusement of young ne'er-do-wells. Hunting on horseback was not a common pursuit except for the highborn, such as members of the imperial family; it was usually condemned as deleterious to the crops of the peasants. Fishing, however, was a scholarly sport. Its practice had been sanctified by many great men of the past, and fishing forms the theme of many famous paintings. The scholar could also watch birds, admire the scenery from a mountain pavilion, play the lute, and compose poetry or paintings.

The scholar never used his hands for work other than calligraphy or painting. He never engaged in any form of hard work after early childhood, when he might wait upon his elders at table. In later life he cultivated the sensitivity of his fingers by rolling smooth stones or metal objects in the hand; this improved his ability to judge the quality of fine porcelain. He also grew the nail of a little finger as long as possible, protecting it with a silver shield, as proof of his unfamiliarity with manual labor. He was encouraged to adopt a stooping gait, known as the scholar's posture. (This posture was always used by actors depicting scholars on the stage.)

In earlier times the scholar's life had not been quite like this. In the T'ang period, and perhaps even more in Han times, the scholar gentry went in for active exercise and for manly sport. Hunting was then a normal recreation for the country gentry. Polo, perhaps introduced from Persia in the seventh century, was played by girls as well as by young men. At the T'ang court certain dances of a ceremonial character were a common feature of festivals. These recreations faded away with the rise of the examination system. As the competition for public examinations grew harder, it was more and more necessary for the student to devote all his time to learning. In earlier times men of means, including scholars, normally traveled about on horseback. In later times the sedan chair and the litter largely replaced the horse.

The system of education strongly reinforced the separation of the military and civil services. Soldiers could not be trained in this way; they had to take exercise—to ride, to draw the bow and wield the spear or sword. Scholars were trained to despise the military life as fit only for rough men of little education: "Good iron is not used for nails nor good men for soldiers," said a proverb; but how old was the proverb? It would have sounded strange in the ears of the T'ang Emperor T'ai Tsung, a soldier of genius at the age of sixteen and later an administrator and calligrapher renowned for his ability and art. An older proverb said: "Generals and ministers are not grown from seed: youth must exert itself." This was still quoted in later times, but its paralleling of generals and civil ministers was totally ignored.

When his education was completed, the young man still had many difficulties before him. He had to face the examination system. By passing the examinations that were held in the provincial capital (and the odds were long against his passing) the young scholar obtained the lowest degree. (If he failed to pass, he could take the examination again and again.) A passing grade made him eligible for appointment to the civil service. The candidate very often had to wait for years to get a post, but he was compensated by a number of privileges, which placed him in a different legal category from ordinary citizens. He could act as an unpaid assistant to an official to gain experience or he could teach in a school. (Many scholars never attained more than a teacher's or assistant's post.) He could also,

every third year, take the examination for a higher degree, which was more likely to secure him an appointment.

The lucky or the able scholar might expect appointment as a magistrate in a small provincial seat. The magistrate was a very important local figure; he bore heavy responsibility for the preservation of order, the collection of revenue, and the maintenance of public works, such as roads, dikes, and irrigation channels. But he was never allowed to serve in his native province; very often he was sent to the other end of China, where the local dialect was unintelligible to him. He would therefore gather a staff of assistants who were not members of the regular service and who knew the country and the language. They often served successive magistrates for years and were the real local government. They were literate, but not "scholars," for they had passed no public examinations. They were paid not by the state, but by the magistrate himself from his own pocket, or from whatever he stole out of the local revenue. This practice was strictly illegal, and an enemy could always use it to denounce a magistrate for embezzlement. Still, all magistrates were forced to embezzle; it was accepted as a necessary evil. If the magistrate's underlings were not paid, they would not work well, and they would sell justice and favors. This was something they always attempted to do anyway, but it was wise for a magistrate to try to keep corruption at a low level in the territory under his control.

The magistrate did not serve for very long in any locality. After two or three years he would be transferred; if he was well connected and had influence, he might obtain an appointment in one of the ministries at the capital. This gave him a much easier life, with less responsibility and fewer hazards. Some fortunate and unusually able men obtained such a post at the beginning of their careers and

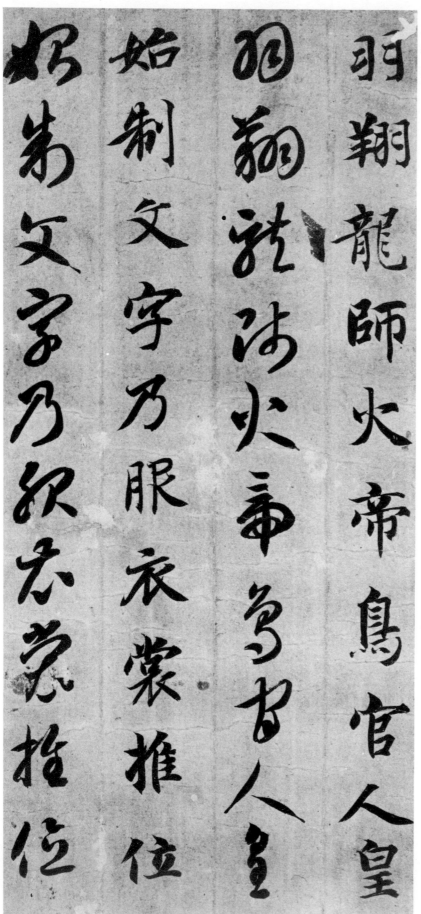

At the age of seven, students began the arduous task of memorizing the Thousand Character Classic, *a portion of which is shown at left. Composed of a thousand different characters, the* Classic *was a rhyming compendium of historical information.*

never acted as provincial magistrates. The more common experience was to be sent off to another distant post, perhaps in a higher rank, such as that of circuit intendant, who was charged with supervising military, fiscal, judicial, or commercial affairs, or as a magistrate of a prefecture. The responsibilities were heavier and the pay not conspicuously better, but the opportunities for lucrative "squeezes" were much improved.

The higher an official rose, the more important connections at the capital became to him. Competitors would be at work to obtain his post for themselves. He had to cultivate the men in power, by family influence if possible and by gifts if necessary. Throughout his long career he had to take and pass examinations, because these were required for the most important posts. If really able, he might reach the highest degree, with access to the throne and appointment to one of the major offices of government. Even then he would be retested every few years. Throughout his career he was never given leave; he had no opportunity to return to his home and no possibility of serving at a post within a reasonable distance of it. When one of his parents died, however, he had to resign office for three years and return to his native place to mourn the loss, tend the tombs, and demonstrate filial piety. He was not paid during these enforced absences.

It is hardly surprising that under such conditions many official families became almost entirely divorced from their native homes. They lived in the capital, if they could, or followed the family head on his wandering career. Sooner or later he might get a post at Peking, and then a more regular family life would be possible. It was common to find families who had lived all their lives in the capital and never so much as seen the place they derived from. There were Cantonese who had never been to Canton and would never serve there; they might, however, be buried in the family tomb at the native place of a grandfather or an earlier progenitor.

This was the life of those who made a success of their careers. Many were not so fortunate, however. Committing a major misdemeanor might well bring a death penalty or cashiering from the service. Cashiering ended all hope of a further career. If the unfortunate, disgraced official was not exiled to some far-off province such as Sinkiang or Yünnan, he had to return to his native countryside. There he usually vegetated for the rest of his days, although he generally used all of his influence at the capital to have his sentence remitted. Even when no offense could be proved, spiteful enemies in high places could destroy an official's career. A man who had incurred ill-will could be appointed, say, to a post near Canton. No sooner had he finished the long, expensive journey to Canton—where he hoped to recoup his expenses from the fruits of office—than he would receive an order transferring him to a post two thousand miles away. He had to set out at once on another long, expensive, uncomfortable, and often dangerous journey. As soon as he arrived at his new post, an order would come transferring him to yet another post, involving perhaps another two thousand miles of difficult travel. At this point the victim recognized what was afoot and usually sent in his resignation, begging to be allowed to return to his native place to recuperate from illness or to care for his aged parents. If the enemy did not really want to kill his victim, but only to ruin him, permission to resign from the service would be graciously accorded.

The perils of an official career were real and great. The rewards seem to us inadequate, often involving cares and discomforts that were hardly less irksome than official disgrace. Yet there was never any shortage of candidates; on the contrary, the scholars sought appointment with ardent concentration. They had spent their lives striving for office, and they would not refuse it when it was offered. Their whole training and family and social pressures drove them on. Only rather late in Chinese history did there appear indications that some men were no longer attracted by the prospect of an official career. They studied the classics, and perhaps passed the examination for the first degree, but thereafter they sought no career, preferring to devote their time to literature or art, or to teaching. Throughout history there were men of real distinction and great talent who did not wish to serve a corrupt court or failing dynasty. They were known as "sleeping dragons" and they were much respected. Sometimes a new ruler would hear of one and endeavor to tempt him to his service. Very often the offer was declined.

Many other abilities must have been wasted; not every man of intellectual power is a humanist, and Chinese society made little provision for using the talents of men whose bent lay toward science, mathematics, and technology or engineering. Such men were probably as numerous as the students of the classics were. If they were well-to-do, they could indulge their interests. They wrote books, which were not much regarded at the time, but which provide us with a precious record of Chinese knowledge in fields outside the domain of Confucian scholarship. Clearly, exceptional ability and dedication were needed to break out of the mold and ignore the overwhelming social pressure to conform and become a Confucian scholar. The civil service system had been fashioned by the T'ang emperor as an instrument to defeat the military aristocracy; it had become a stifling shell, restraining all progress and social change. When, in the nineteenth and early twentieth cen-

The extravagance and debauchery that marked the final years of the T'ang emperor Ming Huang's reign forced the once-revered "Brilliant Emperor," the patron of many of China's greatest poets, to abdicate in favor of his son in A.D. 756. In this Ming dynasty copy of an earlier painting, the emperor is pictured (seated on the dais) instructing the prince, his heir (at lower right).

turies, the system cracked under foreign pressure, it became evident that there were in China a host of men who had the skills and ability to deal with science and technology. It was many years before the social and economic system could provide such men with adequate careers. Once the opportunity was granted, however, the grandsons of Confucian scholar-officials were able to grasp it and become nuclear physicists and engineers.

The scholar-official class had a great sense of unity, even when it was riddled with intrigues and jealousies. Against those who disputed its pre-eminence and privileges, the scholars closed their ranks. The first of these traditional enemies were the eunuchs; every young student learned of their iniquity in his history lessons. From the point of view of the emperor, the eunuchs had important political value; but from the point of view of the regular civil servants, they were a pernicious group of arrogant upstarts, ill-educated, presumptuous, corrupt, and hostile toward scholars. In this opinion the scholars were, for the most part,

correct. Eunuchs came from plebeian families, and although in later centuries some were literate, none were well-trained scholars. Their literary tastes ran to popular novels and the drama. Many had talent as actors, a fact that gained favor with the palace ladies. The Empress Dowager Tz'ŭ Hsi, who was very fond of the popular drama and opera, favored certain eunuchs who were able to stage such works and to act in them. To scholars the eunuchs' dramatic talents merely proved how inferior these creatures were. A wise ruler would ignore the eunuchs and reduce them to their proper status as servants. With the weapon of history in their hands, the scholars, from the time of the Han dynasty onward, pilloried the court eunuchs with scarcely an exception; but the scholars never found a way to get rid of them.

The eunuchs represented a peculiar danger to the scholar-official because they had direct access to the very font of power, the emperor himself. Eunuch influence—a hint here, a word there—could undo the careful and reasoned remonstrances of a minister or high official

Throughout much of Chinese history there was a deadlock between the eunuchs and the civil service; after the disastrous end of the Han dynasty the eunuchs never again attempted to assume full power and destroy the civil service. On their part the scholar-officials, remembering the same traumatic events, never invoked the army to destroy the eunuchs. The emperor could not govern without the civil service; he could not control his palace and his harem without the eunuchs.

The scholars' second opponent—half despised, half feared—was the army. If the army assumed power in times of disturbance and government collapse, scholars lost their authority. Their careers were ended unless they attached themselves to some satrap; he himself would probably have a short career and a violent end, which would destroy his followers too. There was the chance, however, that a general, be he ever so rough and illiterate, might prove to be the founder of a powerful dynasty. It was a dangerous gamble, but if it came off, the scholars who had joined him

at the outset of his career would reap a golden reward of honor, power, and wealth. In times of trouble the scholars needed the army. It alone could repress peasant disorders and rebellion that might strike at the scholars' economic existence by diminishing the rent from their estates. Once a dynasty had fallen, only the army could provide a new dynastic founder. But when peace was restored and a new dynasty was in the saddle, the army was no longer needed and the scholars had no further use for it. Send it away to the frontiers, they urged, and, above all, do not use it to govern the country. That task should be once more the duty and the reward of men who had assiduously studied the Confucian classics.

The merchant class did not exactly represent a danger to the scholars. Nevertheless, it was kept firmly in its place, with little authority. Merchants had money, which was often used to bribe officials in the capital to overrule the power of a local magistrate. Consequently, local magistrates had to walk carefully. Merchants were always derided in the

So assiduously were fine examples of calligraphy and major scholarly texts collected by members of China's aristocracy that one T'ang emperor supposedly ordered the theft of a document that he wished to add to his personal library. At Emperor T'ai Tsung's command, an official named Hsiao I befriended the monk Pien-ts'ai, who guarded the original copy of Orchid Pavilion, a famous work of calligraphy. Above, at center, Pien-ts'ai is shown receiving Hsiao I and a servant. The envoy won the monk's confidence—and stole the precious work.

In this Sung dynasty painting, officials and their servant-assistants
are occupied with the task of collating ancient manuscripts.

historical texts. Scholars were taught to deplore their influence. Merchants wanted to protect their wealth by investing it in land, and if possible, by purchasing rank, which they were unable to obtain by passing an examination. Thus they could gain the protected status of graduates and unemployed officials. The practice of purchasing rank grew fast in the late Manchu period. In many periods throughout history, merchants were forbidden by law to buy farmland; but they managed to evade the rule with surrogate purchasers, who were often penurious members of the scholar-gentry class. The scholars needed the merchants too; they could be squeezed for money in various ways. They could pay handsomely for the honor of marrying the daughters of a needy scholar-official family. Scholars went to merchants for loans and advice on investments, they accepted bribes from merchants who were their clients and protected them against other officials. But scholars tended to repeat the textbook criticisms of greedy merchants who took usury and did not work at the "fundamental occupation" of agriculture or serve the state as officials.

The scholar class was severely critical of the Buddhist and Taoist priesthood, although neither group could be considered a threat to the ascendancy of the scholar gentry. Taoist priests were usually men of the people and rather unscrupulous fortunetellers and magicians. They might stir up trouble among an ignorant and superstitious peasantry, especially in times of drought or famine. By tradition they were anti-Confucian. Buddhist monks shared some of these characteristics. Furthermore, they were adherents of a foreign creed. Buddhist sects also inspired rebellions among the peasants—sometimes formidable ones. Above all, Buddhism had its own learning and literature, which challenged the pre-

dominance of Confucian philosophy, literature, and ethics. Confucian history taught the young scholar to deplore the influence of Buddhist monks at court and attributed many troubles to that influence. The young Confucian scholar could see Buddhist monks chanting the sutras at weddings and funerals; his uncle might well have gone off to live as a hermit in a mountain monastery; his mother and his sisters might have been fervent Buddhists and ardent visitors of the monasteries (one of the few places outside the home open to them). Nevertheless, the pure young scholar had to ignore all this. It might be maintained that the scholars really needed Buddhism as a foil to emphasize their own literary culture.

There was one other opponent, who was usually too highly placed for direct attack, but who was criticized nevertheless through the medium of history. This was the most powerful woman at court, the empress or the reigning monarch's favorite concubine. If she did not try to sway the emperor, influence his policy, and suggest official appointments and dismissals, scholars would praise her in their histories as a model of the true, dutiful, pure Confucian wife. If she used her persuasions on the monarch, then her activities impinged on the power of the scholar-officials and were deplored. At many periods the empress or favored concubine promoted the careers of her relatives at the expense of ordinary officials. Yet she, too, was a necessity for the smooth running of society; the emperor had to have an heir—indeed several heirs if possible—to guard against the risk of a disputed succession with all its potential trouble and disaster. In the last resort the scholars were always on the side of order and authority, however much they disliked some of those who wielded it, for without order and authority there could be no role for them in Chinese society.

12 Artists and Writers

A seated scholar prepares to play his lute for two female students of the arts, one of whom arranges plum blossoms while the other examines a painting.

The record of Chinese literature goes back about two thousand five hundred years; a comparable period in the Western world would extend back to the time of classical Greece. The record of Chinese art extends back even longer, dating to Shang times, which were contemporaneous with the New Kingdom in ancient Egypt and the almost-mythical Mycenaean age in Greece. The bronzes of the Shang era are among the most admired works of Chinese civilization. But no one knows anything at all about the makers of these magnificent vessels—who designed them and who had mastered the considerable technical feat of casting in clay molds great weights of molten bronze, sometimes as much as three quarters of a ton. In many cases the inscriptions on the bronzes simply state that a particular individual made the vessel; "may his posterity cherish it forever," these inscriptions continue. The personage who says he "made" the vessel does not mean by this that he performed the actual task. He was a grandee or great nobleman who commissioned the vessel to commemorate an honor that was bestowed on him—very often an enfeoffment. We have no means yet of knowing what segment of society the makers and designers of the Shang bronzes came from. However, they were doubtless Chinese. From the quality of the work and the technical skill required for its execution, it seems clear that they were not primitive tribesmen enslaved after being captured in war.

The artists of the feudal period and of the succeeding early empire were also anonymous. Surviving bas-reliefs from Han tombs and some remarkably well-preserved mural painting—among the earliest Chinese painting known—are unsigned, and no literary record remains to tell who designed or painted them. The surviving works from the Han period do not depict landscape, but rather human activities: life in the home or episodes from the chase. It seems probable that Buddhism turned attention to nature in the period after the fall of the early empire, inspiring artists to depict landscape and poets to write about it.

According to the Chinese, the first great painter known by name is Ku K'ai-chih, who lived around A.D. 364 and worked at the court of the Tsin dynasty at Nanking. One or two pictures attributed to Ku K'ai-chih still exist, although many modern scholars hold that these are early copies rather than originals. Ku K'ai-chih's style is very unlike that of later artists and closer to that of the anonymous painters of the Han tomb murals. In an age when Buddhism was gaining prestige and influence among the educated class, Ku K'ai-chih painted many religious pictures for Buddhist monasteries. None of these now remains.

Ku K'ai-chih is not the only artist whose works have disappeared. Indeed, Chinese literature preserves the names of many artists whose work has vanished. We have the literature of art—criticism, appreciation, and description of individual works—but not the paintings themselves. Only a meager number of pictures survives from the T'ang dynasty, three hundred years after the time of Ku K'ai-chih, and even these date from the later part of the period. This gives us little whereby to judge T'ang art, which was so well known and highly esteemed in its own era and under the subsequent Sung dynasty.

Men such as the poet-painter Wang Wei and Wu Tao-tzǔ, who was acknowledged as the greatest T'ang master, are only represented by copies. There are a few works attributed to Han Kan, Ming Huang's contemporary (one appears on pages 160–161); there are also some ascribed to Chou Fang, who lived in the next generation. T'ang art is better known from the frescoes on the walls of the cave temples at Tun-huang in Kansu province

than from the surviving works of famous artists. The Tun-huang frescoes are not signed. They probably represent a style that was rather provincial or old-fashioned at the time they were painted. The style has more in common with the art of the Han period than with the sophisticated work that scholar-artists were doing under the T'ang.

Traditionally in China painting was an activity pursued by scholars. Its evolution is doubtless connected with the rise of calligraphy as an art, a rise that depended on the adoption of the brush and ink as writing materials some time in the late Warring States period or under the early empire. The beauty of their script encouraged the Chinese to conceive of calligraphy as an art, and calligraphy acquired an importance and esteem equal to that of painting. The variation of style, the width of the line, the vigor of expression, and subtlety of design are factors that can be appreciated by connoisseurs as much in calligraphic work as in a drawing or painting.

By the T'ang period, art was a major activity of the scholar class, and a great number of paintings were produced. We know that the artists were among the educated elite of the age, sometimes poets, in all cases scholars, and often high officials of the government. This was to remain characteristic of Chinese artistic life up until modern times; no doubt it was founded on the simple fact that to be a painter it was also necessary to be literate and an elegant calligrapher.

It was the scholar-artists who were to determine the direction Chinese painting was to take. Wang Wei is typical. He was a poet of no mean accomplishment as well as an official active in the court life of Ch'ang-an. His great delight, however, was rural solitude, which is emphasized in both his painting and his poetry. It was a theme that would dominate Chinese poetry and painting. The two arts were

The familiar legend of the nymph of the Lo River—the tale of a goddess' futile attempts to entice her mortal lover into her underwater abode—is the subject of a well-known scroll once attributed to the fourth-century artist Ku K'ai-chih. Experts now believe that the scroll is a close copy of Ku's original work; it was probably completed during the Sung dynasty, when ink drawings (similar to the one that can be seen affixed to the ship's cabin in the detail above) became popular.

closely intertwined in Chinese culture. Often poem and painting appeared together on the same scroll, composed with the same brush and ink. The words had visual importance, and the pictures were what Western artists often call literary—meaning that their story-telling aspects became as important as their aesthetic ones.

Wang Wei was later regarded as the founder of the Southern style of painting; and a member of the T'ang imperial family, Li Ssŭ-hsün, is called the founder of the Northern style. The names "Northern" and "Southern" are not to be taken in a strict sense, for an artist who followed one of the styles was not necessarily from the corresponding region. The styles were distinguished by the strength or delicacy of the brush strokes in landscape painting. The south has, a Chinese art critic wrote, "mild and graceful scenery," while in the north there are "grand and ma-jestic landscapes. . . . Art itself is divided into

the two separate schools of the North and South, according as pictures are done in con-formity with the characteristic nature" of each region. (A typical Southern style painting ap-pears on page 33 of this book; the Northern style of landscape can be seen in the picture on pages 60–61.)

Painting was done in ink on silk or fine paper; the use of color was sparing, and no oil paint was used. One reason why such fragile old paintings have survived at all is that the Chinese did not display works in frames upon a wall, but kept them rolled up and wrapped in silk. They were only to be taken from their boxes and unrolled for the apprecia-tion of visitors or for the aesthetic satisfaction of their owner.

The Chinese people believe that the Sung period was the greatest age of painting. No doubt their judgment is partly based on the fact that much Sung painting has survived; but underlying it also is the unquestioned merit of the great Sung painters and the high regard paid to art in the Sung times. The art-ists of the period excelled in landscape paint-ing, which seems to have been their favorite, but not their only, subject. Like the T'ang artists, almost all the Sung painters were re-nowned scholars, and many were high officials as well. The Emperor Hui Tsung—last of the Sung line to reign over north China—was a famous and accomplished artist. He was the founder of the first academy of art, which was organized along the lines of a regular school and which awarded degrees. The emperor took part in the instruction of pupils, set the exami-nation subjects, and judged the works sub-mitted to the academy. He maintained a pic-ture gallery in the palace. The catalogue of his collection, which he had published, is still ex-tant; it includes the titles of 6,396 pictures, some of which were of T'ang date. It is inter-esting to learn from the writings of Sung com-

An album leaf by the Southern Sung painter Li Sung, which takes its title, The Red Cliff, I, *from a prose-poem by the eleventh-century poet Su Shih, depicts the author and two companions floating in a boat along the turbulent Yangtze River, past the cliff that inspired Su's poem.*

mentators that by the early twelfth century T'ang pictures were becoming rare.

Most of the well-known Northern Sung artists were officials and scholars. Li Sung is one of the few painters of renown who is said to have come from a humble situation. He began life as a carpenter, and this training served him well; when a piece of furniture is shown in one of his works, it is rendered with great accuracy and detail. Han Kan, the T'ang artist, is one of the few other painters said to be of non-scholarly origin. Wang Wei found him serving in an inn; impressed by his talent, Wang took him away from the inn and provided for his education. Unless a poor man was given such assistance, he had little chance of developing, no matter how gifted he might be. In China skill with the brush was inseparable from literacy. This was a limitation that must have deprived art of many potential masters.

The Southern Sung period was a great age of painting, even though the Sung court had to retire to Hang-chou in Chekiang province after north China was lost. This period saw the full development of a characteristic form of painting: the long panoramic landscape scroll. Usually, it depicts a vast scene, intended in some instances to represent hundreds of miles.

The criticism is often made that, after the Sung period, Chinese art became less original and more imitative. The Sung painters became the model, and Ming and Ch'ing artists worked only in styles established by their predecessors. This is probably an overstatement. We do owe our knowledge of Sung work in large part to their Ming copyists, but this is no reason to suggest that the Ming artists were incapable of original work. The work of the first masters of landscape painting was always the most admired, and the continuation of their tradition was lively and vigorous in Ming and in early Ch'ing times. Traditional painting flourished

until the end of the empire, and it still survives, although in China today praise is reserved for works inspired by Western models. However, it is unlikely that so long a tradition and such a rich heritage of art will be discarded or forgotten.

A characteristic of art in China has been the sharp division between those mediums that were considered scholarly and those that were regarded as mechanical or, perhaps, simply as non-literary, even though they were cultivated and admired nonetheless. Porcelain and sculpture fall into the latter category. Neither received much literary attention. The names of the sculptors who worked in the famous Buddhist cave temples at Lung-men or Yün-kang remain unknown. No record exists of the artist who designed the magnificent, gigantic heraldic stone lions that still stand at the Liang tombs near Nanking. The making of porcelain, which was perfected in the Sung period, was under imperial patronage; consequently, the names of some potters have been recorded, but other information about them survives only in folk tradition—quite unlike the precise accounts of painters' lives. As the porcelain industry developed to a great scale in Southern Sung, and again in Ming times, porcelain making became divorced from individual responsibility. Technical experts fired the pots, painters decorated them, and other craftsmen performed the various processes required to finish the work. The names of the directors of the imperial pottery at Ching-te-chen have also come down to us; these men did make innovations, experimenting with new techniques and new designs, but they were not responsible for individual pieces.

This division between the scholar-artist and the craftsman, however gifted he might be, was a result of the domination that literary values exercised over the ruling class. Sculp-

Bamboo was a favorite subject of artists, who believed that the plant possessed the virtues of a superior man: pliancy and resilience. Studies of bamboo, executed in ink alone, demand a calligrapher's sureness of hand; the fourteenth-century painting (opposite) shows how similar calligraphy and bamboo painting techniques are.

OVERLEAF: *Frank imitation of another artist's style was common in Chinese art, and it was not considered extraordinary that the Ming artist Ch'iu Ying devoted much of his career to painting works that were derivative, such as this* Landscape in the Manner of Li T'ang. *Li T'ang was a painter of the Southern Sung dynasty.*
SMITHSONIAN INSTITUTION, FREER GALLERY OF ART; SKIRA

303

ture was either in the service of Buddhism or it was funerary; sometimes it appeared on a grand scale in the tombs of emperors, and sometimes on an intimate and delightful domestic scale, as with the clay figures that were buried in tombs. In neither case was sculpture treated as an art. Buddhism and Buddhist art were for the common people (even if scholars did sometimes retire to mountain monasteries for peace). Tomb art was for the dead and had a religious or magical significance. It was therefore ignored by the living, and those who made it were looked on as craftsmen, although, as we now can see, they were accomplished artists. There are no records of the men who were both painters and sculptors, and perhaps also skilled workers in precious metals.

The domination of literature was overwhelming, and no art had cachet unless it was literary. Of all Chinese literature, it was poetry that was most closely related to the visual arts. One of the first poets to be known by name is Ch'ü Yüan, who lived in the fourth century B.C., in the period of the Warring States, and was a minister at the court of the king of Ch'u. He initiated a new form of poetry, which has been called the elegy. The most famous of his works is the *Li Sao*, "Encountering Sorrow," an allegory containing allusions to the poet's fall from favor. This was a theme that would appear again and again in Chinese poetry. Ch'ü Yüan seems to have led a tragic life, and he died by drowning himself in a small river in Hunan. It is popularly believed that the well-known dragon-boat festival, now celebrated in early summer throughout the Chinese world, originated in the search for Ch'ü Yüan's body.

Poetry from the Han period is not very plentiful, but the work of Ssŭ-ma Hsiang-ju, who lived in the age of the Emperor Wu in the second century B.C., has survived and is still

ROYAL ONTARIO MUSEUM

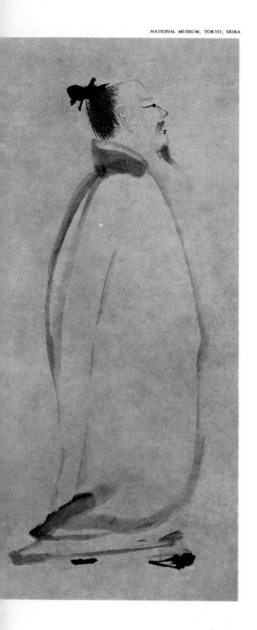

Renowned for his drinking as well as his verse, the T'ang poet Li Po (shown above chanting a poem) is said to have drowned while leaning from a boat in an attempt to embrace the moon's reflection on the surface of a river.

admired. The anthology called the *Ch'u Tz'u,* or *The Songs of Ch'u,* dating from well before the Han period, but compiled in the second century A.D., had a strong influence on later poetry. (One poem from the *Ch'u Tz'u,* "The Summons of the Soul," appears on pages 322–325.)

In the post-Han period, from the late third century to the early seventh century A.D., Buddhism and Taoism exerted a powerful influence on literature, particularly on poetry. Almost all the great poets of this age were under the inspiration of both religions. Taoism, with its concept of the drug of immortality and its belief in the Immortals who lived in the high mountains, turned the minds of men of letters to the beauties and awe-inspiring grandeur of the south China landscape. The poets in whose work these new tendencies are manifest were to have a lasting influence on Chinese poetry. In this period Confucianism was relatively unimportant as an intellectual influence. Times were violent, wars were frequent, and sudden death was the expected fate of the man engaged in the stormy life of politics. Buddhism offered solace and an explanation of the evil of the world. Life was not ended by physical death; reincarnation would bring the wandering soul back to the world of mankind in many successive rebirths. The symbol of the true enduring world was nature, not man and his ephemeral institutions.

In accordance with these ideas, Buddhism, like Taoism, turned to nature as a source of enlightenment and comfort. The poets were drawn exclusively from a small elite, the aristocracy of the warring dynasties. They served the reigning dynasty as officials, achieving positions mainly because they belonged by birth to a powerful clan or faction. Life was precarious; the capital offered delightful recreation and intellectual stimulus, but dangers there were ever-threatening. In the mountains,

far from official pressures, the poet could escape from these dangers and seek that harmony with nature, which Taoism taught was the first step toward immortality and which Buddhism saw as a wise renunciation of "illusion"—the ordinary lives of men.

In Chinese literary tradition the T'ang period, from the seventh to the early tenth centuries, has always held pride of place as the great age of poetry. Today the importance and value of the poets who wrote in the immediately preceding period is increasingly recognized, and their influence on their T'ang successors is better understood. The T'ang period produced not only a great volume of poetry—at least three thousand poets are listed—but also the most famous poets of Chinese literature, Li Po, Tu Fu, the painter-poet Wang Wei, Mêng Hao-jan, and Po Chü-i. The first four were contemporary with the great Emperor Hsüan Tsung, or, as he was called, Ming Huang, and at various times served him at court or in the provinces. Characteristically, most of the poets were also scholar-officials, and some were equally well known as artists. It is at least as much due to the talents of these men as to the emperor's own actions that Ming Huang and his court have left for posterity such a shining reputation for grace and sophistication.

The themes of Chinese poetry differ from those familiar to the Western world. Love poems are rare; romantic love was hardly a normal experience in a society where marriage was arranged by elders and young couples met for the first time at the altar. On the other hand, friendship, which was often based on shared education and shared official careers, was a dominating theme in poetry, as in life. Poems about parting from friends are among the most famous in Chinese literature; characteristic of these is Li Po's "A Farewell to Mêng Hao-jan on His Way to Yang-chou"

The influence that Buddhism exerted upon Chinese art is evident in this vibrantly colored Sung dynasty painting portraying the Buddhist Peacock King, a deity who consumed men's evil thoughts.

(reprinted on page 328). Typically, in these poems an official who received a distant appointment is seen off by his friend, who knows that many years, at best, will pass before they meet again. War poetry is not particularly characteristic of Chinese literature; scholar-officials were not soldiers, and poets were necessarily of the scholar class, for no others were sufficiently literate to write poetry. Chinese poets often lament the devastation of war or the suffering of the people, but the patriotic war was not something they celebrated.

It would be a mistake to conclude that because the T'ang dynasty was adorned by gifted poets, no subsequent period produced poets of equal stature. There were some, but even these were hardly able to escape completely from the T'ang tradition. A history of Chinese literature would certainly not ignore later poetry, but a short survey such as this must concentrate on aspects of literature and the work of writers that typified each age: It is, in general, true that the T'ang is the age of poetry; the Sung, an age of philosophy; and the Ming, a period in which the novel developed. Drama flourished in the rather short Yüan dynasty, and it has prospered ever since.

Belles-lettres, essays, and memorials to the throne, composed in the highest style, were the chosen endeavor of scholars of all ages; among these works many are still admired and were, before the establishment of the People's Republic, taken as models of style. One of the most famous of the memorials was written by Han Yü (768–824) of the T'ang dynasty. An official all his life and a fearless critic of what he considered mistakes in the policy of the court, Han Yü was a champion of Confucian scholarship at a time when it was rather neglected. He condemned the then current patronage of Buddhism and wrote a memorial (reprinted on page 199) opposing the veneration of a relic, which was said to be the finger bone

The twelfth-century philosopher Chu Hsi believed in the perfectibility of man through education. His dictum—that knowledge leads to virtue, and virtue to the "sudden revelation" of universal truth—underlay the philosophical school of neo-Confucianism.

of Buddha. Han Yü was banished to govern a remote and unhealthy region in far-off Kuang-tung. He made it a model district, and some years later returned triumphantly to the capital.

Not all those who opposed court fashions in such an outspoken way were as fortunate as Han Yü, who possessed great literary ability and administrative capacity, both of which were appreciated even if his views were unwelcome. Yet his example of outspokenness was often followed. The memorial to the emperor, criticizing a current policy or suggesting a new one, is one of the established Chinese literary forms. In memorials the scholars express most clearly their underlying philosophy and their moral standards and values, and give evidence of the small consideration that they paid to certain practical aspects of life and government. If they criticize an economic measure or taxation policy, it is on the grounds that it does not conform to ancient practice; if it does happen to have a precedent, then the precedent is labeled a bad one, which

should not be followed. Moral values are stressed—Confucian concepts of virtue, filial piety, loyalty, and sincerity. The vices of luxury, extravagance, and debauchery are condemned, and the woeful results to be expected from these vices are cited.

The Sung period, especially the Northern Sung period, from 960 to 1126, is famous for being the second great age of Chinese philosophy. There seem to have been several reasons why at this time writers and thinkers turned to a re-examination of the Confucian philosophy and teaching. One is the simple, material fact that since the invention and spread of printing, books became easily available. Copies of the ancient texts, and of later commentaries on them, were now acquired by a large and growing class of scholars, the same class that also provided the civil service with its officials. From the very first the new philosophy and the new criticism were involved in the factionalism and changes that were a feature of the political and official world.

The second reason why Sung scholars turned to philosophical studies was the need to revitalize Confucian teaching to meet the challenge of Buddhism. The teaching of Confucianism along lines laid out by the Han commentators and restorers, nearly a thousand years earlier, was considered inadequate in comparison with the indoctrination in the Buddhist theology that was done by learned monks. A third reason for the new interest seems to have lain in the spirit of the Sung period, which was more nationalistic and traditional, and less open to foreign thinking than the T'ang period had been.

Confucius had accepted the religion that was prevalent in his day. The Confucian tradition contained no developed cosmology. It was strong on ethical and moral teaching, but offered little guidance to men seeking to resolve the problem of evil and answer the great

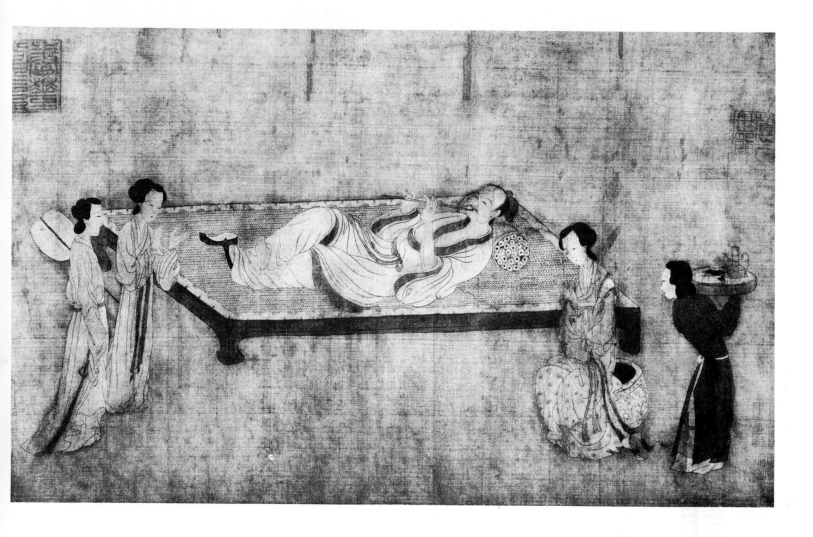

question of the First Cause, the supreme controlling force in the universe. These matters were, on the other hand, the subjects of Buddhist speculation. A series of Sung philosophic writers, many of them officials, addressed themselves to these problems, working strictly within the Confucian system. There was no question of rival schools, such as the hundred schools of the Warring States period. The Sung writers were Confucians, and the subject of their disputes was the true meaning of the classical texts. Their purpose was to distill from this ancient literature a systematic philosophy that could give a Confucian answer to the questions Buddhism had raised.

The story of the Sung philosophic contentions is long and rather technical, but there were three questions debated. The first was the question of the origin of the universe. From obscure passages in some of the old texts the Sung philosophers constructed a cosmology that identified the First Cause, the Supreme Ultimate, with *t'ai chi*. The term had been found

in the ancient *I Ching*. Chou Tun-i (1017–1073) was the first of the Sung philosophers who made use of this concept to build what was, in effect, a new system. Not that the Sung writers ever admitted making innovations. They claimed to be discovering lost meanings, which the neglect of centuries had caused to be overlooked. *T'ai chi* is the primary cause of the existence of the universe, and it is a moral force. The Sung writers made no distinction between the moral and material; to them both were emanations of *t'ai chi*.

The second debate revolved around the question of whether *t'ai chi* had any personality. It was finally resolved by the Southern Sung philosopher Chu Hsi, who was antideist. "There is no man in Heaven judging sin" was his dictum. In this sense the new doctrine certainly departed from the belief of the ancients to whom *t'ien*, "heaven," was personified. Chu Hsi saw the Supreme Ultimate as *li*, the moral law, and this term was taken as an equivalent of *t'ai chi*, stressing the moral as part of the

The eighth-century Emperor Ming Huang is shown within his imperial palace, contentedly reclining on a couch, playing a flute, and attended by a group of youthful concubines. Ming Huang was a great patron of the arts, most notably of the new art of drama.

311

First Cause. In so far as the ancient deities *t'ien* or *shang ti* were accepted by the Sung thinkers, they were identified with *t'ai chi*, and in practice denied personality. Debate over whether there was what might be called a supreme deity or a moral force that acted without personality continued into the Sung period. The debate was ended by Chu Hsi, who decided in favor of the latter interpretation, which has been orthodox Confucian doctrine ever since.

The third subject of debate was the nature of man. This was closely related to the concerns of the Confucian writers of the late classical period. Mencius had taught that the nature of man was good, and Hsün Tzǔ had taken the opposite view. In the Sung period a third alternative was debated, called the whirling water doctrine by Chu Hsi and others. This had its origin in the work of an

ancient opponent of Mencius called Kao Tzǔ, who argued that the nature of man at birth was neither good nor bad, but, like water whirling in a rocky gorge, would take any outlet it could find, which might be good or bad, according to circumstances. Education to guide the unformed nature was thus all important.

Chu Hsi condemned this doctrine and Hsün Tzǔ's idea that the nature of man is originally bad; he conferred his approval on the teachings of Mencius. The Su School, named after Su Hsün and his more famous son, the poet Su Tung-p'o, argued that the nature of man was not composed of innate virtues; man must choose virtues by an act of will. Unless he did so, his nature could not be considered moral. This view came close to the whirling water doctrine. The Hu School, following the teachings of An-kuo (1074–

1138), claimed that if the nature of man was called good, this implied that it could also be bad, since good exists in relation to its opposite. The Hu School further contended that nature can be defined as a faculty of liking or disliking. The moral man liked virtue and chose it; the inferior man was swayed by base desires and chose vice.

The original teaching of Chou Tun-i was transmitted by disciples, of whom the most famous were Ch'êng Hao, his brother Ch'êng I, and Shao Yung, who was the first to raise the problem of the nature of man. In the late Sung era the philosophic debate became entangled in politics, and the doctrines of various thinkers were praised or condemned on partisan rather than on philosophic grounds. Chu Hsi himself did not receive the accolade of unquestioned orthodoxy until some years after his death, which occurred in 1200.

The neo-Confucian movement, which so deeply engaged the minds of the Sung scholars, left an enduring mark on Chinese civilization. The teaching of Chu Hsi became, in effect, the orthodoxy of the Confucian system. One consequence of its triumph was the spread of agnosticism among the educated classes of China, until belief in gods or the supernatural came to be regarded as rustic and unsophisticated. The new Confucianism, like the old, dominated the schools and the examinations for public office, and later generations were brought up in its principles. The decline of Buddhism from Sung times onward may be due in part to the force of the new Confucian teaching, which was not seriously challenged until Western influences penetrated Chinese culture.

In China, unlike Greece, different arts did not flourish at the same period or originate at

The Sung dynasty painting (above) is one of a series depicting a popular story in Chinese literature—the kidnapping, captivity, ransom, and release of the Lady Wên-chi. Taken prisoner in A.D. 195, and married against her will to a Tatar chieftain, Lady Wên spent twelve years among the Mongols and bore her barbarian husband two children. Her reluctant leave-taking of her Mongol family is seen in the detail above, which shows Lady Wên bidding goodbye to her grieving husband, her handmaidens, and her clinging children before the tent at right.

313

the same time. Drama, for example, came very late to China. It did not, as in the West, develop from early religious observances, but first appeared in the form of short pieces in which only two actors performed. The T'ang Emperor Ming Huang, at whose court these pieces were, it seems, first performed, is still the patron spirit of actors; he is credited with starting the first school of drama, called the Pear Garden from its location in one of the gardens on the palace grounds. Apparently this was more a training center for musicians and singers than for actors, and early T'ang dramatic performances, apart from the short two-character pieces, were comparable to ballets and masques. The T'ang was a period very much open to foreign influence and ready to adopt foreign innovations. It can not be proved that the seeds of Chinese drama came from abroad; but the fact that actors and singers are almost always depicted as foreigners in the clay tomb figures seems to suggest that foreign influences were strong.

Under the Yüan dynasty, which ruled China from 1260 to 1368, drama thrived; the plays of the Yüan period are the earliest in Chinese literature and are considered to be among the best. It has been suggested that the reason for the theatre's sudden rise to importance was the Mongol preference for non-Chinese officials and the consequent unemployment of the Chinese scholar class. Left out of government, they turned to art and wrote plays. This seems a little inadequate as an explanation. But it does seem very possible that foreign influence—the movement of envoys, of servants of the Mongol emperors, and even of traders from all over Asia—may have introduced throughout China a taste for plays—a taste that before then had not extended beyond the court. Foreign influence did not effect the subjects of the drama itself. The Yüan plays are devoted to Chinese topics; his-

torical episodes of dramatic quality provided a rich source of plot. Legendary folk tales, such as the adventures of the monkey, Sun, in search of the Buddhist scriptures, and other tales inspired by Buddhist and Taoist lore, also provided plots.

In the Ming period a new literary form, the novel, developed fully and gained popularity. Its origins can be traced to earlier times. The storyteller was probably a figure of great antiquity in China. It may be possible that the invention and diffusion of printing, and a perceptible rise in the level of popular education, enabled the storytellers to increase their public. They refreshed their memories and trained their students by means of short précis called *hua pen*, or "story roots." These form the core of the first great novels. In many, if not all, early novels, the chapters open with the invocation, "Official reader, you will remember that in the last chapter . . ." and end with, "Official reader, if you want to know what happened to so-and-so in these circumstances, please listen to the next installment." These phrases clearly echo the words of the storyteller as he gathers or dismisses his audience. "Official reader" is the Chinese equivalent of our own "gentle reader" of an earlier age. In the West a literate person was presumably of gentle blood; in China he was presumably an official.

The Ming novels display in their subject matter the changing outlook of the age. The first novel, *San Kuo Chih Yen I*, or the *Romance of the Three Kingdoms*, is a fictional version of the history of the fall of the Han dynasty and the wars of the subsequent Three Kingdoms period. The hero is Liu Pei, founder of the smallest of the Three Kingdoms and an alleged descendant of the imperial family of the Han. Ts'ao Ts'ao, the founder of the kingdom of Wei, is the villain. The book has a strong "legitimist" standpoint. Written in the early

OVERLEAF: *In a scene from a production of the opera* The Lady General, *players wear the richly brocaded costumes and elaborate headgear that are traditionally associated with the Chinese theatre.*

李紈

Ming period, it reflects a desire for peace, national unity, and strong government, as might be expected after the turmoil of the last years of Mongol rule. On the whole, the main story sticks close to history, but the tale is also embellished with many dramatic episodes for which there is no authority. For more than five hundred years the novel has enjoyed an undiminished popularity, and although it was forbidden reading for the young, it was undoubtedly read by every literate person in his schooldays. The same can be said of all the great novels of the Ming and Manchu periods. This literature, written in the colloquial not in the classical language, was despised and condemned, although scholars themselves wrote the books and everybody read them.

Aside from their colloquial style, there was another reason for official disapproval of the novels. The *San Kuo* may be loyalist and unexceptionable to authority, but its successors, *Shui-hu*, *Chin P'ing Mei*, and *Hung-lou Meng* (the last dating from the early Manchu period), are either subversive or licentious, or both. *Shui-hu*, which has been rendered as *The Fringes of the Marsh*, makes a gang of outlaws its heroes and describes the injustices and cruelties that drove these once-honest men beyond the law. The heroes wage a constant guerrilla war against the rascally and cowardly provincial authorities, until the dynasty (supposedly the Sung, but obviously the reigning Ming) is overthrown by foreign invaders. Its overthrow does not trouble the author in the least. He acclaims the restoration of order and good government by a "true Son of Heaven."

From one episode in *Shui-hu* a later author drew the story of *Chin P'ing Mei*, an untranslatable title since it consists of parts of the names of the three heroines. This novel has many passages that, as used to be said, "can only be rendered in the obscurity of a learned language"; it very faithfully follows its char-

The Voice of the Poet

The cavorting skeletal figure, opposite, is supposed to represent K'uei-hsing, the Chinese god of literature. Appropriately, K'uei is composed of several Chinese characters, which are, unfortunately, too stylized to be easily recognized. The bold composition is only one of a series of depictions of the god done by Ma Tê-chao, a nineteenth-century government official.

Translating Chinese poetry into any Western language is an astonishingly difficult task. There are fewer than a thousand monosyllables, and each of them has many meanings. The exact meaning of each is determined by its tone, by the character with which it is written, and by the context in which it appears. Dealing with the complexities of the language presents Chinese poets and their translators with a number of formidable problems. In Chinese poetry, for example, the length of a line is measured not in stressed syllables but in characters, each of which is a separate "idea." A poem of four five-character lines inevitably contains precisely five "ideas" in each line; those lines can rarely be translated with only five words. Such limitations are self-imposed as well as inherent. By long-standing precedent, Chinese poets have attempted to avoid repeating so much as a single monosyllable, even in poems that are several thousand characters long. Moreover, in one style of Chinese poetry, called ruled or modern (although some examples are thirteen centuries old), it is traditional for the poet to pair words in adjoining lines according to part of speech. If the third word of one line is a verb, the third word of the next line must be a verb too. If the poem opens with an adjective denoting size, then the first character in the second line of the poem must also be an adjective denoting size.

Such mathematical precision is possible only because of the absence in the Chinese language of articles and prepositions, and of distinctions among the tenses. This verbal economy makes it quite possible for Chinese poets to write a meaningful poem using only twenty characters, each of which makes an equal and important contribution to the story. Each character also depicts the "idea" it denotes, giving the poem a dimension that is almost unknown in Western literature. Scholars, eager to impart the meaning and, as much as possible, the feeling of Chinese poetry to their readers, have necessarily produced translations that render the sense but not the style of the originals.

The Ancient Tradition

Compiled by the scholar Wang I in the second century A.D., *the* Ch'u Tz'u, *or* The Songs of Ch'u, *is a poetry anthology of enormous literary and historical significance. As a result of Wang's commentary, which accompanies the* Songs, *the work is a vital source of information about the customs of the people of Ch'u in central China. Poems in the anthology are of two types: songs, which are quite brief, and lengthy first-person narrative poems. In many of the poems in Wang's anthology every line contains a meaningless mid-line word,* hsi, *which functions as a musical carrier sound, encouraging the reader to chant the poem. The narrative poems take the form of incantations, and the principal speaker in them is frequently a shaman, a member of that group whose purported mystic powers were held in particular awe by the Ch'u people. The long poem, "The Summons of the Soul," is uttered by such a shaman, to recall his dying sovereign to life.*

THE SUMMONS OF THE SOUL
from The Songs of Ch'u

The Lord God said to Wu Yang;
"There is a man on earth below whom I would help:
His soul has left him. Make divination for him."
Wu Yang replied:
"The Master of Dreams. . . .
The Lord God's bidding is hard to follow."
The Lord God said:
"You must divine for him. I fear that if you any longer decline, it will be too late."
Wu Yang therefore went down and summoned the soul, saying:

O soul, come back! Why have you left your old abode and sped to the earth's far corners,
Deserting the place of your delight to meet all those things of evil omen?
O soul, come back! In the east you cannot abide.
There are giants there a thousand fathoms tall, who seek only for souls to catch,
And ten suns that come out together, melting metal, dissolving stone.
The folk that live there can bear it; but you, soul, would be consumed.
O soul, come back! In the east you cannot abide.
O soul, come back! In the south you cannot stay.
There the people have tattooed faces and blackened teeth;
They sacrifice flesh of men, and pound their bones to paste.
There are coiling snakes there, and the great fox that can run a hundred leagues,
And the great Nine-headed Serpent who darts swiftly this way and that,
And swallows men as a sweet relish.
O soul, come back! In the south you may not linger.
O soul, come back! For the west holds many perils:
The Moving Sands stretch on for a hundred leagues.
You will be swept into the Thunder's Chasm, and dashed in pieces, unable to help yourself;
And even should you chance to escape from that, beyond is the empty desert,
And red ants as huge as elephants, and wasps as big as gourds.
The five grains do not grow there; dry stalks are the only food;
And the earth there scorches men up; there is nowhere to look for water.
And you will drift there for ever, with nowhere to go in that vastness.
O soul, come back! lest you bring on yourself perdition.
O soul, come back! In the north you may not stay.
There the layered ice rises high, and the snowflakes fly for a hundred leagues and more.
O soul, come back! You cannot long stay there.

O soul, come back! Climb not to the heaven above.

For tigers and leopards guard the gates, with jaws ever ready to rend up mortal men,

And one man with nine heads, that can pull up nine thousand trees,

And the slant-eyed jackal-wolves pad to and fro;

They hang out men for sport and drop them in the abyss,

And only at God's command may they ever rest or sleep.

O soul, come back! lest you fall into this danger.

O soul, come back! Go not down to the Land of Darkness,

Where the Earth God lies, nine-coiled, with dreadful horns on his forehead,

And a great humped back and bloody thumbs, pursuing men, swift-footed:

Three eyes he has in his tiger's head, and his body is like a bull's.

O soul, come back! lest you bring on yourself disaster.

O soul, come back! and enter the gate of the city.

The priests are there who call you, walking backwards to lead you in.

Ch'in basket-work, silk cords of Ch'i, and silken banners of Cheng:

All things are there proper for your recall; and with long-drawn, piercing cries they summon the
wandering soul.

O soul, come back! Return to your old abode.

All the quarters of the world are full of harm and evil.

Hear while I describe for you your quiet and reposeful home.

High walls and deep chambers, with railings and tiered balconies;

Stepped terraces, storied pavilions, whose tops look on the high mountains;

Lattice doors with scarlet interstices, and carving on the square lintels;

Draughtless rooms for winter; galleries cool in summer;

Streams and gullies wind in and out, purling prettily;

A warm breeze bends the melilotus and sets the tall orchids swaying.

Crossing the hall into the apartments, the ceilings and floors are vermilion,

The chambers of polished stone, with kingfisher hangings on jasper hooks;

Bedspreads of kingfisher seeded with pearls, all dazzling in brightness;

Arras of fine silk covers the walls; damask canopies stretch overhead,

Braids and ribbons, brocades and satins, fastened with rings of precious stone.

Many a rare and precious thing is to be seen in the furnishings of the chamber.

Bright candles of orchid-perfume fat light up flower-like faces that await you;

Twice eight handmaids to serve your bed, each night alternating in duty,

The lovely daughters of noble families, far excelling common maidens.

Women with hair dressed finely in many fashions fill your apartments,

The Ancient Tradition

In looks and bearing sweetly compliant, of gentleness beyond compare,
With melting looks but virtuous natures and truly noble minds.
Dainty features, elegant bearing grace all the marriage chamber:
Mothlike eyebrows and lustrous eyes that dart out gleams of brightness,
Delicate coloring, soft round flesh, flashing seductive glances.
In your garden pavilion, by the long bed-curtains, they wait your royal pleasure:
Of kingfisher feathers, the purple curtains and blue hangings that furnish its high hall;
The walls, red; vermilion the woodwork; jet inlay on the roofbeams;
Overhead you behold the carved rafters, painted with dragons and serpents;
Seated in the hall, leaning on its balustrade, you look down on a winding pool.
Its lotuses have just opened; among them grow water-chestnuts,
And purple-stemmed water-mallows enamel the green wave's surface.
Attendants quaintly costumed in spotted leopard skins wait on the sloping bank;
A light coach is tilted for you to ascend; footmen and riders wait in position.
An orchid carpet covers the ground; the hedge is of flowering hibiscus.
O soul, come back! Why should you go far away?
All your household have come to do you honor; all kinds of good foods are ready:
Rice, broom-corn, early wheat, mixed all with yellow millet;
Bitter, salt, sour, hot and sweet: there are dishes of all flavors.
Ribs of the fatted ox cooked tender and succulent;
Sour and bitter blended in the soup of Wu;
Stewed turtle and roast kid, served up with yam sauce;
Geese cooked in sour sauce, casseroled duck, fried flesh of the great crane;
Braised chicken, seethed tortoise, high-seasoned, but not to spoil the taste;
Fried honey-cakes of rice flour and malt-sugar sweetmeats;
Jadelike wine, honey-flavored, fills the winged cups;
Ice-cooled liquor, strained of impurities, clear wine, cool and refreshing;
Here are laid out the patterned ladles, and here is sparkling wine.
O soul, come back! Here you shall have respect and nothing to harm you.
Before the dainties have left the tables, girl musicians take up their places.
They set up the bells and fasten the drums and sing the latest songs:
"Crossing the River," "Gathering the Caltrops," and "The Sunny Bank."
The lovely girls are drunk with wine, their faces flushed and red.
With amorous glances and flirting looks, their eyes like wavelets sparkle;
Dressed in embroideries, clad in finest silks, splendid but not showy;
Their long hair, falling from high chignons, hangs low in lovely tresses.

Two rows of eight, in perfect time, perform a dance of Cheng;
Their *hsi-pi* buckles of Chin workmanship glitter like bright suns.
Bells clash in their swaying frames; the catalpa zither's strings are swept.
Their sleeves rise like crossed bamboo stems, then they bring them shimmering downwards.
Pipes and zither rise in wild harmonies, the sounding drums thunderously roll;
And the courts of the palace quake and tremble as they throw themselves into the Whirling Ch'u.
Then they sing songs of Wu and ballads of Ts'ai and play the Ta Lü music.
Men and women now sit together, mingling freely without distinction;
Hatstrings and fastenings come untied: the revel turns to wild disorder.
The singing-girls of Cheng and Wei come to take their places among the guests;
But the dancers of the Whirling Ch'u find favor over all the others.
Then with bamboo dice and ivory pieces, the game of Liu Po is begun;
Sides are taken; they advance together; keenly they threaten each other.
Pieces are kinged and the scoring doubled. Shouts of "Five White!" arise.
Day and night are swallowed up in continuous merriment of wine.
Bright candles of orchid-perfumed fat burn in stands of delicate tracery.
The guests compose snatches to express their thoughts as the orchid fragrance steals over them.
And those with some object of their affections lovingly tell their verses to each other.
In wine they attain the heights of pleasure, and give delight to the dear departed.
O soul, come back! Return to your old abode.
    Envoi:
In the new year, as spring began, I set off for the south.
The green duckweed lay on the water, and the white flag flowered.
My road passed through Luchiang and to the right of Ch'ang-po.
I stood on the marsh's margin and looked far out on the distance.
My team was of four jet horses; we set out together a thousand chariots strong.
The beaters' fires flickered skyward, and the smoke rose like a pall.
I trotted to where the throng was, and galloped ahead to draw them;
Then reined as we sighted our quarry, and wheeled around to the right hand.
I raced with the King in the marshland to see which would go the faster.
The King himself shot the arrow, and the black ox dropped down dead.
"The darkness yields to daylight; we cannot stay much longer.
The marsh orchids cover the path here: this way must be too marshy."
On, on the river's waters roll; above them grow woods of maple.
The eye travels on a thousand li, and the heart breaks for sorrow.
O soul, come back! Alas for the Southern Land!

A Man and a Woman

SONG OF A CHASTE WIFE
by Chang Chi (c.768–830)

You knew sir, that I had a husband,
When you sent me this pair of shining pearls.
Grateful for your skein-soft thoughts,
I wore them over my red gauze bodice.
But my home is a tall house built beside the
                              Imperial grounds,
And my good man bears arms in the Palace of
                              Radiance.
I know, sir, that your heart is pure as the
                              sun and the moon.
But in serving my husband I have vowed to be
                              with him in life and death;
So I now return your two shining pearls with
                              a tear on each,
Regretting that we did not meet while I was
                              still unwed.

THE LANTERN FESTIVAL
by Ou-yang Hsiu (1007–1072)

Last year at the Lantern Festival
The flower-market lights were bright as day;
When the moon mounted to the tops of the
                              willows,
Two lovers kept their tryst after the yellow
                              dusk.

This year at the Lantern Festival
The moon and the lights are the same as then;
Only I see not my lover of yesteryear,
And tears drench the sleeves of my green
                              gown.

TO MY WIFE
by Ch'in Chia (first century)

Man's life is like the morning dew:
In this world he has misfortune in plenty.
Griefs and hardships oft come early;
Glad unions oft come bitterly late.
Mindful that I had soon to leave on service,
Farther and farther away from you every day,
I sent a carriage to bring you back;
But it went empty, and empty it returned.
I read your letter with feelings of distress;

At meals I cannot eat;
And I sit alone in this desolate chamber.
Who is there to solace and encourage me?
Through the long nights I cannot sleep,
And solitary I lie prostrate on my pillow,
                              tossing and turning.
Sorrow comes as in a circle
And cannot be rolled up like a mat.

Eager, eager the charioteers prepare to
                              journey;
Clang, clang, resound the bells.
At dawn they will lead me afar;
I fastened on my girdle to await cockcrow.
I peered into the empty room,
And my mind seemed to see your face and
                              form.

One separation breeds ten thousand regrets;
Rising and sitting I am unquiet.
How am I to express my heart?
It is by these gifts as sincere tokens.
The precious hairpin is fit to add luster to
                              your hair;
The bright mirror will reflect your face;
The perfumes will help to cleanse;
And the plain lute holds clear notes. . . .

Frequently promised in marriage at birth and generally married by the age of fourteen, a Chinese woman spent the major part of her life in total subservience to her husband and to the members of his family, particularly his mother. Bound by marital mores that precluded the very possibility of dalliance, as "Song of a Chaste Wife" suggests, Chinese women were obliged to tolerate concubinage. Once widowed, they were expected to refrain from remarrying. Despite inequities, these marital customs survived unaltered until this century, inspiring, as poems such as Ch'in Chia's "To My Wife" clearly suggest, constancy, obedience, and protective tenderness in both the husband and his wife.

THE RIVER MERCHANT'S WIFE: A LETTER

by Li Po (705–762)

translated by Ezra Pound

While my hair was still cut straight across my
            forehead
I played about the front gate, pulling flowers,
You came by on bamboo stilts, playing horse,
You walked about my seat, playing with blue
            plums.
And we went on living in the village of
            Chokan:
Two small people, without dislike or
            suspicion.

At fourteen I married My Lord you.
I never laughed, being bashful.
Lowering my head, I looked at the wall.
Called to, a thousand times, I never looked
            back.

At fifteen I stopped scowling.
I desired my dust to be mingled with yours
Forever and forever and forever.
Why should I climb the look out?
At sixteen you departed,
You went into far Ku-to-yen, by the river of
            swirling eddies,
And you have been gone five months.
The monkeys make sorrowful noise overhead.

You dragged your feet when you went out.
By the gate now, the moss is grown, the dif-
            ferent mosses,
Too deep to clear them away!
The leaves fall early this autumn, in wind.
The paired butterflies are already yellow
            with August
Over the grass in the West garden;
They hurt me. I grow older.

If you are coming down through the narrows
            of the river Kiang,

Please let me know beforehand,
And I will come out to meet you
            As far as Cho-fu-Sa.

AI AI THINKS OF THE MAN SHE LOVES

Ting Liu Niang (*sixth century*)

How often must I pass the moonlight nights
            alone?
I gaze far—far—for the Seven Scents Chariot.
My girdle drops because my waist is shrunken.
The golden hairpins of my disordered head-
            dress are all askew.

A MESSAGE

by Chang Pi (*eleventh century*)

I go in a dream to the house of Hsieh—
Through a zigzag porch with arching rails
To a court where the spring moon lights for
            ever
Phantom flowers and a single figure.

Parting and Meeting

A FAREWELL TO MENG HAO-JAN
ON HIS WAY TO YANG-CHOU
by Li Po (705–762)

You have left me behind, old friend, at the
Yellow Crane Terrace,
On your way to visit Yang-chou in the misty
month of flowers;
Your sail, a single shadow, becomes one with
the blue sky,
Till now I see only the river, on its way to
heaven.

A BRIEF BUT HAPPY MEETING
WITH MY BROTHER-IN-LAW
by Li I (*died* 827)

"Meeting by accident, only to part"
After these ten torn wearisome years
We have met again. We were both so changed
That hearing first your surname, I thought you
a stranger—
Then hearing your given name, I remembered
your young face. . . .
All that has happened with the tides
We have told and told till the evening bell. . . .
Tomorrow you journey to Yo-chou,
Leaving autumn between us, peak after peak.

INVITING A FRIEND
TO SPEND THE NIGHT
by Kuan-hsiu (832–912)

Silvered earth without dust, and the golden
chrysanthemum in bloom,
Purple pears and red dates falling on the
lichen moss;
A shaft of Autumn water, and a round moon—
On such a night, my old friend, are you not
coming?

PARTING AND MEETING
by Kao Shih (*died* 765)

She left her love
A young and red-cheeked girl.
When next they met,
Her hair was white.

Vanished
Was her beauty,
But the tears of parting
Still seemed to linger
In her eyes.

A HEARTY WELCOME
by Tu Fu (712–770)

North of me, south of me, spring is in flood,
Day after day I have seen only gulls . . .
My path is full of petals—I have swept it for
no others.
My thatch gate has been closed—but opens
now for you.
It's a long way to the market, I can offer
you little—
Yet here in my cottage there is old wine for
our cups.
Shall we summon my elderly neighbor to
join us,
Call him through the fence, and pour the jar
dry?

In an effort by the government to ensure impartiality in official decisions, members of China's enormous bureaucracy were forbidden to serve in their home territories. This practice of obligatory exile separated government officials—most of whom were poets who had secured office on the basis of their familiarity with classical Chinese texts—from their families and friends. Many officials continued to write poetry while in office, and their verses frequently and quite logically dealt with the departure, absence, or impending return of a close friend or relative. The speaker might be a young girl, a veteran of the civil wars, or a widow, but the loneliness was plainly that of the official dwelling among strangers, far from home.

STOPPING AT
A FRIEND'S FARMHOUSE
by Mêng Hao-jan (689–740)

Preparing me chicken and rice, old friend,
You entertain me at your farm.
We watch the green trees that circle your
village
And the pale blue of outlying mountains.
We open your window over garden and field,
To talk mulberry and hemp with our cups in
our hands.
. . . Wait till the Mountain Holiday—
I am coming again in chrysanthemum time.

A FAREWELL
AT FENG-CHI STATION
by Tu Fu (712–770)

This is where your comrade must leave you,
Turning at the foot of these purple moun-
tains. . . .
When shall we lift our cups again, I wonder,
As we did last night and walk in the moon?
The region is murmuring farewell
To one who was honored through the three
reigns;
And back I go now to my river-village,
Into the final solitude.

TO A FRIEND BOUND NORTH
AFTER THE REBELLION
by Ssǔ-k'ung Shu (*eighth century*)

In dangerous times we two came south;
Now you go north in safety, without me.
But remember my head growing white among
strangers,
When you look on the blue of the mountains
of home.
. . . The moon goes down behind a ruined fort,
Leaving star-clusters above an old gate . . .
There are shivering birds and withering
grasses,
Whichever way I turn my face.

A NOTE ON A RAINY NIGHT
TO A FRIEND IN THE NORTH
by Li Shang-yin (813–858)

You ask me when I am coming. I do not
know.
I dream of your mountains and autumn pools
brimming all night with the rain.
Oh, when shall we be trimming wicks again,
together in your western window?
When shall I be hearing your voice again, all
night in the rain?

329

The Chaos of the World

A VIEW OF THE WILDERNESS
by Tu Fu (712–770)

Snow is white on the westward mountains
    and on three fortified towns,
And waters in this southern lake flash on a
    long bridge.
But wind and dust from sea to sea bar me from
    my brothers;
And I cannot help crying, I am so far away.
I have nothing to expect now but the ills of
    old age.
I am of less use to my country than a grain
    of dust.
I ride out to the edge of town. I watch on the
    horizon,
Day after day, the chaos of the world.

SPRING HEART-BREAK
by Liu Fang-p'ing (*eighth-ninth centuries*)

With twilight passing her silken window,
She weeps alone in her chamber of gold;
For spring is departing from a desolate garden,
And a drift of pear-petals is closing a door.

ON THE LAKE
by Chêng-yen (*seventeenth century*)

I come and go amidst the mists and waves;
In this life I call myself "Master of the West
    Lake."
With a light wind and a small oar
I paddle out from the rushy creek.

In high spirit I raise my song,
And in the quiet of the night my voice is
    wondrous clear.
But there is no one to enjoy it,
So I myself applaud,
As the song echoes from a thousand hills.

EXPRESSION OF MY GRIEF
by Yüan Chên (779–831)

Her father loved best his youngest daughter;
After she married me in poverty she had a
    hundred devices.
When I lacked clothes, she sought in her
    wicker-box;
When I wanted to buy wine, I coaxed her to
    pull out her golden hairpin.
Wild plants were our food, and long beans
    tasted sweet;
Fallen leaves from an old locust-tree added
    to our fuel.
Today my official pay is more than a hundred
    thousand,
But for you I can only make pious offering.

In the past we jested of widowhood;
Today it has come before my eyes.
Your clothes have nearly all been given away;
But the needlework still remains that I cannot
    bear to uncover.
I yet remember the old affection, and am kind
    to maids and men,
And for that dream I have given away money.
I know that this sorrow is the lot of all,
But when man and wife have shared poverty a
    hundred things bring grief.

Idly I sit in grief for myself and in grief
    for you,
How much time is a hundred years?
Têng Yu, childless, understood his fate;
P'an Yüeh, mourning for his wife, still wrote
    poems to her.
To share a grave's darkness where is my hope?
In another life to meet again is yet harder
    to expect.
Only for the whole night my eyes are ever
    open
To requite you for a lifetime of knitted
    brows.

During times of anarchy and strife, the family was the one stable struc-
ture. Each family kept its own records, punished its wayward members, preserved
its history, and educated its young; each was, in a sense, an autonomous govern-
ment, ruled by a patriarch. In troubled times a man looked upon any prolonged
separation from his family with greatest trepidation; the family was the law,
and gave order to one's life. Outside it, as the T'ang dynasty poet Tu Fu declares
in "A View of the Wilderness," one was exposed to "the chaos of the world."

AUTUMN THOUGHTS

by Chang Chi (c.768–830)

Here in Loyang City as I felt the Autumn
wind,
I longed to write home, but my thoughts were
countless.
I feared that in my haste I had not said all,
And, as the messenger made to go, I broke the
seal again.

DRINKING ALONE
WITH THE MOON

by Li Po (705–762)

From a pot of wine among the flowers
I drank alone. There was no one with me—
Till, raising my cup, I asked the bright moon
To bring me my shadow and make us three.
Alas, the moon was unable to drink
And my shadow tagged me vacantly;
But still for a while I had these friends
To cheer me through the end of spring. . . .
I sang. The moon encouraged me.
I danced. My shadow tumbled after.
As long as I knew, we were boon companions.
And then I was drunk, and we lost one
another. . . .

ENJOYING THE PEONIES AT
THE TEMPLE OF GOOD FORTUNE

by Su Shih (1036–1101)

In my old age I adorn myself with flowers, but
blush not;
It is the flowers that should blush for deck-
ing an old man's head.
Half tipsy I fumble along home, and men must
be laughing at me,
For along the road half the folks have hooked
up their blinds.

A SONG OF GRIEF

by Pan Chieh-yü (first century B.C.)

Glazed silk, newly cut, smooth, glittering
white,
As white, as clear, even as frost and snow.
Perfectly fashioned into a fan,
Round, round, like the brilliant moon,
Treasured in my Lord's sleeve, taken out, put
in—
Wave it, shake it, and a little wind flies from
it.
How often I fear that Autumn Season's
coming
And the fierce, cold wind which scatters the
blazing heat.
Discarded, passed by, laid in a box alone;
Such a little time, and the thing of love cast
off.

FAREWELL TO GENERAL CHAO

by Ch'ên Yu-ting (fourteenth century)

The length and breadth of all within the seas
he will traverse,
But no signs of grief at separation are on
his face.
The thought of years of lonely wandering
Is as the wind of Autumn and the chill of his
sword-blade.

The Serenity of Nature

RETURNING TO
LIVE IN THE COUNTRY
by T'ao Yüan-ming (365–427)

In my youth I was out of tune with the
        common folk:
My nature is to love hills and mountains.
In my folly I fell into the net of the world's
        dust,
And so went on for thirty years.
The caged bird longs for its old woodland;
The pond-reared fish yearns for its native
        stream.
I have opened up a waste plot of the south
        moor,
And keeping my simplicity returned to garden
        and field.

A homestead of some ten acres,
A thatched cottage with eight or nine rooms;
Elms and willows shading the hinder eaves;
Peach and plum trees ranking before the hall.

DRINKING WINE
by T'ao Yüan-ming (365–427)

I built my hut amid the throng of men,
But there is no din of carriages or horses.
You ask me how this can be.
When the heart is remote, earth stands aloof.
Culling chrysanthemums by the eastern hedge,
I see afar the southern hills;
The air of the hills at sunset is good;
The flying birds in company come back to
        their nests.
In this is the real savour,
But, probing, I can find no words.

A BUDDHIST RETREAT BEHIND
BROKEN-MOUNTAIN TEMPLE
by Ch'ang Chien (*c.*727)

In the pure morning, near the old temple,
Where early sunlight points the tree-tops,
My path has wound, through a sheltered
        hollow
Of boughs and flowers, to a Buddhist retreat.
Here birds are alive with mountain-light,
And the mind of man touches peace in a pool,
And a thousand sounds are quieted
By the breathing of a temple-bell.

QUESTION AND ANSWER
AMONG THE MOUNTAINS
by Li Po (705–762)

You ask me why I dwell in the green
        mountain;
I smile and make no reply for my heart is free
        of care.
As the peach-blossom flows down stream and
        is gone into the unknown,
I have a world apart that is not among men.

Chinese poetry appears totally lacking in epic scope, and, indeed, China's great poets have commonly been men whose subject matter is mundane and quite accessible. Chinese poems are anecdotal and personal. Their brevity and simplicity are no accident, but are, rather, a deliberately cultivated reflection of the poets' philosophy. The poems attempt to duplicate in both visual and verbal composition the serenity of the natural order, whose veneration has been a familiar feature of Chinese thought and teaching since a full century before the time of Confucius.

A BOAT IN SPRING
ON JO-YA LAKE
by Chi Wu-ch'ien (*c.* 726)

Thoughtful elation has no end:
Onward I bear it to whatever come.
And my boat and I, before the evening breeze
Passing flowers, entering the lake,
Turn at nightfall toward the western valley,
Where I watch the south star over the
                                      mountain
And a mist that rises, hovering soft,
And the low moon slanting through the trees;
And I choose to put away from me every
                                      worldly matter
And only to be an old man with a fishing-pole.

NORTH AMONG GREEN VINES
by Li Shang-yin (813–858)

Where the sun has entered the western hills,
I look for a monk in his little straw hut;
But only the fallen leaves are at home,
And I turn through chilling levels of cloud.
I hear a stone gong in the dusk,
I lean full-weight on my slender staff . . .
How within this world, within this grain of
                                      dust,
Can there be any room for the passions of
                                      men?

HSU YU'S GOURD
by Wang Chi-wu (1645–1725)

The gourd hangs on the tree,
Light as single leaf;
The wind blows it click-clack in the night.
It were best to cast it away that my dreams
                        may be pure.
The whole world is not so great, the gourd is
                        not so small;
All things beyond the body are an
                        encumbrance.

333

Mortality

Mao Tse-tung's regime has systematically discouraged ancestor worship, but a few families still observe a once nearly universal ceremony honoring forebears. In mid-autumn of each year an elaborate rite was celebrated at the family shrine. There, in the presence of the members of the extended family, the patriarch intoned the names of every deceased relative. This ceremony, which often lasted for several hours, served two functions: it reassured each listener that in the future his name too would be remembered and his spirit be invoked, and, perhaps unintentionally, it reminded him of how inconsequential his own life was. That double sense of history and mortality is emphasized in the group of poems below.

ON THE CITY WALL
by Tzŭ-lan (*ninth century*)

The ancient tombs lie thicker than grass;
The new graves encroach even on the
highway.
Outside the city-wall there is no vacant
ground;
Inside the city-wall men are still growing old.

THE PENALTIES OF RANK
by Po Chü-i (772–846)

Three score and ten! A slave to office yet!
In the Li Chi* these luminous words befall:
"The lust for honors not at all,"
Here is the golden line we most forget.

Alas! how these long years afflict a man!
When teeth are gone, and failing eyes grow
dim.
The morning dews brought dreams of fame to
him.
Who bears in dusk the burdens of his clan.

His eyes still linger on the tassel blue,†
And still the red sedan of rank appeals,
But his shrunk belly scarce the girdle feels
As, bowed, he crawls the Prince's Gateway
through.

Where is the man that would not wealth
acclaim?
Who would not truckle for his sovereign's
grace?
Yet years of high renown their furrows trace,
And greatness overwhelms the weary frame.
The springs of laughter flow not from his
heart,
Where bide the dust and glamour of old days.
Who walks alone in contemplation's ways?
'Tis he, the happy man, who dwells apart.

*the Book of Rites
†a symbol of office

THE INLAID HARP
by Li Shang-yin (813–858)

I wonder why my inlaid harp has fifty strings,
Each with its flower-like fret an interval of
youth.
. . . The sage Chuang-tzu is day-dreaming,
bewitched by butterflies,
The spring-heart of Emperor Wang is crying
in a cuckoo,
Mermen weep their pearly tears down a moon-
green sea,
Blue fields are breathing their jade to the
sun . . .
And a moment that ought to have lasted for
ever
Has come and gone before I knew.

SONG OF A LIFE
by T'ang Yin (1470–1523)

Man's life from of old has rarely reached
seventy;
Take away the early childhood years and the
late years of old age;
Between these a man's time is not long.
And even so there is heat and frost, trouble
and vexation.
Once past Mid-autumn the moon is less
bright;
Once past April the flowers are less beautiful.

THE ANCIENT WIND
by Po Chü-i (772–846)

The peach blooms open on the eastern wall—
I breathe their fragrance, laughing in the glow
Of golden noontide. Suddenly there comes
The revelation of the ancient wind,
Flooding my soul with glory; till I feel
One with the brightness of the first far dawn,
One with the many-colored spring; and all
The secrets of the scented hearts of flowers
Are whispered through me; till I cry aloud:—
"Alas! how gray and scentless is the bloom
Of mortal life!" This—this alone I fear,
That from yon twinkling mirror of delight
The unreal flowers may fade; that with the
            breath
Of the fiery flying Dragon they will fall
Petal by petal, slowly, yet too soon,
Into the world's green sepulchre. Alas!
My little friends, my lovers, we must part
And, like some uncompanioned pine that
            stands,
Last of the legions on the southern slopes,
I too shall stand alone, and hungry winds
Shall gnaw the lute-string of my desolate
            heart.

THE COLOR OF LIFE
by Ssü-K'ung T'u (834–908)

Would that we might for ever stay
The rainbow glories of the world,
The blue of the unfathomed sea,
The rare azalea late unfurled,
The parrot of a greener spring,
The willows and the terrace line,
The stranger from the night-steeped hills,
The roselit brimming cup of wine.
Oh for a life that stretched afar,
Where no dead dust of books were rife,
Where spring sang clear from star to star;
Alas! what hope for such a life?

STAYING THE NIGHT
WITH FRIENDS
by Yüan Mei (1715–1797)

Seventy-seven, such an old fellow!
In three years I get one look at the West Lake
            rains;
Back I come, place after place, for a short
            visit,
Troubling family after family to cook me
            chicken and millet.
My friends, forbear to ask the date of my next
            coming,
For this is an uncertain thing not for my
            ordering;
I keep saying I will never return and then
            returning,
And it is shameful to keep cheating folk like
            this.

The Soldier's Life

United against invading barbarians or divided against one another, the Chinese over the centuries fought an almost unbroken succession of dynastic, defensive, and expansionist wars. In regular succession dynasties arose north of the Yangtze River, grew bold enough to invade the south, ruled for a time over a unified empire, and were overthrown. Such cyclical warmaking required the conscription of millions of common soldiers and resulted in uncounted casualties. Poems such as Chang Pin's "Lament" and Li Po's "The Moon at the Fortified Pass" emphasize that "not one battle famous in history [has] sent all its fighters back again."

LAMENT FOR
TEN THOUSAND MEN'S GRAVES
by Chang Pin (*ninth-tenth centuries*)

The war is ended on the Huai border, and the
     trading roads are open again;
Stray crows come and go cawing in the wintry
     sky.
Alas for the white bones heaped together in
     desolate graves;
All had sought military honors for their
     leader.

THE MOON AT
THE FORTIFIED PASS
by Li Po (705–762)

The bright moon lifts from the Mountain of
     Heaven

In an infinite haze of cloud and sea,
And the wind, that has come a thousand miles,
Beats at the Jade Pass Battlements. . . .
China marches its men down Po-têng Road
While Tartar troops peer across blue waters
     of the bay . . .
And since not one battle famous in history
Sent all its fighters back again,
The soldiers turn round, looking toward the
     border,
And think of home, with wistful eyes,
And of those tonight in the upper chambers
Who toss and sigh and cannot rest.

A TROOPER'S BURDEN
by Liu Ch'ang-ch'ing (*eighth century*)

For years, to guard the Jade Pass and the River
     of Gold,
With our hands on our horse-whips and our
     sword-hilts,
We have watched the green graves change to
     snow

And the Yellow Stream ring the Black
     Mountain forever.

LUNG-HSI SONG
by Ch'ên T'ao (*ninth-tenth centuries*)

They vowed to sweep away the barbarians
     without regard of self;
Five thousand in their furs and brocades
     perished in the Tartar dust.
Alas! their bones, lay beside the Wu-ting
     river;
They still live in their ladies' dreams in
     Springtime.

THE WILD GEESE
by Lu Kuei-mêng (*ninth century*)

From South to North, how long is the way!
Between them lie ten thousand bows and
     arrows.
Who can say, through the mist and fog,
How many birds can reach Hêng-yang?

WHAT PLANT IS NOT YELLOW?
from the Book of Odes

What plant is not yellow?
What day is without a march?
What man is not on the move
Serving in the four quarters?

What plant is not black?
What man is not wifeless?
Heigho, for us soldiers!
We alone are not treated as men.

Not rhinoceroses, not tigers,
Yet we are loosed in this mighty waste.
Heigho, for us soldiers!
Day and night we never rest.

The fox with his broad brush
Lurks among the gloomy grass;
But our wagon with its bamboo body,
Rumbles along the road of Chou.